SENIOR PORTRAITS

By Larry Peters,
M. Photog. Cr.

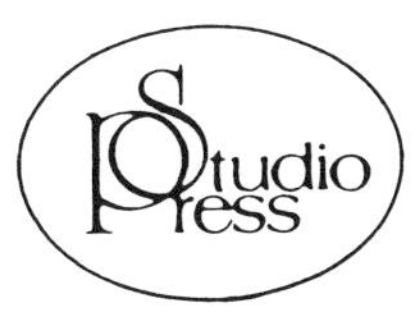

TWAIN HARTE, CALIFORNIA

Published by STUDIO PRESS
Twain Harte, California 95383-1268, USA

Printed in the United States of America.

ISBN 0-934420-10-6

Contents

Dedication

This book is dedicated to the diversified, working photographer who wants to point his business in the very profitable direction of doing high school seniors, or doing more of them. Seniors may be a large or a small part of your business, but the methods I present in this book will help you develop this market even further and do it much faster.

Thank You

I don't say it often enough, but I hope my wife, Karen, knows how much she is loved and appreciated. She's the one who showed me that hard work is basic to the accomplishment of anything.

My older daughter, Melinda, compiled all the data and photographs and worked on the editing. I thank you, Melinda.

My younger daughter, Janine, gave me a reason to write - just to show it can be done. Thanks for the nudge, Janine.

Thank you, Diane Stahl, for reading my handwriting and typing the first draft, and you, Jeff Tabit, for your photographic assistance.

Betty and Tim Wilson created a working draft and helped and supported in numerous ways and I am forever grateful.

I thank Gary Jentoft for his inspiration, Charles Lewis for selling principles, Gene Butler for marketing ideas and support, and Dick Stevens for knowing that business principles are the same, no matter what the business.

And God, I thank you for giving me direction and the ability to do whatever I decide to do.

Introduction

It is my firm belief that anything you want can be yours if your mental attitude is right. To get it you must create an intense burning desire from deep within. We all know the difficulties of everyday life, but there are so few who know both how to cope with life's daily frustrations and how to use their feelings to succeed in what they want. I strive to make this my story because I have seen success elude many who work for it, yet come easily for others.

Yes, success is an attitude and, if you are happy and contented with your portion, who can say that you are not successful?

A book should tell you a little about the author, so let me begin by saying that I live in the small, midwestern town where I was born. London - population 8,000, more or less - is about half way between Columbus and Springfield, Ohio, and is still surrounded by farms.

I had no formal training in photography until I was already earning money from portraiture and wedding photography, but I have always had a burning desire to make my life as much a success as I can. After high school I attended a small college in Columbus and - because I had to work part time - I commuted the twenty-five miles daily.

Then I taught high school for six years about fifteen miles from London and it was here that I had my first real exposure to photography. As the advisor to the high school newspaper, I had to oversee the photography and related processing, so I was soon processing b/w negatives and printing them. As I began to show some skills in photography, students began to ask me to do their weddings and, soon after, their senior portraits.

In 1974 I attended Winona School of Professional Photography and took the Basic Portraiture course. Two years later I took the Advanced Posing and Lighting course, and these two courses were the only formal training I have had. Before then, I found it necessary to duplicate posing and lighting techniques learned from other photographers.

I didn't make a lot of money from those portraits and weddings, but each assignment became a learning experience and I gradually improved. The teaching job was replaced by work in my father-in-law's manufacturing plant, and for the next five years I worked two jobs at once. During the days I sat at a desk making invoices, producing catalogs, and managing personnel, while at nights I cultivated the love of photography.

In 1980 I photographed 240 high school seniors who came to me mostly by word-of-mouth supplemented with a little newspaper advertising.

Two weeks before Christmas, 1981, I left the comfort of a secure job with my father-in-law to start a full-time photography studio in a small town that had been without a studio for more than twenty-five years. The first few months were tough, so I filled in the slow times with substitute teaching until I met Gary Jentoft at a seminar he conducted in Columbus.

Karen went with me and we learned things we will never forget, things such as, "All the business you can possibly want is right in front of you - but you have to ask for it!" Isn't that simple? Yes, and very profound.

Another thing Gary said that still sticks with us is, "How busy do you want to be? How much income do you want from your occupation? What do you want to achieve from your profession in dollar rewards and peer acceptance? It is this simple: decide what you want and go for it! If you're not sure, sit back and maintain your current attitude; I can assure you that nothing will happen to change things."

This book is being written for those who are willing to try, for those who are filled with a burning desire and those who will be grateful for what they achieve.

In 1989 we photographed 1325 seniors with orders averaging over $525. That's just under $700,000 in seniors alone We now have an effective direct mail program in place that pulls in more than our share of seniors, and we have become the leading company in the U. S. in developing and marketing new backgrounds and props for senior portraits. We have achieved success in both these areas and now my desire is to teach other photographers the nitty-gritty things about this field so you and your family can also enjoy the same success my family and I have experienced.

In this book I will show you how to generate business, how to do posing and lighting that are dynamic and exciting, how to satisfy the school requirements for yearbook photography and how to sell your product. Let's do it! Senior portraits really can be both fun and profitable.

Chapter I

School Contracts

In the past most schools had a recommended photographer and all the students were supposed to use that studio for their portraits. The schools enforced this rule by refusing to allow photos by other studios in the annual. Why would the schools do this? They did it because the studio owners "paid" for the contracts in any of several ways, most often by doing activity photos at no charge or by giving free supplies and the use of cameras to the school photo class. I have heard of outright bribes being given, the worst of which was loaning the year- book advisor a new car for the year.

One large contract studio owned a deluxe vacation home at a famous mountain ski resort where each year he would hold a weekend bash for school principals and yearbook advisors. He also made the home available to the advisors for selected weekends during the ski season and for longer times during the summer vacation. It's very hard for the small studio owner to compete with that sort of enticement, so I am very glad that the day of the contract photographer is beginning to disappear.

When I first started doing senior photography, I believed the only way I could compete was with a contract, so I repeatedly sought to meet with school officials to make my proposal to them. It was all in vain because everyone was comfortable with the current arrangement. How many of you know that most of us are extremely reluctant to make any changes that may rock the boat and we are much happier just drifting with our present arrangements? (School teachers may be the worst at this.)

In addition, the studio owners who have these cozy little agreements are very comfy with the situation and they will do all they can to maintain the status quo. They almost have to totally screw up, go out of business or die for the contract to open up again. Even then, it's usually open only long enough for another studio to make the same sort of deal.

If you are planning to start in senior photography with a school contract, you had better forget that idea unless your father is the principal! The schools don't know who you are, the students don't know who you are and - worst of all - nobody even cares who you are. Forget the contracts and go after the students directly with superior photography and posing.

If you will do this, you can't help but succeed as most contract studios deliver a second rate product, poorly posed, sloppily lighted and done in an assembly line method. If it were not for the contracts, most of them would be out of business tomorrow and I say, "good riddance".

There are exceptions, however, to even the worst situations. We now have three contracts that were handed to us. They were given up by other photographers and the schools asked us to step in. There were no bribes involved and we've never had to bid on the contracts. They were offered to us with no strings, we accepted them gladly and we give the contract students (about 300-350 total) the same high quality we give our non-contract students. Everyone seems happy with the arrangement: the contracts are renewed verbally each year.

School contracts are as different as each school system. In their simplest form they will include all or most of the following:

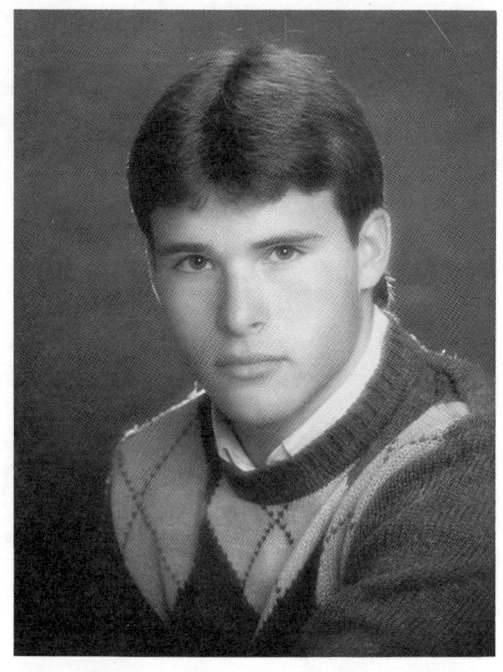

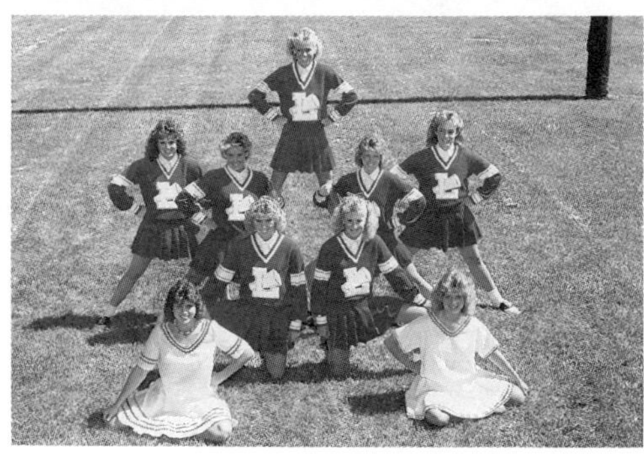

19 88

LONDON HIGH SCHOOL

1) You agree to photograph each senior and furnish to the year book a b/w or color glossy photo of each one. In return, the school gives you the name and address of each student so you can easily contact them. Occasionally, however, a school's lawyer will prevent your getting the senior roster for fear of violating the right to privacy of the students, but this is only rarely a problem.
2) You agree to supply the yearbook with b/w film so students can take candid photos of each other. You will probably be expected to process and print the film at no charge. Don't leave this open-ended; limit the rolls to a set number. For instance, in a nearby school with a senior class of about 130 we give forty rolls of b/w film, plus processing and printing to 3½x5.
3) You agree to make a certain number of trips to the school, usually during the day, to photograph the organizations the school wants to include in the year book. These photos are usually taken in b/w and delivered as 5x7s, but this may vary.
4) During the year you will have to cover one game (both boys and girls) for each major sport the school participates in and perhaps several of the big football games. You will usually be expected to supply b/w 3½x5s of these. However, you can often turn both this and Item #3 above into profit- making ventures by photographing the students in color and promoting the sale of memory mates, statues or buttons to the individual students. Properly promoted, these items will just about pay for the time you spend on activities pix.
5) The actual times for photography and the photos for the book are set at this time. Actually, the deadline for photographs is set by the year book printing company, but do your best to allow for outdoor photography during Autumn.
6) Prom photos can be very lucrative; as the school photographer you should be allowed to cover the major dances - Homecoming, Winter Festival, Valentine's Day, Junior-Senior Prom, and others. Design an array of packages from - say - eight dollars to forty dollars (1989 prices) so you can turn a real profit from this photography. You won't sell too many $40 packages, but they will make the other medium priced packages seem less costly by comparison and persuade many kids to spend $25 or $30 rather than just $8.
7) Some smaller schools may require a class composite which is put together by you and given to the school. It shows all the students you photographed from that school. If you use only the portraits you created, students who want to be included in the comp must come to you.
8) If you do get a contract, it's wrong to tell students their photos will not appear in the yearbook unless they are photographed by you. This is called a "closed yearbook" because it's closed to portraits from any other photographer. I believe this to be unduly restrictive and that it should be outlawed. That's my opinion and that's the way we work it at the schools we service.

In addition, closed yearbooks have been a source of legal cases for some years. Parents, students and photography studios believe the closed yearbook forces a student to go to a certain photographer and that this constitutes discrimination and restraint of trade.

It gets even worse if the contract studio has a sitting fee that must be paid before the portraits are made. Many of the large chain studios get around this by charging nothing for the sittings that are done on the school premises, but the quality of photography done under these circumstances is wretched. There is no variety, only headshots, there are no clothing changes, no out-door poses and no exciting props. The students deserve better and they know it, and many of them will use the contract studio just for the yearbook pose and go elsewhere for the photos they buy.

Try to avoid contracts that require you to loan or give equipment and supplies for the use of student photographers. The students know they have no responsibility for the cameras and will inevitably abuse them. If you lend the cameras, you'll get back junk at the end of the year: if you give them, they will still be trashed and you'll have to supply another set next year. Sign a contract that asks for cameras and flashes only as a last resort.

If a school asks for a cash rebate from senior photography, RUN, don't walk, for the door. Many schools do receive kick-back money from underclass (grades one through eleven) photography, but this is different from senior portraits. These photos are usually taken in a single day and school personnel provide a lot of the organizing and management effort. It's quite proper to pay for all this free help.

You do not get that kind of help with seniors, however, so you need to keep all the money if your business is to be profitable. Avoid any contract that calls for cash money because that will prove to be very expensive to you.

Properly handled, school contracts can be pleasantly profitable and I enjoy attending the activities of my three schools, doing their dances, and mingling with the students. I believe that a few good contracts are an excellent base for a studio owner to build his business on, but the day they become a hassle, I'll drop them. I know the quality and variety of my work is good enough that I can attract seniors without a contract and make a good profit.

HAVE YOU RECEIVED MAILERS SAYING
"Freedom of Choice"

HAVE YOU WONDERED WHY?
Many will try to tell you that you have the right to choose a photography studio . . . **WHY?** ***To get your business!!***

DID YOU KNOW:
You have always had that choice!!! Even though we are the school photographer, **WE** asked all of our schools to give the students the choice for their yearbook photograph.

—Please Beware Of The Ploy To Pull Your School Spirit Apart—

YES, WE DO THE CLASS COMPOSITE:
The composite portrait of all your fellow classmates hangs in the lobby or hallway of your school for all to see for years to come.

Please know that this photograph is a grouping of all the portraits made by Peters' Main Street Photography. It is framed or reduced to the size specified by your school and given **FREE TO YOUR SCHOOL!!**

We want to include you on this composite but most of all, we would be honored to be your senior photographer.

HIDDEN COSTS:
At other studios, you cannot order your composite picture. **Why would you pay twice?** One for the other photographer's fee and an other time for a composite session with us. Add these together and you pay more in the long run by going to two places.

CHECK IT OUT:
Being your school photographer is a privilege. We realize that your Senior Portrait is a "Once In A Lifetime" experience so why not choose the best! It makes sense. You only have to pay one sitting fee and get your yearbook and composite picture in one sitting.

DON'T BE MISLED. YOU HAVE THE FREEDOM OF CHOICE **NOW** AS YOU HAVE HAD IN THE **PAST** AND WILL CONTINUE TO HAVE IN THE **FUTURE!**

Don't let **FALSE** advertising confuse you. Don't let an untrue statement guide your decision. Why would someone make these false statements? ***Just To Get Your Business!!***

Choose with care, please visit the photography studio, (theirs and ours) and let us show you and your parents our slide show.

This is an important decision, make it a wise one!!

Peters **Main Street Photography, Inc.**
314 North Main Street
London, Ohio 43140
(614) 852-2731 or 1-800-446-1922

This mailer and the one on the next page were sent to the seniors of our contract schools in response to a competitor's mailing. Both give a very good reason for coming to Main Street Photography: they won't be included in the school composite if they go elsewhere.

YOUNG EDITIONS '89

(614) 852-2731

Dear Member Of the Class of 1989:

It's a pleasure to help you plan one of the most memorable years of your life, **YOUR SENIOR YEAR.**

We are glad to be part of your year and plan on starting it off with a **BANG!** All winter, we've developed new backgrounds, poses and props that are truly going to make your photo session something to remember.

This is written to you to give you ideas about deadlines and other important information.

Important Things You Should Know!

Take Advantage Of Our Early Season Specials they are real **MONEY SAVERS!!**

All portraits should be finished before **January 1, 1989**, to insure you a spot in the yearbook and on the class composite. **SPECIAL NOTE:** *Madison Plains Students must be photographed before September 15th.* **You have an early deadline!!**

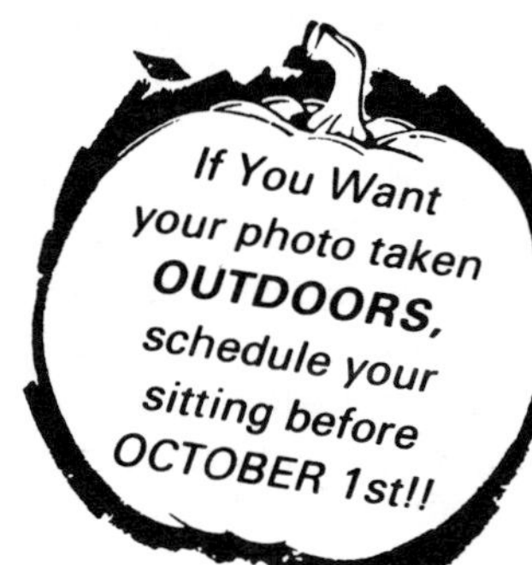

A word of warning to all fall athletes. You will have a hard time scheduling after your practices begin. You will be better off having your pictures taken during the summer months.

YOUR HIGH SCHOOL '89

We will provide your school with the yearbook photograph and only those created by Main Street Photography will appear on class composites. Sorry, but the quality of many area photographer yearbook picture is far below average work.

Schedule your appointment at your convenience. Hours: Mon-Fri, 9-5, Sat. 9-12. **Call 852-2731.**

Reserve your date if you want your appointment at a certain time. Scheduling is done on a first come basis and this year is shaping up to be a busy one.

Plan on being here at least an hour for your sitting. Some take longer than others.

Unique poses are something we love, **BE CREATIVE WITH YOUR CLOTHING AND PROPS.** *You've earned this bit of freedom so enjoy and be yourself.*

LIFETIME GUARANTEED COLOR PHOTOGRAPHS

Peters Main Street Photography, Inc.
314 N. MAIN
LONDON, OHIO 43140

YOUNG EDITIONS '89

IMPORTANT INFORMATION ABOUT YOUR SENIOR PORTRAIT

Chapter II

How to Attract Seniors

The high school senior market can be a very lucrative business, although its seasonal qualities may make it hard to fit into your present way of doing business. More and more studio photographers are looking toward seniors for a substantial part of their overall business because of the part-timers who have invaded the wedding market and taken over a good bit of it. The part-timers who have no doubt about their abilities to do weddings are often hesitant to take on portraits because they lack the studio facilities to do a competent job of it.

In the past, high schools were often locked up by "contract" photographers. Portraits by non-contract studios were not accepted for the yearbook and the students were literally forced to buy from the officially sanctioned studio. Today that monopolistic practice has largely passed from the senior scene and most of the large contract studios have lost their grip on the business. The result is that smaller studios offering better services and photographic quality have moved in to fill the vacuum. You can do it, too.

When you start a senior promotion there are several things to keep in mind. The first is how many high schools are there within a thirty-five mile radius? A good senior photographer can pull students from as far as thirty-five miles away (more or less, depending on things like population density and the nearness of cities and large towns), so this distance is a realistic goal you can work towards. It won't happen at once, but you can expect to see it within three to five years if your photography is fresh and exciting and your advertising is carefully thought out.

Second, how many studios in your area are presently doing Senior Photography and what territorial arrangements exist? Sometimes a studio owner will erect an imaginary shell around himself and the schools he is currently photographing and deceive himself that no other studio will go after "his" schools. In other circumstances, several studios may agree not to compete in those schools each photographer designates as his territory.

This is foolish thinking: high school seniors are old enough to know what they like in portraiture and the kids will go where they want. It's a mistake to set territorities and I am convinced that free competition based on quality of work and variety of poses decides how far students will travel to have their portraits made.

Even if there are limits already set and agreed upon, you can still jump over the non-compete territorities and promote beyond them. In Ohio's Madison County where we live there are only fifteen thousand people, but every day we serve students who have driven past other good studios to come to us, many of them from the Springfield area and even more from the Columbus market. Why? It's because we offer what they want and we actively promote and advertise to reach and persuade them.

Third, I believe that a market area composed of small towns and farms is the very best for senior photography. At least I can relate to that sort of market because it's what I grew up with and enjoy: I would be lost in a big city. We live and work in a small town surrounded by farms where the people are warm and friendly by nature. There is little wealth here and most of our business comes from the children of factory workers, farmers and small business owners. We have found that our

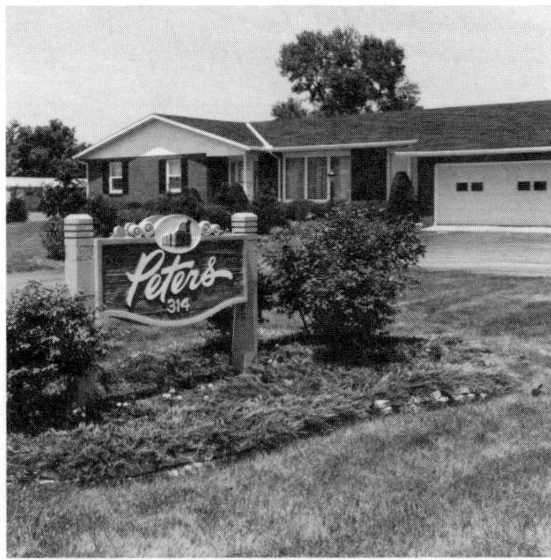

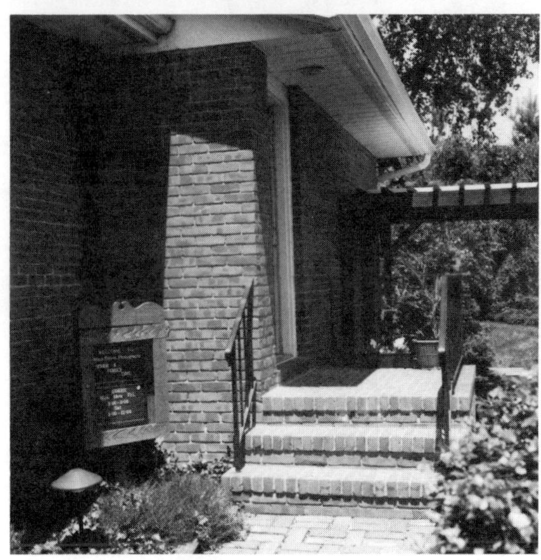

Our studio is located in the back and basement of our home on the outskirts of small-town London, Ohio. We added on to accomodate the studio.

orders for Senior Photography are - on average - larger from this group than the orders we get from the students who come to us from Springfield or Columbus. After a lot of thinking and some consultation with other photographers, we think we know why this is:

1) Classes are smaller in the small town schools, the students all know each other and they want to exchange photos with every one of their classmates.
2) The family units are tight because the grandparents and most of the aunts, uncles and cousins live nearby. All of these people receive portraits of the grads at Christmas and the more of them there are, the more portraits we sell.
3) People from this market rarely have large, formal homes in which an interior decorator has taken the family portraits from the walls and relegated them to the dresser "where they belong", so we sell more wall portraits.

The students who come to us from the wealthy areas of nearby cities are more demanding of special services and more prone to complain of traveling so far and of how much they have to pay. They always seem to doubt that our small town, in-home studio can be that much better than studios closer to them and they almost always buy fewer photographs than the country kids.

So if you are looking for an area to start a studio in, my advice is to locate on the fringes of a larger town or market area. Look for an area that is showing natural growth so you can expect the number of sittings to increase and your business to grow with the area.

I was born in a small town and feel most comfortable here; I am lucky to have many small towns and farms nearby, plus a couple cities not too far away, that provide a mixture of potential clients. You'll do yourself a favor if you establish your studio where there is the same kind of clients and income levels. I believe this will make life simpler for you and give you some very helpful advantages. It is definitely easier to build a foundation in a small town where competition may not be as stiff and then work outwards to selected portions of the larger towns. Even the city people will drive to your studio if you have something worth while to offer.

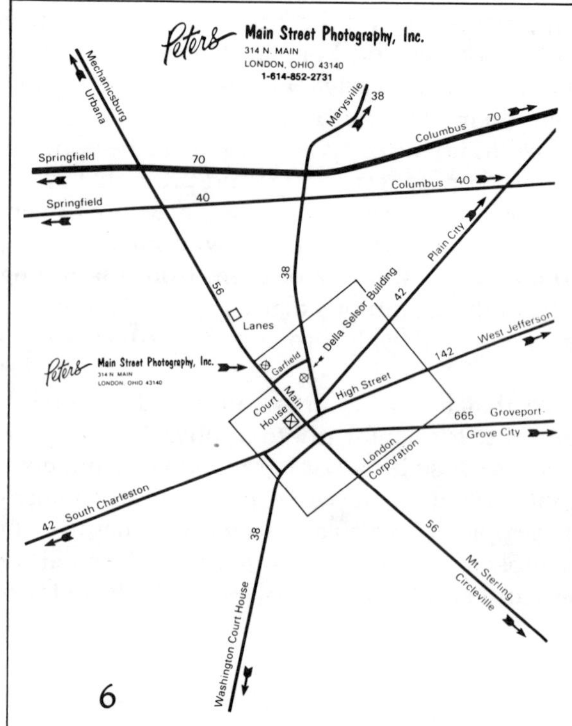

This map (8½x11) is mailed to each student making an appointment. We also send the "Guidelines" sheet shown on page 50.

Chapter III

Methods of Promoting Business

HOW TO ATTRACT NON-CONTRACT SENIORS TO YOUR STUDIO

A student who comes to your studio from a school where you have no contract is a "non-contract" senior, and these students can enhance your profit picture tremendously. It is the non-contract senior that has made our business what it is today.

Some photographers have landed contracts with one or two very large schools that supply them with all the business they want or can handle, and they have based all their plans and projections on these schools. What happens, however, if they lose the contracts? They have left themselves open to very large problems; losing a big contract can be a real shock.

That's the reason we promote to every senior in our area whose name and address we can obtain. Right at this moment those non-contract seniors make up two-thirds of our business and they represent real peace of mind for us. If we should lose our three small contracts, we haven't lost it all. The two principal ways we use to successfully attract these seniors are through a student representative program and a strong direct mail advertising program. Let's look at the student rep program first.

DESIGNING A STUDENT REPRESENTATIVE PROGRAM

Before you can design such a program, you should know what it actually is. Let me give you our definition. A student representative is a boy or girl you select to help promote your studio in his/her school. The use of a student representative is fundamental advertising. Clients will not come to your studio unless they are aware of your product, so the student representative program is designed to assist your advertising in two ways.

First, the rep will gather the names and addresses of other junior students so you have at least a partial mailing list of the kids at that school. With that list you can now send direct mail advertising to the homes of the incoming seniors.

There are two ways to gather the names and addresses. One of them is to have a sign-up sheet that the reps can pass around between periods or during home room. Other juniors sign up on this sheet and you use this information as your mailing list.

A better way and the one we employ is to have a perforated card made up with a half-price sitting fee offer on the top half; the bottom has spaces for the name and address to be filled in. The student keeps the top half to present when coming in for the sitting, while the rep retains the name-address portion and returns it to the studio after writing his/her own name on it. When that student places an order, the rep is paid on the basis of a sale.

Second, you do complimentary sittings of the reps and they take their portraits (they're proof size and mounted in folios) to school to show others what you are capable of. In this way they promote your studio by word-of-mouth, the very best advertising there is. If your work is good, this enthusiastic showing should generate lots of business all by itself.

Don't expect these students to be tremendously talented sales people: the goals to expect from the program are a mailing list and word-of-

This is the double postcard used by our Ambassadors. The top half is given to the senior, while the completed bottom is retained by the Ambassador and returned to the studio.

YOU'VE WAITED A LONG TIME FOR YOUR SENIOR PORTRAIT
SO
CHOOSE YOUR PHOTOGRAPHER WITH CARE

Bring the certificate the day of your sitting and receive 50% OFF the sitting style of your choice. Make sure your friends get this offer from ______________________, our representative at your school.

When you place a portrait order, we will add 8 FREE WALLETS to your order.

1-614-852-2731 Peters Main Street Photography, Inc.
314 N. MAIN
LONDON, OHIO 43140

One offer per student (expires 1/1/87)

- -

Please send me information about Senior Portraits.

Name______________________________

Address ___________________________

City, State and Zip Code ______________

School ____________________________

Phone Number ______________________

Give this to____________________, your student representative or mail to us. DON'T BE LEFT OUT!

Main Street Photography, Inc.
314 N. Main St.
London, Ohio 43140

mouth advertising. Some people who have tried a student representative program expected it to be a cure-all for their business woes and they were greatly disappointed when this one idea did not solve their problems. They blamed the program rather than their imperfect execution of it.

That's not the way to evaluate any program. You must recognize that not every rep will do as well as you hoped, while others will exceed your expectations. The correct evaluation is to look at the program at the end of the season and see if you got any more students from the target schools than you did the year before. If you see an increase, or if you got into a school where you have never been before, the program should be considered at least a qualified success. You can build on that the next year as you improve and refine both your student rep program and direct mail efforts. Never give up after just one year!

In setting up an ambassador program, the hardest part is finding the first student representative. Here are a few suggestions that may help.

1. Search your files for clients you have photographed already. If they live in a town or school system where you want to promote, call them up just to see if they know a student (or have one in the family) in the junior class that might be interested in such a position. The more popular and outgoing the student is, the better rep he or she will be, so look for kids of that sort. (The first recommendation you get may not be your ideal for a number one pick, but it's a place to start. Later, as you get sittings from this school, you can be more selective. After the first year you might ask a student who seemed very active in school affairs, or who placed a large order, to help you choose a representative for the next year.)

2. Place an ad in the classified section of the local newspaper soliciting a student from a certain school. Here's a sample ad: "Wanted: Junior from XYZ School for part-time modeling. Requires good appearance, ability to communicate and some typing. Phone number." An ad like this should produce several applicants from whom you can select the best for the job.
3. Knowing a teacher or someone who works in a particular school system is a productive way of finding student reps. Frequently, friends can be very helpful in finding someone for the program. Have you ever noticed that almost everyone is willing to help you if you just ask? It's a curious American trait to pull for the underdog and this time it can be you. But remember - you have to ask for the help you want.
4. Sometimes a person such as the school guidance counselor will suggest someone energetic who needs a part-time job. Do not be afraid to ask.
5. Some studios work a neat promotion to honor junior class members for achievement, perhaps for their work on the prom committee or in the student government. These studios give a complimentary sitting and feature the kids in a newspaper write-up that is actually a studio ad. Promotions like these put you in contact with students who are well known and active, exactly the sort to be excellent student reps.
6. If all else fails, you can buy a mailing list from a list broker. Do not rely on these lists to be accurate, and do not expect as good results as you will get by working with a representative. Our experience and that of other photographers is that the lists are compiled from drivers' licenses, from the names of those who have taken SAT or ACT tests and from other similar sources. Some juniors don't get drivers' licenses or take the college entrance tests so their names don't get on the purchased list. In addition, some of the names are only sophomores, some have moved, while others are duplicates caused by different spellings of the last name.

Not only is there inaccuracy in the lists, but when you mail your offer to these names, you are essentially coming to them cold. They have not seen samples enthusiastically shown by a rep and they have no idea who you are. The motivation to come to you is very low, so compiled lists that you purchase are really a last choice. Better than nothing, but not a lot.

Our experience says have two students per school, regardless of the school's size; more than this is confusing. Try to get quality people. If your portraits are exceptional, the quality students will be eager to represent your studio.

If you have to use direct mail to a cold rented list the first year in an area, you can expect a response rate of one and one-half to two per cent at the outside, which should stimulate you to get a student rep program in place for next year.

HOW TO PRESENT THE PROGRAM TO PARENTS IN A NON-THREATENING WAY

Unfortunately, not all photographers have the best ethics and the news is filled with reports of child pornography and child abuse. Because of this, responsible parents want to know something about the people their kids are involved with when they take a job. The job you are offering is quite different than the usual kids' jobs at Colonel McWendy's so my recommendation is that you take the initiative and call the parents of every student you are considering for the rep job and spend a few moments explaining the program.

Parents should know what is going on with their children and it would be very wise of you to build good will with the parents by inviting them to attend a student representative program with their children. Then they can see your operation and become familiar with the type of photography you are offering students. Many times the parents will be even more enthusiastic about your work than the kids and will do a great job of selling other parents. They will also see that the kids do their job of showing the sample prints and getting names. And in the end, it is often the parents who make the decision whether their children can work for you or not.

REPRESENTATIVE MEETING

We try to pick an evening or two in the middle of March for getting these students together. This gives them time to have their photographs taken before the end of April and begin to accumulate names and addresses. This way they will have most of the month of May in school to hand out promotional material and to show their photographs to fellow classmates.

We invite parents to attend the representative meeting. We are finding that more parental participation means more success for the whole project. The meeting lasts one and one-half hours during which we show an audio-visual program about Senior Photography. We use two projectors with a professionally prepared music and commentary tape and this program is the clincher. If they had any doubts about participating in the program, they are all mine after they see this presentation. You can feel the excitement as these students get caught up in the fact that they soon will be part of these exciting photographic images.

After the slide presentation we talk about the student representative handbook. This handbook explains what is expected of the student reps and how they are paid. We need to give them aids in collecting names and addresses such as the one-half off courtesy card enclosed. Sign-up sheets that can be circulated in home rooms or in classes are other methods that can be used to collect names and addresses.

Now is also the time to talk about clothing. We encourage these students to bring five entirely different outfits from dressy to sporty, plus everyday wear. We want each one of them to have an extraordinary collection of poses and backgrounds to share with their classmates.

One idea that has been catching on is a color analysis session with each of these students where we help them decide what colors are best for them to be photographed in. This added attention to detail shows that we care about their photo sessions and it drives home the point that the photographs I make of them will be outstanding in every way.

Once the reps have their portraits, we send them out to collect names and addresses and we have found putting a deadline on their name

MAIN STREET PHOTOGRAPHY, INC.

STUDENT AMBASSADOR GUIDEBOOK

FOR EFFECTIVE REWARDS

by Larry Peters, C.P.P.

SQUARE ONE

One of the most important parts of a business is promotion and this is where you come in by preparing a list of names and addresses of those students in your class.

Here's how:

1. DO NOT use school files. The school has the right to protect the privacy of each student and doesn't like it when someone violates their right so use other methods in address collections.

2. Student Directories may be an easy answer if available in your school system.

3. Class yearbooks provide names, then working as a team in splitting the alphabet and using a phone directory and zip code directory.

4. Circulating a list in either homeroom or a free period allowing each student the right to request information is a good way to collect names.

5. Circulating and later collecting student information cards is also a good way to collect.

6. The assimilation of your school's mailing list is very important, so don't leave anyone out.

WHAT DO I GET.......

For securing the best possible mailing list from which you and we work all year.

$.25 per name submitted (duplicates will be eliminated from second list submitted)
$10.00 Cash Bonus if you secure 1/2 of your class in ONE WEEK
$20.00 additional CASH BONUS if 100% of your class in ONE WEEK.

PLEASE ALPHABETIZE YOUR CARDS AND LISTS.

Collection of a mailing list is not illegal because we could use a mailing list broker. We chose to have the Student Ambassador for the personal touch and to get a more accurate list.

WHAT DO I GET.......?

Pictures

You will be photographed and given 2 folios with approximately 2Ø prints which you will use to show around your school and pass out your 5Ø% off Sitting Cards. THIS IS A GREAT WAY TO GET PEOPLE EXCITED ABOUT THEIR SENIOR PICTURES.

You will also have a Posing Guide to carry with you which is always a handy reference to show others the style of our photography.

More Cash.

Each time your 5Ø% off Sitting card is presented or someone refers to you when they have their pictures taken, you will receive additional cash bonuses.

REWARDS OF GOAL SETTING..........

You will be rewarded for your effort. Each time the 5Ø% off sitting card or your name is written on the sitting cards, you will receive credit.

For the first 1Ø referrals, you will automatically receive $15Ø.ØØ worth of Senior Photography. This will be credited to your account.

For between 11 and 2Ø referrals, you will receive $1Ø Cash Bonus.

For between 21 and 5Ø referrals, you will receive $15 bonus.

For all referrals over 5Ø, you will receive $2Ø each.

IF YOU REFER 75 students, you will receive $5ØØ.ØØ ADDED BONUS which you can take in cash or apply to a spring break trip.

(The trip would be secured by our office for you and you would use the $5ØØ bonus to pay for the trip. The remainder of the cost would be your expense.

THIS REALLY IS A GREAT WAY TO GET HELP FOR A GREAT SPRING BREAK TRIP.

Tips for Ambassadors

* Call those who have not made appointments at home.

* When you know a friend has an appointment, suggest that they take a friend with them to share the photography session.

* Write a letter or postcard to them making comparisons of our photography with others.

* Ask them if they got a particular mailing and offer.

* Remind them that we do yearbook glossies at no charge and tell them when their yearbook deadline is.

* Talk about variety, posing and props.

* Tell them about our goal to give them the best portrait that they have ever had created.

* If they have had a sitting by the school photographer, before they place their order, tell them to check to make sure they have received the best in posing variety for the price.

* Tell them that we offer other special promotions such as Wallet Sales, Friends Special and Family Specials.

What about the photography..........?

This is the fun part as a student representative of MAIN STREET PHOTOGRAPHY, THAT YOU WILL BE GIVEN FOLIOS THAT CONTAIN A VARIETY OF POSING TO SHOW YOUR FRIENDS.

This is a fun photography session that is meant to show all the ways you can be photographed. Borrow clothing, show as many styles as you can think of. Remember your hobbies and other interests besides school. The more unusual props that you bring, the more variety we can do. BE CREATIVE. Offer suggestions to us, give us your ideas for what you consider to be good. If you are interested in modeling, include an outfit for the fun of it. Example - shorts, swim suit or contemporary styles. What we do for you at this session is going to be your tool when your portraits are yours so include as much variety as possible.

PROMOTION...........

Show your folios to EVERYONE. Some of your friends will like certain styles and some will prefer others. This is why variety is so important in your clothing. As you show your friends, freely pass out your 50% cards and ask them to consider MAIN STREET PHOTOGRAPHY FOR THEIR Senior Portraits. If they are on the mailing list, tell that they will get additional information at home for their parents to consider.

accumulation is best. They are told to complete gathering the names within a specific time and we reward extra diligence, too. If they turn in all of the names and addresses within one week, we pay a cash bonus.

Do not expect that every student rep will bring you one hundred per cent of their classmates' names; it just won't happen, but use what they bring you wisely. If a rep brings in too few names, you may have to purchase additional names from a list broker. Do not, however, get upset with your representatives: they still have two very important tasks to perform for you.

1. Showing their photographs to their friends.
2. Passing out any special promotions you set up for early business promotions.

If they do these things well, you'll see a lot of business from your Ambassador Program.

The top coupon is passed out by the Ambassadors; the other is included in some of our mailings so each senior knows who the Ambassador is at his/her school.

AMBASSADOR SPECIAL

***This card entitles its holder to a 10 pose photo session* FREE!!**

GIVEN TO (Senior Name): ____________________

GIVEN BY (Ambassador Name): ____________________

HIGH SCHOOL: ____________________

You must be photographed by March 30, 1989. Not redeemable for cash. May be used as partial payment on a larger Senior portrait session. **CALL 1-800-446-1922 or (614) 852-2731.** Hours: Monday through Friday 9:00 a.m.-5:00 p.m. or Saturday 9:00 a.m.-12:00 Noon.

Peters Main Street Photography, Inc.
314 North Main Street
London, Ohio 43140

Pick Up Your FREE 10 Pose Portrait Session From Our Ambassador At Your School - *See Them Today!*

BRIGGS	Gina Sheridan
BISHOP READY	Lolita Bowman, Mindy Jones
CEDARVILLE	Cindy Ankeney
CIRCLEVILLE	Gretchen Weller, Andi Spekman
COLUMBUS WEST	Robin Taylor
DUBLIN	Linda Jaynes, Kristin Williams
FRANKLIN HEIGHTS	Mindi Ventola
FAIRBANKS	Jenny Smith
GROVE CITY	Becky Walisa, Angie Cook
GROVEPORT	Lisa Miller, Sean Robare
GRANDVIEW	George Tabit
HILLARD	Laura Collins, Heather Gall
HAMILTON TOWNSHIP	Angie Workman
JONATHAN ALDER	Angie Wilson, Kathy Phillips
KENTON RIDGE	Hope Allison
LOGAN ELM	Beth Duvall
MECHANICSBURG	Kristin Winland
MIAMI TRACE	Justine Shaw, Andrea Gruber
MARYSVILLE	Brian Hutchins, Becky Hutchins
NORTHEASTERN	Lisa Callicoat
NORTHWESTERN	Kristin Watson
SHAWNEE	Heather Schuler
SOUTHEASTERN	Paula Gravenkemper
TRIAD	Heather Westfall
TEAYS VALLEY	Angie Adkins
URBANA	Scott Instine
WESTFALL	Camille Roush, Jared Mullins
WESTLAND	Jill Billman, Rick Lewis
WESTERVILLE SOUTH	Amanda Reynolds

DIRECT MAIL ADVERTISING

For years many of the nation's top retailers have used the mail as the primary means of advertising their merchandise. Many businesses are unable to fully exploit this medium for promotion, but for a photography business just getting started it is not only the cheapest form of advertising, it is also the most effective and easily predictable method.

The senior market is young, influential and impressionable; if you are operating in that market, make sure you will be remembered by your appearance and your name. If you want students to react positively to your mailing pieces, your material must be first class in every respect. At this time, students are often receiving responses from the colleges where they applied and they can hardly wait to open any mail bearing their name. You might say receiving mail is a sign of incipient maturity.

One thing I have noticed about the mailings many photographers send is the lack of photographs, the very thing they are trying to sell. They send a brochure that gives every evidence of being the work of an amateur, together with a price list that seems designed to confuse, and then wonder why no one calls to accept their offers. A brochure that's short and to the point and heavily illustrated with photographs is ideal. Add to that a price list that is simple and features both easy-to-understand packages and an a la carte menu, and you have something that will work for you.

How much to spend for advertising your photography business is hard to determine, especially if you are new. Some of the experts in photography insist that a new studio has to spend from five to ten per cent of gross on advertising, while others says it should be fifteen or twenty per cent, which seems high to me. Usually the new studio owner doesn't have the freedom to spend that kind of money on an advertising program. Traditional thinking says you must advertise to get clients and the clients supply the money to advertise. That's rather like the old question, "Which came first, the chicken or the egg?", but five per cent of your gross should give you a good start.

I suggest that you advertise cautiously and very selectively at first. For example, if you can get a list of the seniors in your immediate area, that is probably all you need to start. If you accumulate at least 200 names, you should seriously consider using third class (bulk rate) mail because it's cheaper. If you use first class mail, your literature will go faster and delivery is about 100%. Bulk mail is distributed when the mail person feels like it (more or less) and the amount that actually gets delivered is more like eighty per cent. Despite the defects of third class (don't call it "junk"), we use it exclusively. Because we mail each student eight to ten times, every one will get many mailings even if an occasional piece gets lost. As your business grows and you become more adept at what you are doing, each year you should reach out a little farther beyond your immediate area until you are satisfied that you are getting the market share you need for a profitable business.

WHAT DO I SEND?

Experience tells us that we get the best response when every mailer we send contains a definite offer and asks for specific action. Mailings that make many different offers usually succeed only in confusing the customer.

Therefore it is more important to send out repeated mailings, each one dealing with a specific thing, than it is to load your clients with too much information in a single mailing. One expert says you will get ten times the business by advertising to one hundred people ten times than you'll get by advertising to one thousand people once.

We start mailing literature in the middle of April and continue through August. Some years it has been necessary to send flyers in September and October, but this is something that has to be determined by each individual studio.

The types of mailing pieces vary. They may include:

1. Using color wallet photographs taped to a letter so it shows through a window in the envelope.
2. Using flyers printed on a four color printing press. Use glossy wallet color prints to create inexpensive full color advertising materials.
3. Designing a newspaper style advertising piece that contains testimonials of clients telling why they chose our studio over others.

Please remember not to give up if you can't send out full-color, eye-catching literature the first time. That's not your only option. I believe any carefully designed and professionally prepared flyer, even in black and white, is better than sending nothing at all. Be prepared. During the off-season, you should prepare layouts and rough ideas for your mailing pieces. It is important to develop a schedule for mailing an offer, then evaluate its effectiveness so you can decide for yourself whether to continue with that particular style of mailing piece.

Some of the offers we use are:

1. A five dollar sitting charge for a twenty pose sitting, regular value thirty dollars, if your portrait is created in May.
2. A saving on your portrait order if you place an order before July first, because you can use the previous year's price list.
3. One-half off the sitting fee on selected sittings for having your portrait taken in the month of June.
4. A ten dollar discount in the form of a gift certificate or check for having your portrait taken in the month of July.
5. A coupon for a five dollar discount on your portrait order just for turning in the coupon.
6. An offer that states, "We Are Giving Away $500.00 Worth of Photography Free!" The smaller print explains that this is a ten dollar discount for the first fifty people who turn in the coupon.

Many of our offers are on full color postcards and brochures. This one and the two on the next page are samples of offers made on postcards.

We're Giving Away

$500.00

Of Color Photography

Yes,

The First **50 Seniors** to use this flyer for their sitting charge will receive **$10.00 off!!**

This Flyer must be presented at time of sitting

Offer Void After 50

Peters **Main Street Photography, Inc.**

314 N. MAIN

LONDON, OHIO 43140

1-614-852-2731

BULK RATE
US Postage Paid
LONDON, OHIO
Permit No. 27

Don't Be Left Out!!

LIFETIME GUARANTEED
COLOR PHOTOGRAPHS

SAVE ½ IN JULY

Great Photography At Reduced Prices!!

★ Receive our **DELUXE** Portrait Session ★

Including: ***20 POSES***—10 indoor and 10 outdoor with 4 changes of clothing *(Bring 6, we'll help you pick what's best)* - Regular Price $30.00

★ If Photographed in July ★

ONLY-$15.00 — *Save 50%*

(Present this flyer at time of session-one per client)

Times Are Scheduling Fast So Don't Be Left Out!

CALL - (614) 852-2731

Peters

BULK RATE
US Postage Paid
LONDON, OHIO
Permit No. 27

Save In August Before School Starts

There's still time to save on your senior portrait!

Bring this card the day of your portrait session and ***deduct $5.00*** *off your session fee as long as you are photographed in August!*

IT'S SIMPLE

Bring In This Card And

★★ SAVE ★★

Or collect up to 6 of these August Discount Coupons from your friends, and receive a **Deluxe or Larger Portrait Session at a Real Savings. *Maximum Value $30.00.***

Peters **Main Street Photography, Inc.**
314 North Main Street
London, Ohio 43140
(614) 852-2731 or 1-800-446-1922

Peters

BULK RATE
US Postage Paid
LONDON, OHIO
Permit No. 27

LIFETIME GUARANTEED COLOR PHOTOGRAPHS

August Only!!

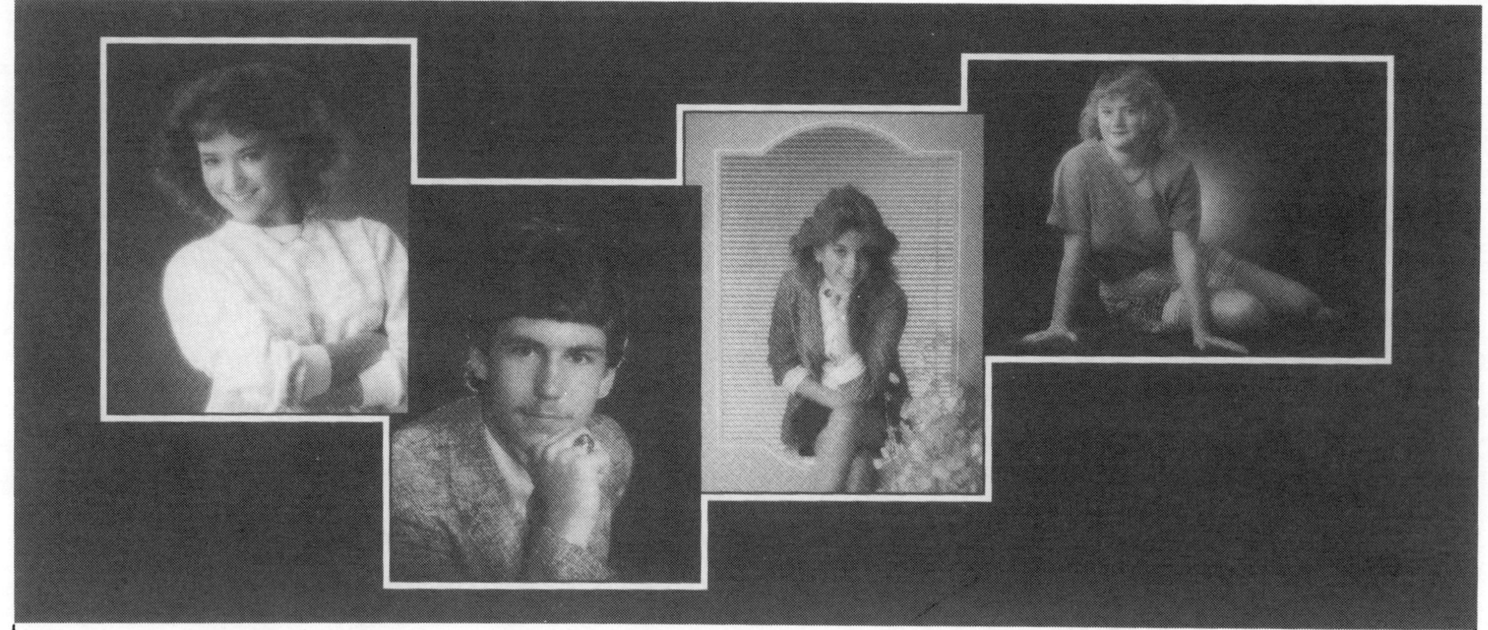

Only In May Can You Save So Much!!!

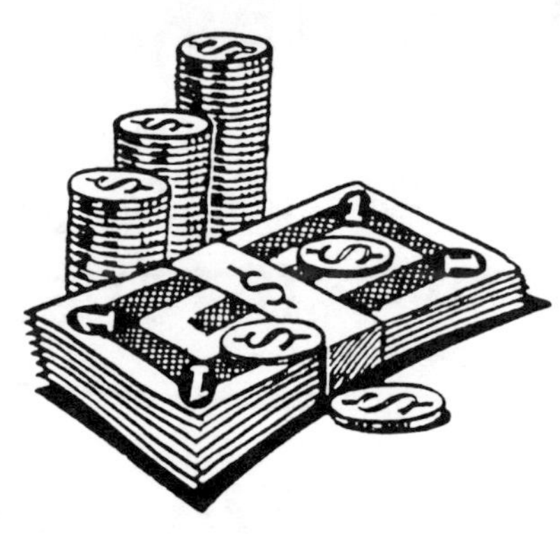

Seniors Of 1989, Special Price For **MAY**, Only:

★★89¢ SITTING FEE★★

12 Pose Sitting — 3 Clothing Changes

Call Today! (614) 852-2731/1-800-446-1922

This offer is valid if portraits are taken in May
If your order is placed by June 30th, you will receive **the Class Of 1988 prices.**

Peters

This 8½x11 brochure features full color photos on both sides, plus a great offer. It was letter folded and sent in an envelope.

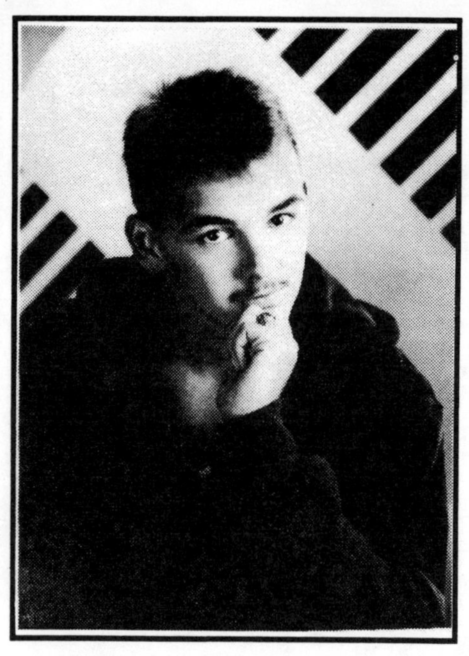

YOUNG EDITIONS '90

—*Save Big For May*—

ONLY $5.00

For A Deluxe Session

- ★ Receive a 20 pose portrait session
- ★ Up to four (4) clothing changes - bring six (6), we'll help you decide
- ★ 10 indoor and 10 outdoor poses from which to choose from
- ★ The Deluxe *"Our Most Popular"* photo session
- ★ All portraits must be taken in May, 1989 to receive the special price
- ★ Regular cost $30.00 - *Save $25.00* for early sessions

Read Carefully About All The Money Saving Specials New For '90

—Early Bird Package—
—Reduced Charges For Having Photographs Taken Early—
—New Music Vests—
—Last Years Prices For Early Orders—
—Extraordinary Photography—
—Ambassador Savings—
—Pre-Appointment Counseling—

Not all brochures are full color. This one was black ink on blue paper, four pages folded to fit a 6x9 envelope.

Who Said You Have To Spend Lots Of Money For Our Photography!

★ Check Out Our "Early Bird" Package ★

1 8x10
80 Wallets
Regular - $150.50
SALE — $75.25

This "Early Bird" package is for all placing orders before July 1. No minimum size orders - *we let you order what you desire!!*

Save ½ Off!

NEW RADIO VEST FOR EARLY SESSIONS

We have over 120 Radio Vests to give away **FREE** to the first students placing portrait orders. (Sizes may vary)

★$30.00 VALUE FREE★

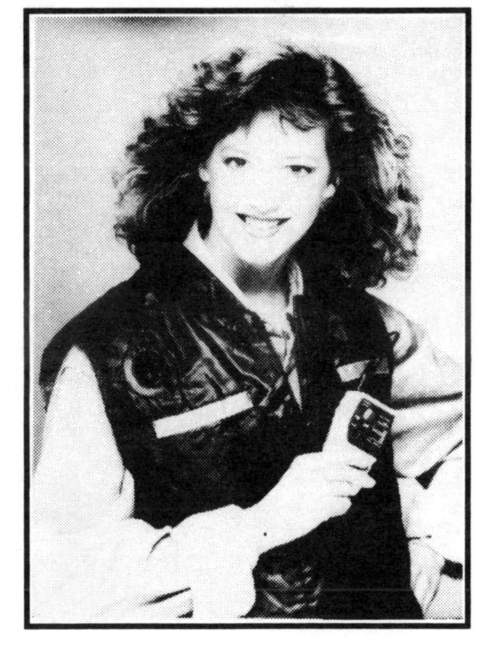

About the vest: Each vest is made of insulated nylon material. There are speakers made into the shoulders. All you do is plug in any portable walkman type radio or tape recorder and the sound is incredible - *your friends will love it!!* Music for everyone! Larger speakers than earphones to enjoy your favorite tunes. ***But, supply is limited.***

Peters

Don't Be Left Out!

Choose A Photography Session That Suits YOUR Needs!

★ Complete List of Photography Sessions ★

Payable at Sitting Time Scheduled

I **THE SENIOR** .... **$24.50 + tax**

8-10 poses indoors, including head and shoulder, close-up, ¾ length, 1 additional clothing change (2 total). Time: - ½ hour.

II **THE DELUXE *"Our Most Popular"*** .... **$30.00 + tax**

18-20 poses, including 10 indoor and 10 outdoor. Head & shoulder poses, close-up, ¾ length, environmental in our garden setting, bring your imagination, bring 6 clothing changes (We'll help you pick the best 4 which are included in the sitting). Time: 1½-2 hours.

III **BLACK AND WHITE GLAMOUR *"Our Newest"*** .... **$55.00 + tax**

Not intended to replace the color portrait, but to be a unique experience. Make-up session to be a corrective make over, 20 poses, 4 changes of clothing (Black and white prices on separate price list). Time: 2 hours

IV **LOCATION (Color or Black and White)** .... **$75.00 + tax**

24-30 poses, including 10 indoor poses at the studio in color and 20 poses in color at your choice of location within 20 miles of London **or** 20 poses in Black and White (no make-up) within 20 miles London. Great for modeling, urban locations, alleys, beaches or wherever you would like to be photographed - 6 clothing changes. Time: ¾ hour at the studio, and 1½ hour at the chosen location.

V **COMBINATION COLOR AND BLACK & WHITE** .... **$80.00 + tax**

18-20 poses in color to include traditional poses and unusual backgrounds. 10 indoor and 10 outdoor (weather permitting) PLUS 10 poses in a contemporary black and white including a make-over for a real image change. 6 clothing changes - 30 poses. Time: 3 3½ hours

VI **JUST FOR THE FUN OF IT** .... **$2.00 per pose (minimum 5 poses) + tax**

Add to any 20 pose session. Bring clothing styles that you've always dreamed of, modeling poses or use our hats for ***"Off The Wall Crazy Poses"*** 2 Clothing changes per 5 poses. Time: additional ¼ hr. per 5 poses.

VII **THE 'ELITE' *"Our Very Best"*** .... **$95.00 + tax**

The Senior girl interested in the best we have to offer. First session begins with a color analysis of client to determine the best colors suited for her complexion. Second session is our make-up session in which we apply the correct colors and amounts for a photography session. Last, a photo session to remember, including 10 outdoor poses and 20 indoor poses. Special poses, lighting, fans and props that anyone serious about photography will appreciate. Two appointments required (6 clothing changes) Time: 2½-3 hrs.

Peters

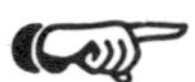
BEWARE — Schedule your appointment at least 8 weeks before you want it inorder to guarantee your date.

ASK our Ambassador at your school on how to save on your session charge.

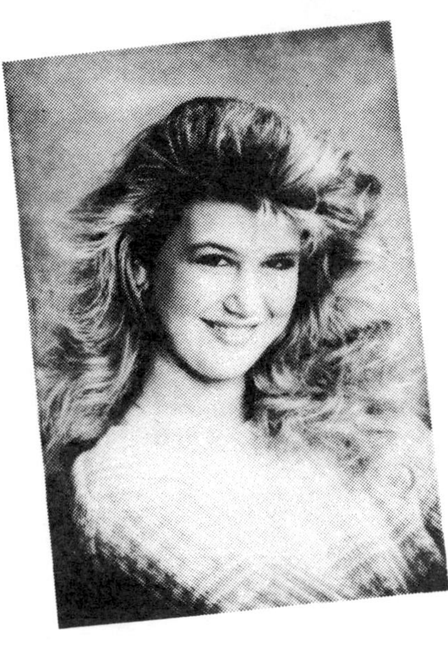

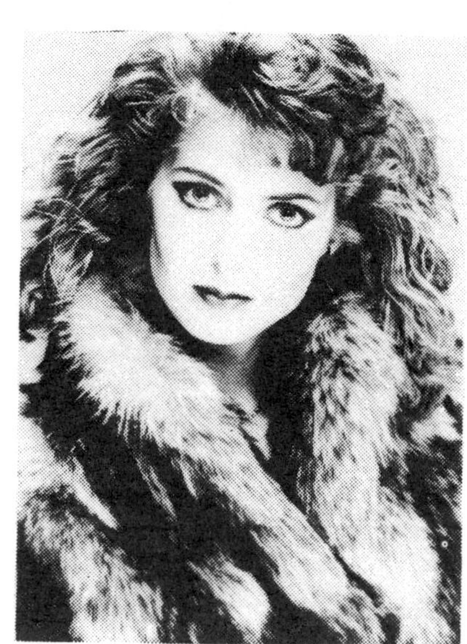

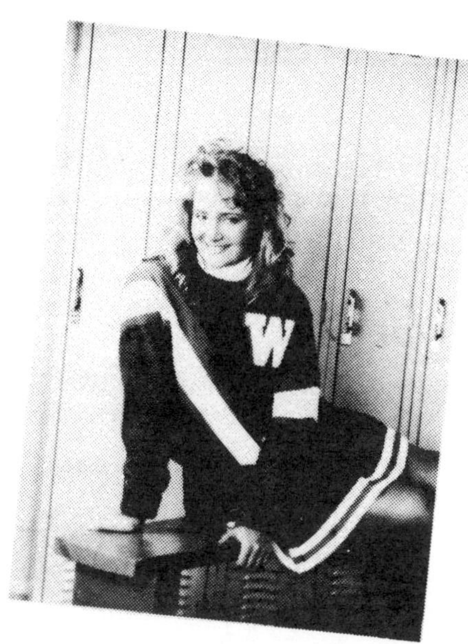

Early Customers Save Big!!

As an additional saving on our regular senior prices place your portrait order before June 30th and we'll use last year's prices. Orders must be placed before June 30th.

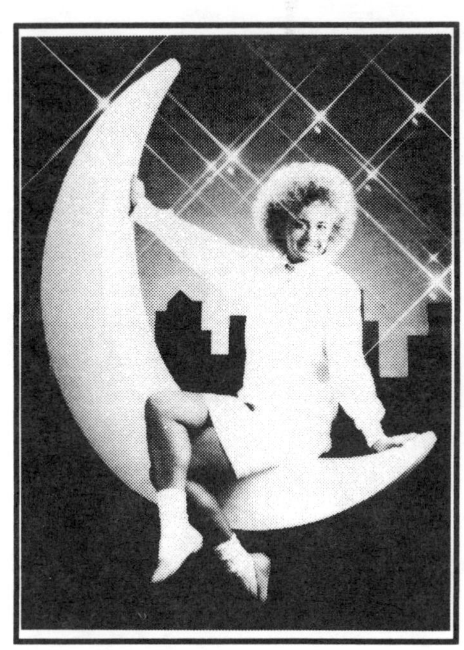

A special service, for each student to visit our studio, we'll give you a tour and show you a 15 minute dynamite slide show so you'll be better prepared. Stop in anytime!

What Do I Do To Take Advantage Of This Offer?

1. See your Ambassador for a complimentary card. You can only get this offer from them (see enclosed list).
2. Call **1-800-446-1922** as soon as you have your card, we are open Monday through Friday 9:00 a.m. to 5:00 p.m. and Saturday 9:00 a.m. to 12:00 Noon.

DO IT — HAVE FUN!

Don't Miss Out On A Photograph You'll Love!!!

No Obligation To Purchase

This brochure was black on yellow twenty pound bond and it was letter folded. As you can see, we were using it to get early sittings in February and March.

Peters Main Street Photography, Inc.
314 N. MAIN
LONDON, OHIO 43140

BULK RATE
US Postage Paid
LONDON, OHIO
Permit No. 27

Ambassador Special

It's Still Not Too Late!!

Peters **Main Street Photography, Inc.**
314 North Main Street
London, Ohio 43140
(614) 852-2731 or 1-800-446-1922

This Offer Is For:

1. All those who already have had their Senior portrait taken and did not like them.
2. Those who called and could not get an appointment in time for their yearbook deadline.
3. Everyone wanting something different. Do your photographs look like Everyone elses? Are they special to you?

Let us create unique and special poses just for you and have some fun doing it!!

You Have To Have Wallets For Your Announcements!

Why not make them something different?

THERE'S STILL TIME!!

You Get-FREE:

Ask your Ambassador for a free 10 pose portrait session coupon, good only at Peters Main Street Photography, ***the leader*** in Senior portraits.

You have nothing to lose and everything to gain!!

****BRING YOUR FRIENDS****

****SPECIAL CLOTHING****

You've Always Wanted To Be Photographed In!

****GRADUATION CAP AND GOWN****

We have many in our wardrobe - one for your School

****ADDITIONAL CLOTHING CHANGES****

With this flyer you can add additional clothing changes and poses.

DO IT RIGHT - ***You're Only A Senior Once!!!***

This is a very limited offer. Each Ambassador has only a limited number of free sessions. In order to insure delivery before Graduation, photographs must be taken in February or March.

OUR BEST FOR YOUR SPECIAL YEAR

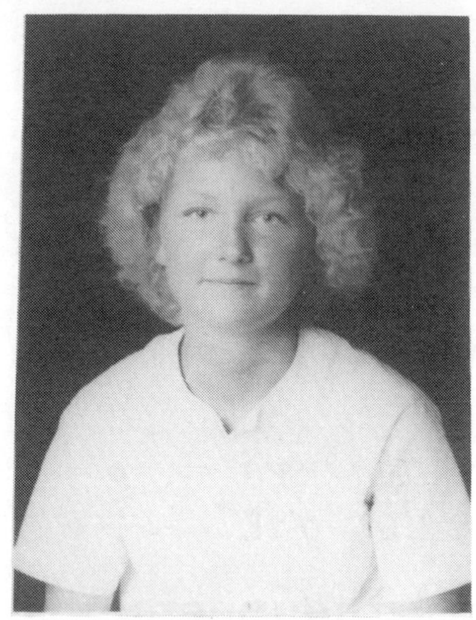

THE

ELITE

SITTING

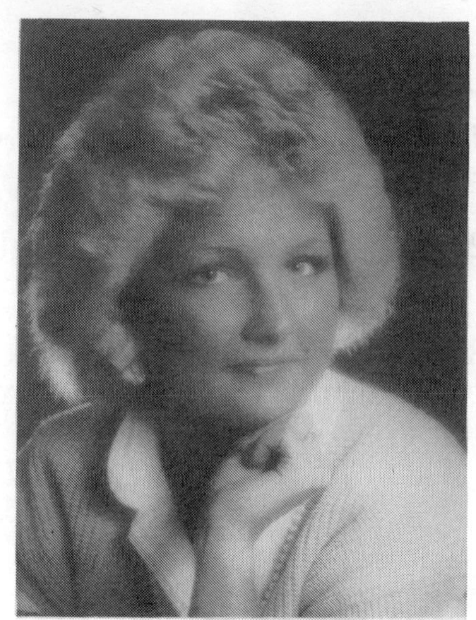

BEFORE ***AFTER***

NOT JUST ANOTHER SENIOR SITTING BUT A TOTAL MAKEOVER!

PRICE INCLUDES:

1. A COLOR CODING SESSION before your portrait sitting.
2. A MAKE-UP SESSION to choose the Right Colors, and Correct Amounts.
3. A HAIR STYLING SESSION "No Cutting" just a Great New Shaping of your present length.
4. A 30 POSE PORTRAIT SITTING, "Yes 30 Poses" with 6 Changes of Clothing.
5. ENTIRE SESSION takes at least 4 hours.

TOTAL COST $80.00

Peters **Main Street Photography, Inc.**
314 N. MAIN
LONDON, OHIO 43140

Here's a sample of a home made flyer. Pasted up on a pale blue grid which disappears when the printer's negative is made, it was made from rub-off lettering, striping from a roll, and typed with a carbon ribbon. The return address was snipped from an envelope and cemented in place. See page 42 for more details.

YOUNG EDITIONS '89

Peters Main Street Photography

314 North Main Street • London, Ohio • (614) 852-2731

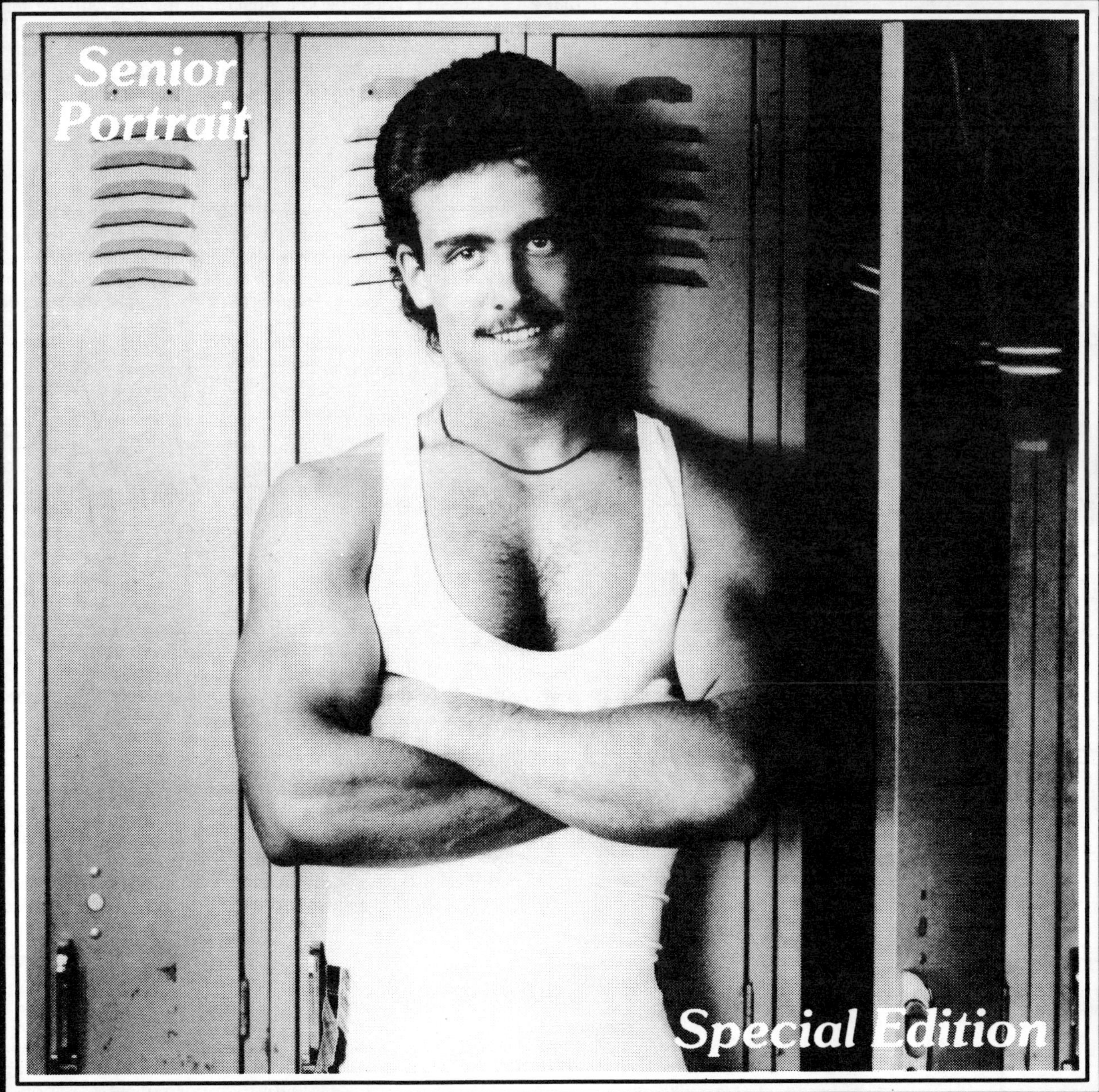

"Young Editions" has become a virtual trademark for our studio. In '89 we did this twelve page book of brags and testimonials in black ink on seventy pound gloss stock and mailed it flat. A great success.

The Main Street Photography Staff

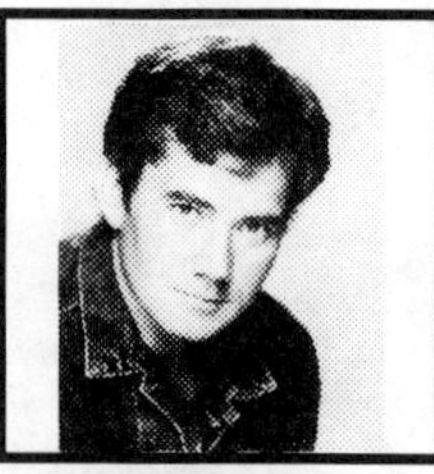

LARRY PETERS

Larry originally started photography as a hobby and his interest grew until he learned portrait technique by attending various schools. As a love for the photography profession grew, Larry developed a style all his own. He believes that each person is unique and should be photographed that way. Because of the tremendous acceptance of High School Seniors to his photography style, Peters' name has become known throughout the entire nation. He is actively sought by photography groups to teach senior photography. You can be sure that you're getting one of the best portraits available. Just ask someone who's had their portrait made by Peters.

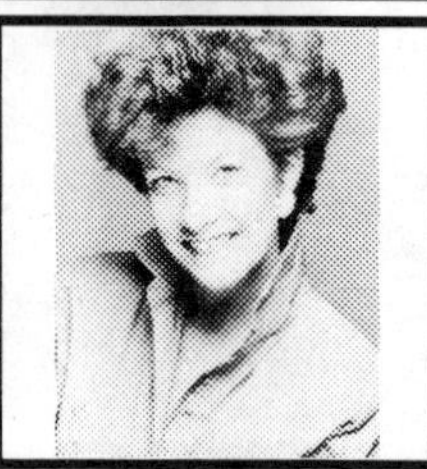

KAREN PETERS

Every business would fall apart without the proper organization and Karen gives her best here. She has a strong business background and knows how to solve problems and organize work. The studio is a family owned and operated business so there is a feeling of pride to everthing that the Peters' do. Karen believes that customer satisfaction is paramount. Too many times today, businesses are interested in collecting your money and never wishing to see you again. Karen believes a satisfied customer is the key to success and wants to make sure that everyone who purchases from the studio will get unequalled treatment.

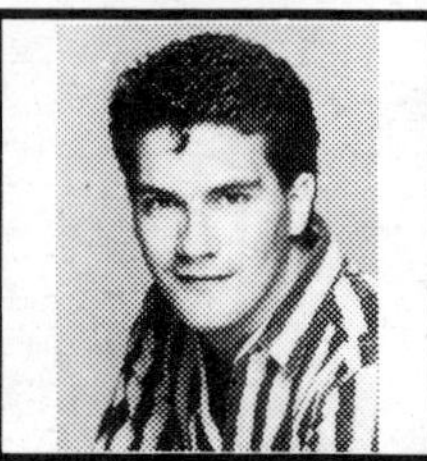

JEFF TABIT

As business grows, it needs more people to make it successful. These people must do all the jobs with the same care that the owners would. Therefore, Jeff was chosen with care. He is a college graduate and has worked directly with Larry for 6 years. Only after all of this experience has Jeff taken on a share of the photography. The result of his indepth training has produced a qualified portrait photographer. It's rare that a photography studio has 2 so talented photographers. Therefore, you are a winner. Two photographers keep you from being rushed through your session and the ideas they share give you even more variety.

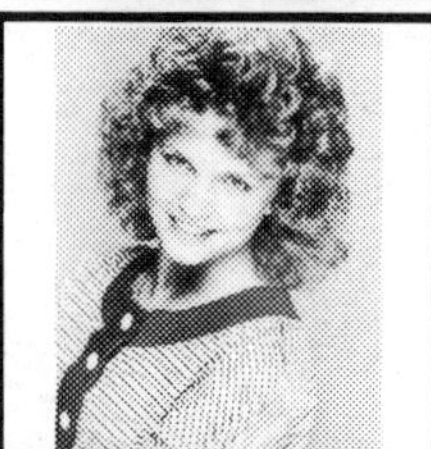

DIANE STAHL

Every business needs employees who are willing to adapt to whatever jobs are needed to be done and this is what Diane has done. Diane's primary responsibility is as a computer operator. Keeping track of appointments, mailing addresses and order tracking are all part of her daily activities. As the Peters' studio has grown, she has become an excellent make-up artist. Her skills in make-up have made for extremely satisfied customers. Diane will also be found as a sales representative and telephone receptionist. She has been employed by Main Street Photography for approximately 4 years.

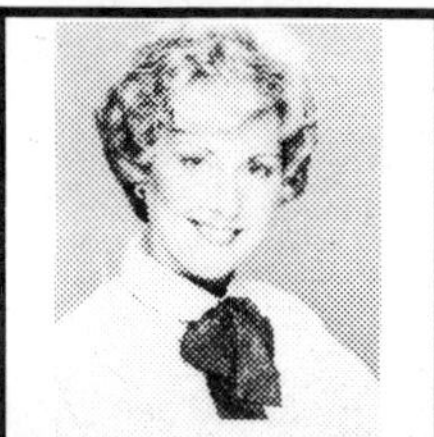

JOANN KERR

It is an incredible job to keep track of your orders as they are received from the lab. For this reason, the person assuming the responsibility of making sure that your order is correct, colors are good and everything is properly framed is a tremendous job. JoAnn has been handling this position for approximately 4 years. The quality of our finished images are JoAnn's responsibility and you can be assured that you will receive the upmost in quality. JoAnn also shares the responsibility of being a sales representative and telephone receptionist.

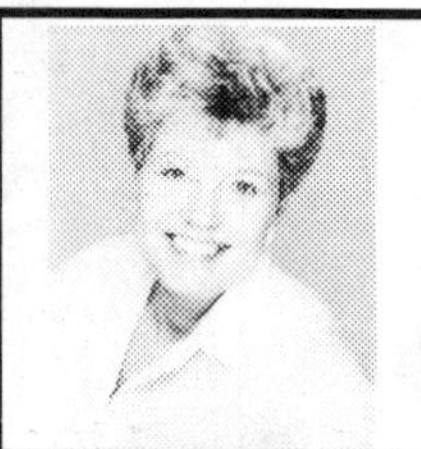

JOYCE BOLLINGER

Many students are very nervous about having their senior portrait made so it is one of Peters studio's primary jobs to relax everyone. This is Joyce's job. Joyce will probably be the first person who you come in contact with when you enter the studio and her smiling face and greeting will immediately let you know that you've chosen the correct studio for your portrait sitting. Friendliness is something that everyone appreciates and Joyce will make you feel right at home. She also shares the sales representative and telephone responsibilities.

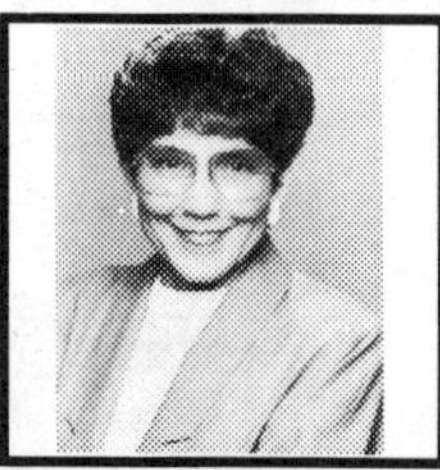

DORIS MINNER

There are many areas in the completion of a portrait that you are unaware. These behind the scene facits of a studio and their accurate completion is what makes a studio a good one. Doris has the responsibility of placing your portrait order. This involves making sure each order is retouched, cropped, sized and ordered correctly. This is the first step in the chain which ultimately gives you a quality finished product. Doris is also a sales representative and telephone receptionist.

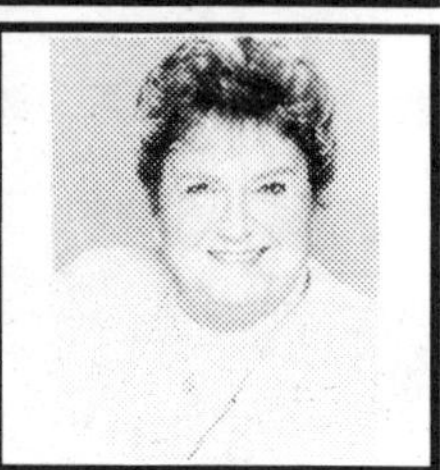

BEA MCNAMARA

Everyone wants their original photograph or previews to be available for viewing as soon as possible. Everyday, throughout the year, Peters receives hundreds of images that need to be sorted and placed in folios for viewing. Bea takes pride in her work and enjoys seeing all of the different poses that seniors do for their portrait sitting. Truly, each senior takes on a distinctive look and when the original previews arrive at the studio, Bea is the first one to view your image. It is her responsibility to notify each person that their photographs are ready. This is an exciting time for you and you can be sure that Bea gives that personal touch to all so that you get the best variety of poses in your folios.

Revolutionary New Video Equipment Tested By Peters

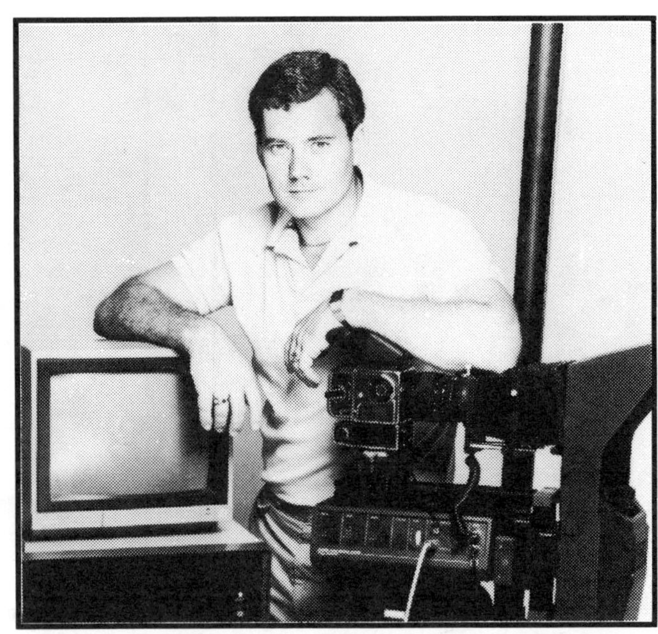

Because of Peters' reputation for variety and its known dependability, Main Street Photography was selected by Kodak to be one of 3 studios in the entire USA to test its new product.

Kodak has developed a new Video Imaging System that if made available to the professional photographer, will revolutionize the way portraits are created in the studio.

Here's how it works. As you have your portrait taken, the image is simultaneously recorded on a video disc and film at the same time. The fact that the image is being recorded on a magnetic disc permits the client being photographed the opportunity to view his session at the end of the sitting.

Many people who are in a hurry to meet a particular deadline will find this system a real source for time saving.

At the end of the photography session (indoor poses) we take the customer into a viewing room and let them pick the images that they wish to order from. (They are able to place their order the same day they are taken!)

Please realize that this is only a test of equipment. We will be testing from March through May.

As stated before, this is a new technique, if sold for public use, it will change the way a portrait studio operates. Instant images for viewing have been well received by all customers who have used the system.

The Peters' Studio is proud that Kodak selected them as a test sight. Because of the confidence the Kodak Company has displayed in their studio in the past 3 years confirms the fact that Peters' can be relied on to create the most unusual sittings available.

Peters

Listen To Your Friends And What They Feel About Peters Main Street Photography!!

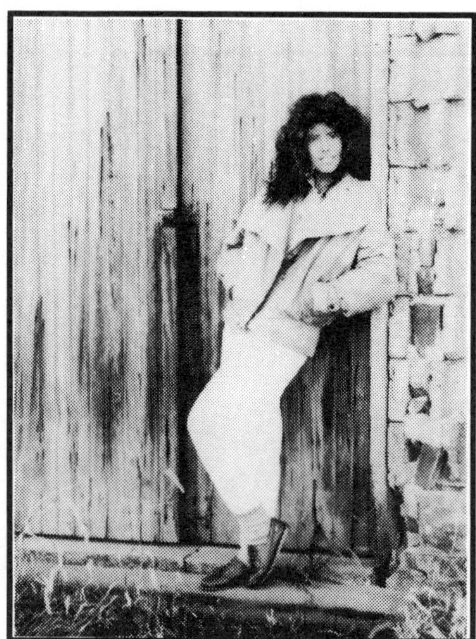

Brenda Eberhard—Westland

I selected Main Street Photography to take my senior pictures because they permit the student to express their individual personality and their photographer has the unique ability to capture that personality in the pictures.

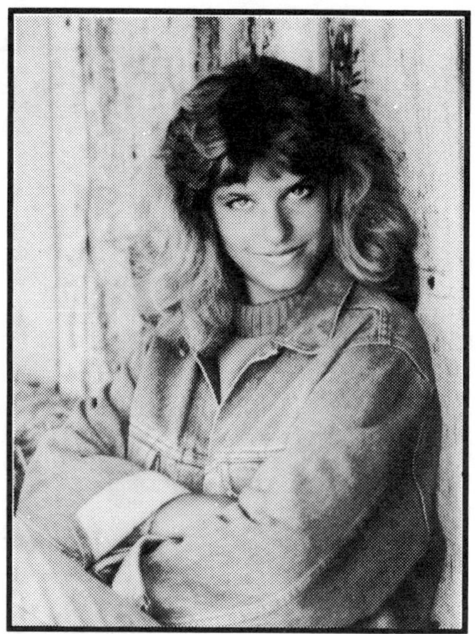

Kim Carter—West Jefferson

I chose Main Street Photography for my senior pictures because I'd seen their work and knew what a wonderful job they do. They are so professional and yet, they make senior pictures so much fun

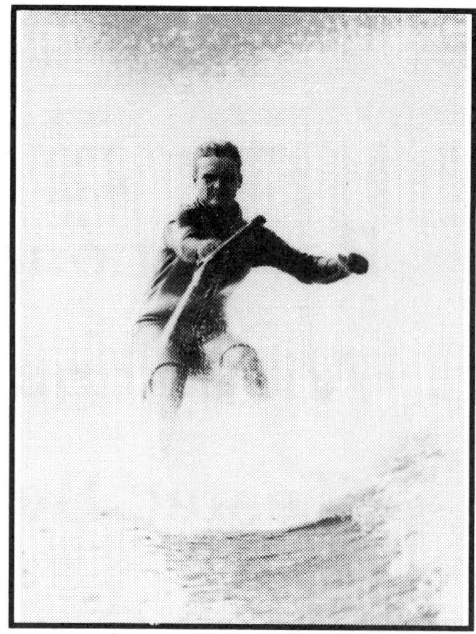

Aaron Orihood—Miami Trace

I was very pleased with my pictures. I wanted my picture taken of me water skiing and Larry took a lot of time to make sure they were great. Everyone compliments on what a wonderful job he did on my traditional and special poses.

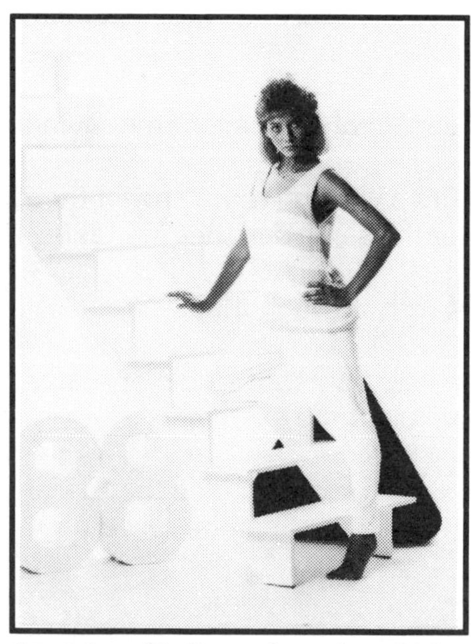

Jerri Ann McGee—Jonathan Alder

I came to Peters to have my pictures taken because I had heard they were the best and I wanted the best for my senior year. They did a terrific job and I know my family and I will enjoy my pictures for years to come.

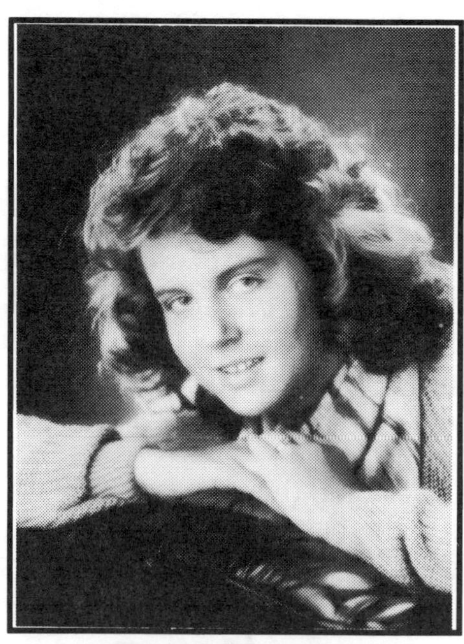

Laura Hyatt—Dublin

I chose Main Street Photography because they were original. I did not want my senior pictures to look like everyone else's. I am very happy with the results.

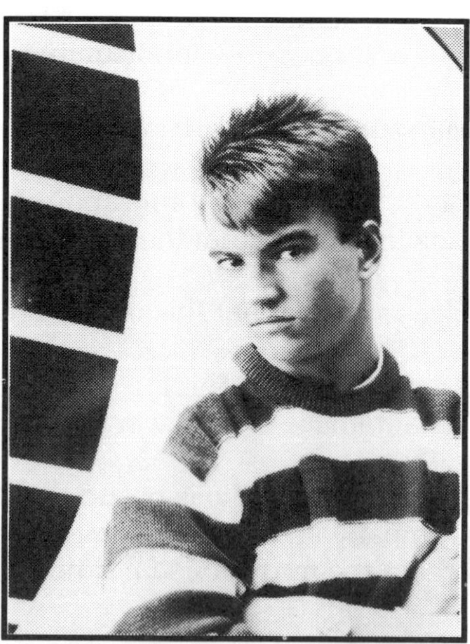

Matt Seesholtz—Hilliard

Main Street was recommended by older friends. I'm glad I went to Main Street Photography because Mr. Peters took time to get photos that didn't look like everyone elses. He made me feel comfortable and at ease.

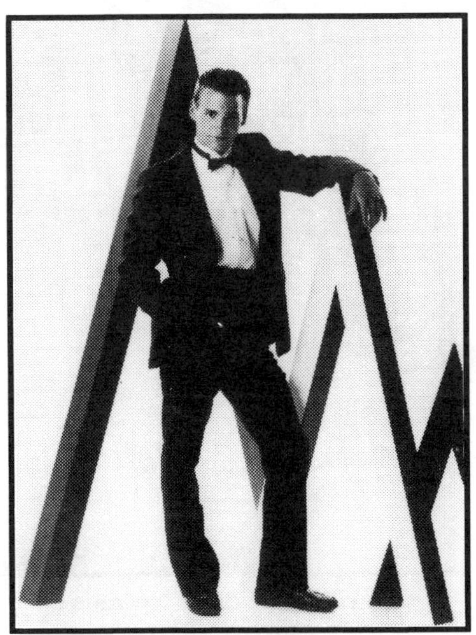

Chris Poglitsh—Worthington

I chose Main Street because I had seen all the variety in poses and backgrounds that Peters uses. I recommended him to my friends because of all the say-so I had in my sitting.

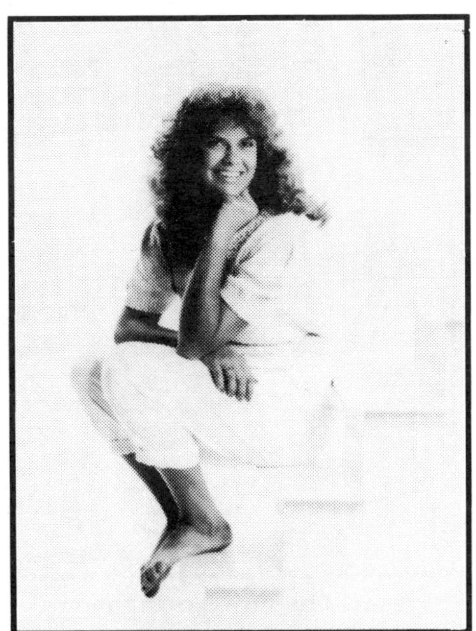

Amy Lathem—Franklin Heights

I chose Peters because of the originality and variety I had seen in his work. The personal and individual attention I received was appreciated. I recommend Peters!

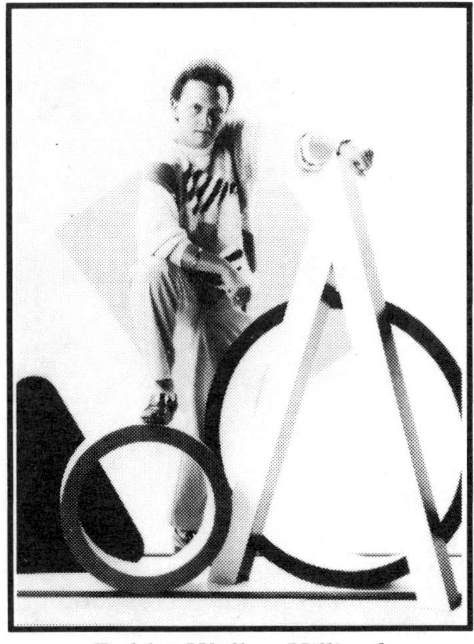

Robby Wells—Hilliard

The expertise and quality of the work at Main Street Photography was outstanding. Each customer is attended to individually and satisfaction at Peters is a main priority. Senior pictures are a major investment and Peters makes it worthwhile.

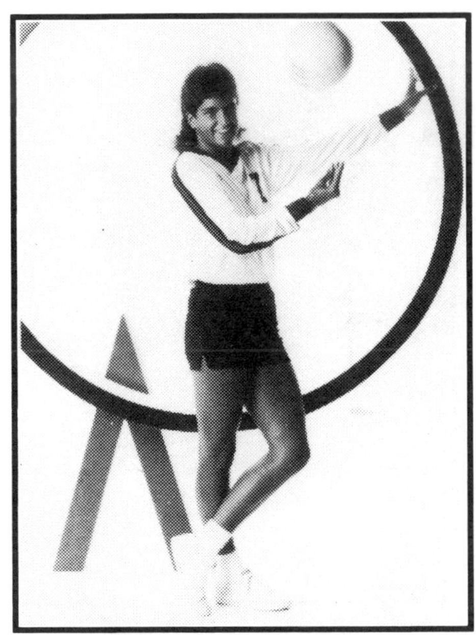

Debbie Alkire—Miami Trace

I personally chose Peters because I knew they would give me the best pictures possible, and they did. It was a lot of fun and they really treated me great. I encourage everyone to get their pictures at Peters.

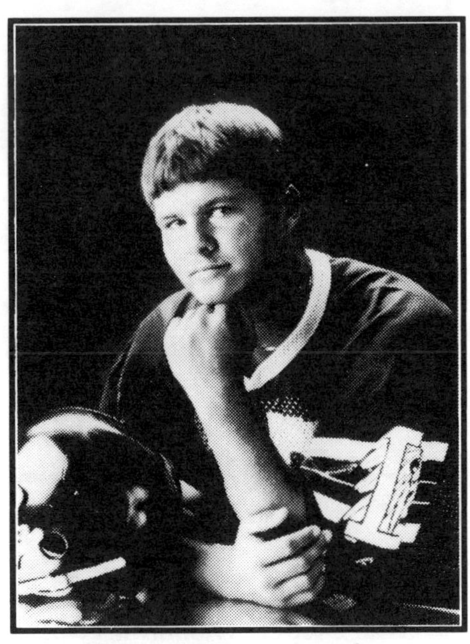

Dwayne Little—London

I chose Peters because he had previously photographed my sister and brothers. I knew he could do a great job!
Thanks Peters!!

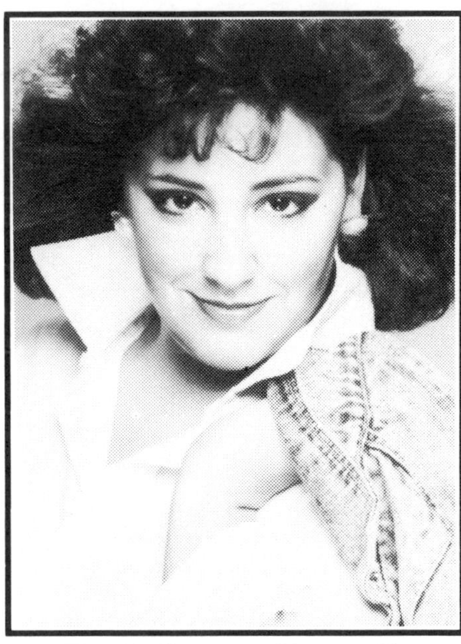

Tina Bollmann—Marysville

The reason I chose Peters was the pictures I saw before mine were all so different but they each captured that one certain personalality each of us had!

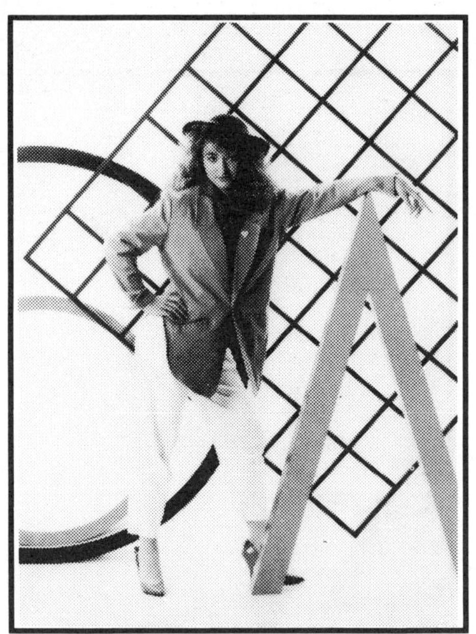

Robin Phillips—Westland
Curiosity was my reason for choosing Main Street Photography. I wanted to see if it was really possible to have a picture taken and be proud of it. So I went to Peters, and now I guess you could say I'm just another satisfied customer.

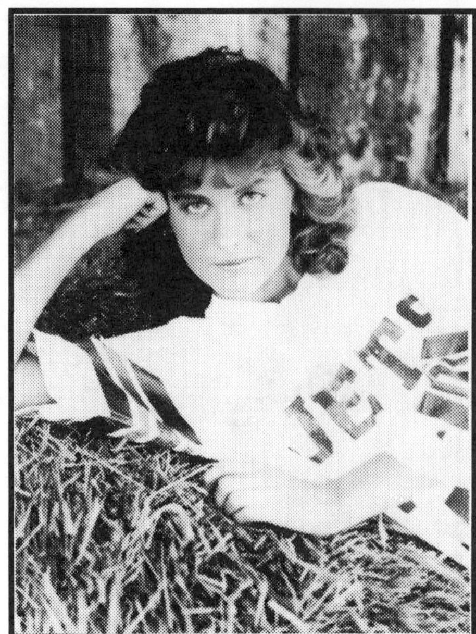

Alana Queen—Northeastern
I decided to go to Peters because I liked the pictures I had seen. He uses fun props, fun poses, and plays good music. It was like a modeling session; one pose this way, the next a little different. You can bring your own special props if you want. It went so fast but I had a lot of fun.

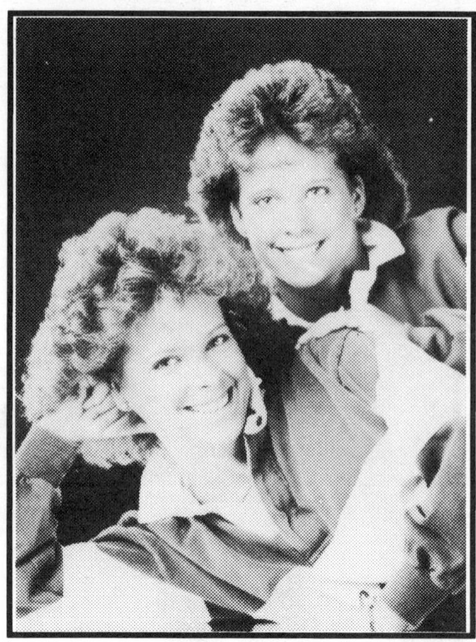

Tricia & Tonya Holmes
Grove City
Peters gives you exactly what you want in your senior pictures. Not only do you get a vareity of indoor pictures but also a variety of outdoor pictues. We would definitely recommend Peters to the class of '89.

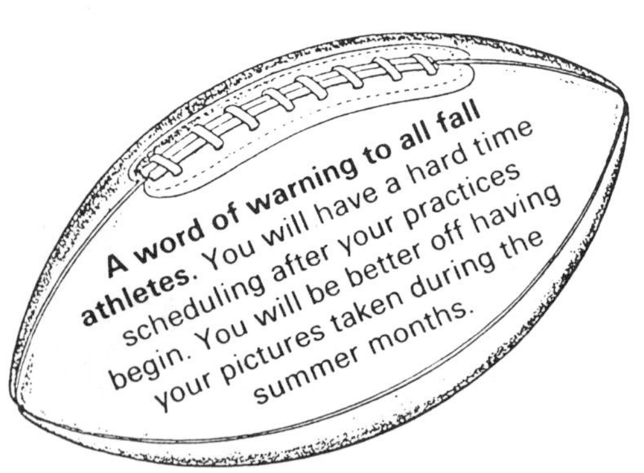

Schedule your appointment at your convenience. Hours: Mon-Fri, 9-5, Sat. 9-12. **Call 852-2731.**

Reserve your date if you want your appointment at a certain time. Scheduling is done on a first come basis and this year is shaping up to be a busy one.

Plan on being here at least an hour for your sitting. Some take longer than others.

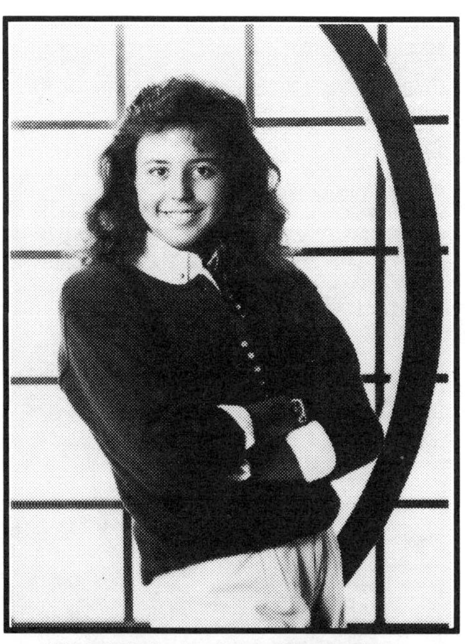

Kim Diebel—Hamilton Twp.
I chose Main Street Photography for their backgrounds and sittings. Unlike the usual studio with the basic two or three sets, Peters has a set for just about every mood. You can even request certain sets or bring in props to make your own. The people at Peters are great, they care about making your Senior pictures the best possible.

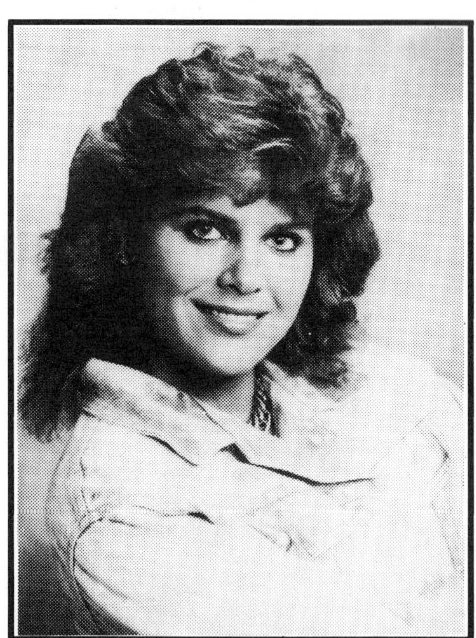

Elizabeth Rodgers
Springfield Northwestern
I chose Main Street Photography two years ago to have some modeling pictures taken. After seeing the great results, I knew that was where I would get my senior pictures taken. The end result was great senior pictures, plus modeling pictures that have won local, state and national awards.

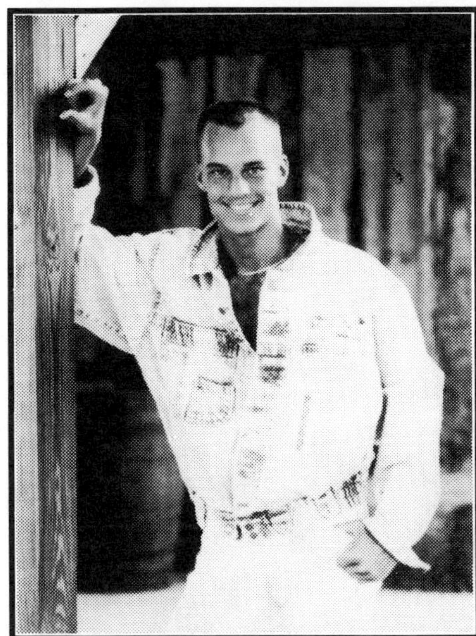

Kelly Bush—Hamilton Twp.

I prefer Peters because they had no restrictions on clothing or backgrounds. They allowed me to be myself and photographed according to my own personality, instead of staying with past year traditions for Senior pictures. I found the staff there so friendly and they made me feel very relaxed. I would, and have recommended them to my friends.

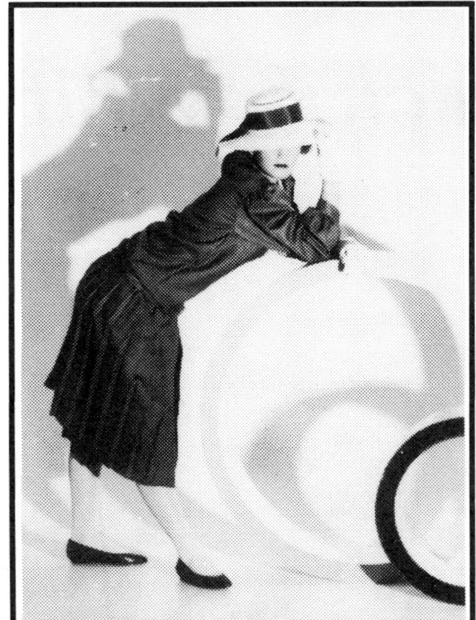

Christie Buckwalter—Urbana

I chose Peters for my senior pictures because of the personal attention you are given. At the time of my sitting, I felt that I was the center of attention and that the photographer's focus was completely on me. Also, at Peters you choose what you want and do as you wish. Both of these factors are important for pictures of any kind and were the reasons that drew me to Peters' for my senior pictures!

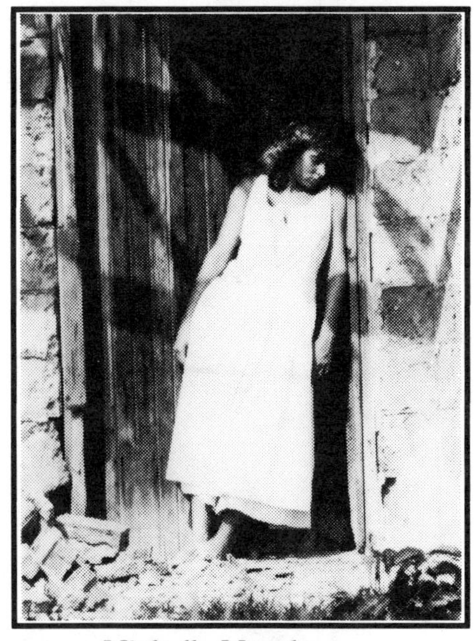

Michelle Mossbarger
Washington C.H.

I had seen other senior pictures taken at Peters and I thought you offered a wider variety of sittings and the pictures were of better quality! From what I had heard Peter's provide a comfortable atmosphere which made you feel at home and the photographers were friendly and fun to work with. I was very pleased.

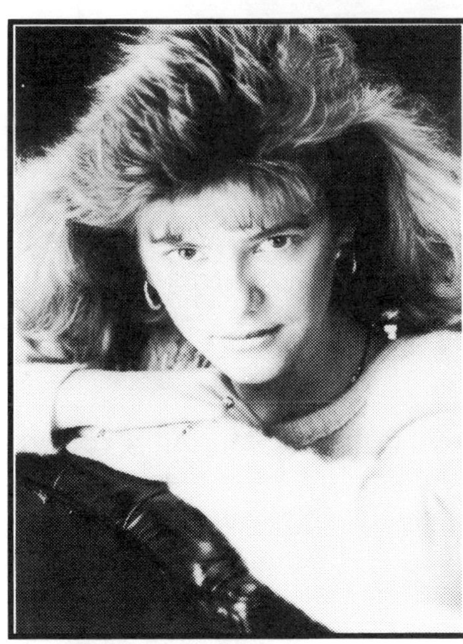

Kelli Hart—Columbus West

As a past representative for Peters', I had worked with Larry before. I knew Larry had a great imagination and would give my senior pictures that special care that everyone wants. He spent time with me and made every picture he took unique. My pictures turned out better than I imagined! My preview of my pictures was even great, they displayed any picture I wanted to see on an enlarged screen and explained every price and package down to the smallest frame. I'm glad I chose Peters' for my Senior Pictures, they made my Senior year something to look back on!

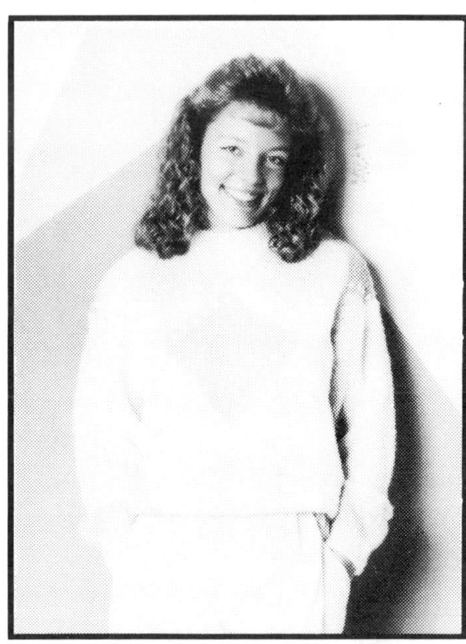

Cheryl Depugh—Miami Trace

I chose Main Street Photography for a number of reasons. First, senior pictures are a once-in-a-lifetime, so I wanted them to be the best they could be. I've seen the great quality of work Peters' has done on many of my friends and relatives pictures who have gone there. Peters' also has a very friendly staff and atmosphere which make getting your pictures taken a lot of fun. Another feature is Peters' originality. They create a style and look that is all your own, not just another pose like everyone else's. Main Street Photography did an excellent job on my senior portraits and I would highly recommend them to future seniors.

Black & White?

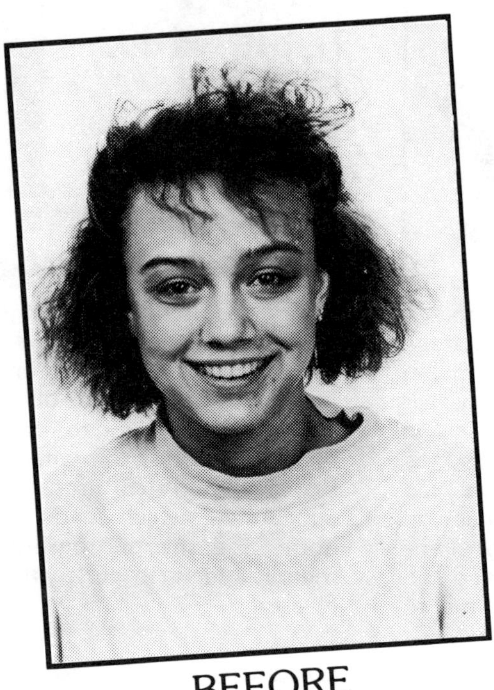

BEFORE

AFTER

Black & White?

Yes, black and white photography has never looked so good. A year ago we started a concept for high contrast black and white photography with seniors that has been sweeping the west coast as glamour photography for adults. This black and white photo session is definitely turning heads, its been attracting the attention of everyone who views it.

Through a heavy and corrective make up session, outstanding photography and close controls of photo finishing, Main Street Photography is satisfying every customer who has a black and white session. This session can give you several looks from a fashion look to a glamourous look. It's guaranteed to knock your socks off while providing a fun photo session. This session is not intended to take the place of a traditional color portrait, it is designed to give you an opportunity to have a new image created, a look you never even knew that you had. We suggest that you add it to one of the other sessions. This way you will have an even greater selection of previews from which to choose your finished order. Go ahead, have fun!! You definitely won't regret your efforts.

Making Your Dreams Come True

Peters black and white glamour pictures.

For the pictures you only dream of taking. Larry Peters can do it for you too. If you want the best pictures for professional use or just for the fun of it, and you thought you could never take good pictures before, come to Peters for the newest look of tomorrow. Its a lot of fun and the results are very rewarding.

Thanks again!!

Melynda Inks
Ready H.S. '88

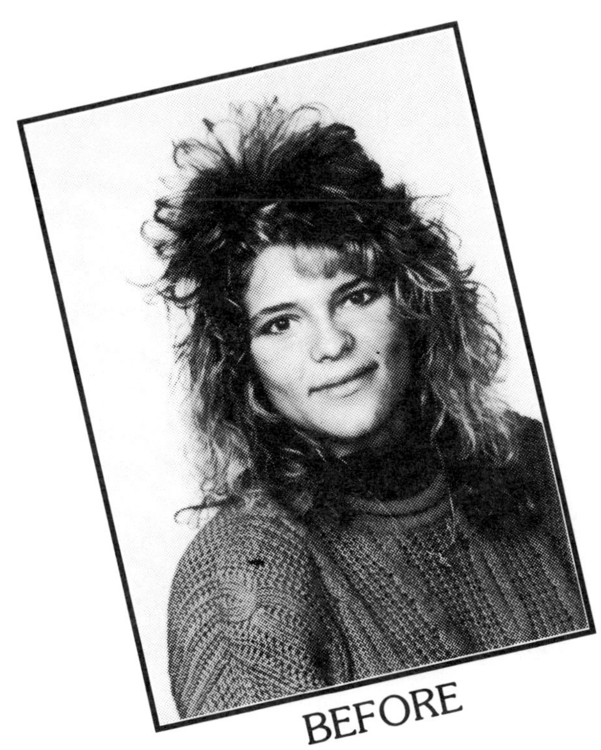

BEFORE

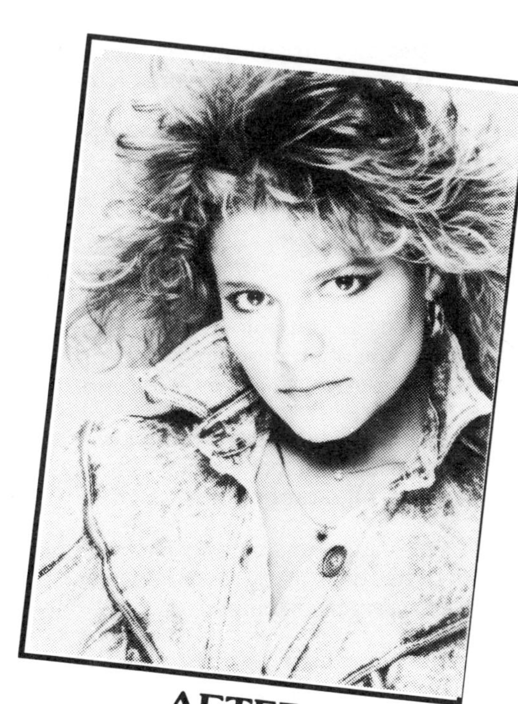

AFTER

Information That You Should Know

For the past few years, Kodak has developed an advertising program titled "For the times of your life", and for the first time ever they are now including Senior Portraits as part of their campaign.

Inorder to show contemporary posing on their brochure, Kodak contacted several nationally known senior photographers and asked them to submit photographs for consideration to be used in their flyer titled "A class act".

This brochure contains 11 different photographs of which 5 were images created by Larry Peters. The brochure is designed so any professional photographer can purchase it from Kodak and then use their own name and and studio logo on the rear cover so that they can use this attractive mailing piece to promote their own senior photographer.

Peters is very excited that they were asked to submit photographs for such a project and very pleased that so many images were selected for use in the flyer. By choosing Peters Main Street Photography you can be assured of receiving many of the best images available in the United States. Don't you deserve the best for your senior year.

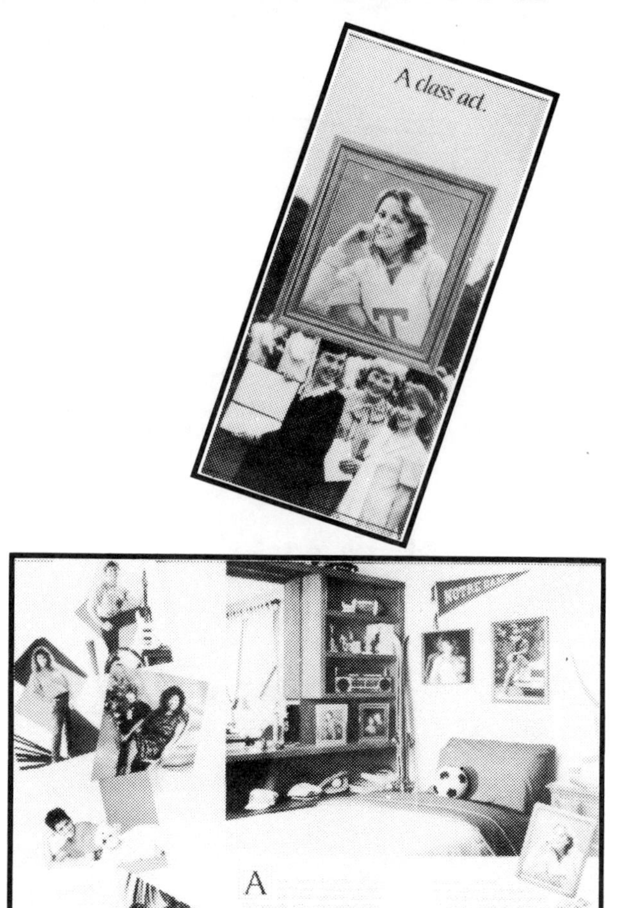

Read What Other Professionals Have To Say About Us?

"I was absolutely amazed by your ability for creating such striking and graphic backgrounds".
Glen Nakamichi Photography - Selma, California

"Peters Main Street Photography is a trend setter in Senior portraiture. His style is very fresh and innovative. I intend to use many of his creative posing ideas in my senior photography".
Ken Lunderby - Lunderby Photography-Buffalo, Minnesota

"I plan to use many of your ideas. I'm very impressed with your work and your studio".
Michael Bell - Cross Lanes - West Virginia

"Larry Peters' program on senior photography is a creative variety of high quality images that seniors can't pass up. His 'get out of the same old stuff' rut convention program is well presented and very professional in all respects".
Joanne and Jay Murray - Seattle, Washington

"I see thousands of senior portraits from photographer across the country and find Larry Peters to be one of the very best . . . He has a real knack for capturing the personality of today's seniors!"
Beth Castildi - Burrell Colour Labs., Crown Point - Indiana.

"Larry's photos are refreshing, dynamic and exciting. He is the most innovative photographer that I have seen in a number of years. I'm going to use lots of his ideas in my studio this year".
Lyle Huisken - Edgerton, Minnesota

"I must thank you for opening up my imagination. Putting your ideas and theory into practice in my own studio has freed me from what was becoming a dull and boring profession".
Don Chaffe - Primrose Studio, Reading, Pennsylvania

Effective - February, 1988

CAMERA CHARGES

Payable at Sitting Time Scheduled

Select the Proper One For You!!

I **THE SENIOR** .... **$15.00 + tax**

8-10 poses indoors, including head and shoulder, close-up, ¾ length, 1 additional clothing change (2 total). Time: - ½ hour.

II **THE DELUXE *"Our Most Popular"*** .... **$30.00 + tax**

18-20 poses, including 10 indoor and 10 outdoor. Head & shoulder poses, close-up, ¾ length, environmental in our garden setting, bring your imagination, up to 6 clothing changes (We'll help you pick the best 4 which are included in the sitting). Time: 1-1½ hour.

III **BLACK AND WHITE GLAMOUR**
"Our Newest" .... **$49.50 + tax**

Not intended to replace the color portrait, but to be a unique experience. Make-up session to be a corrective make over, 20 poses, 4 changes of clothing (Black and white prices on separate price list). Time: 2 hours

IV **COMBINATION BLACK AND WHITE AND COLOR** .... **$65.00 + tax**

10 poses in color to include traditional poses and unusual backgrounds PLUS 10 poses in black and white including a make-over for contemporary Black and White. 4 Clothing changes. Time: 2½ hours

V **LOCATION** .... **$60.00 + tax**

24-30 poses, including 10 indoor and 20 at your choice of location within 20 miles of London, 2 appointments required. Time: ½ hour studio, 1½ hours at location.

VI **JUST FOR THE FUN OF IT** .... **$2.00 per pose**
"Off The Wall" Poses **(minimum 5 poses) + tax**

Add to any 20 pose session. Bring clothing styles that you've always dreamed of, modeling poses or use our hats for ***"Off The Wall Crazy Poses"*** 2 Clothing changes per 5 poses. Time: additional ¼ hr. per 5 poses.

VII **THE 'ELITE' *"Our Very Best"*** .... **$110.00 + tax**

The Senior girl interested in the best we have to offer. First session begins with a color analysis of client to determine the best colors suited for her complexion. Second session is our make-up session in which we apply the correct colors and amounts for a photography session. Next, a hair stylist will enhance your present hair style or design a new look for your photo session. Last will be a photo session to remember, includes 10 out-of-door poses and 20 indoor poses. Special poses, lighting, fans and props that anyone serious about photography will appreciate. Two appointments required (6 clothing changes) Time: 2½-3 hrs.

LIFETIME GUARANTEED COLOR PHOTOGRAPHS

Peters Main Street Photography, Inc.
314 N. MAIN
LONDON, OHIO 43140

BULK RATE
US Postage Paid
LONDON, OHIO
Permit No. 27

Check Out The Savings

Money Saving Offer

$5.00 OFF

Your Portrait Order

Peters Main Street Photography, Inc.
314 N. MAIN
LONDON, OHIO 43140

1 Per Client ***Clip and Save***

Save On Frames

Present This Coupon And Save On Beautiful Frames

$15-$25 worth of frames .... **$3.00 off**
$26-$35 worth of frames .... **$5.00 off**
$36-$50 worth of frames .... **$7.50 off**
$51 & Over worth of frames .... **$10.00 off**

Does Not Apply To Sale Frames

Peters Main Street Photography, Inc.
314 N. MAIN
LONDON, OHIO 43140

1 Per Client ***Clip and Save***

YOUNG EDITIONS '90

Peters Main Street Photography

314 North Main Street • London, Ohio • (614) 852-2731

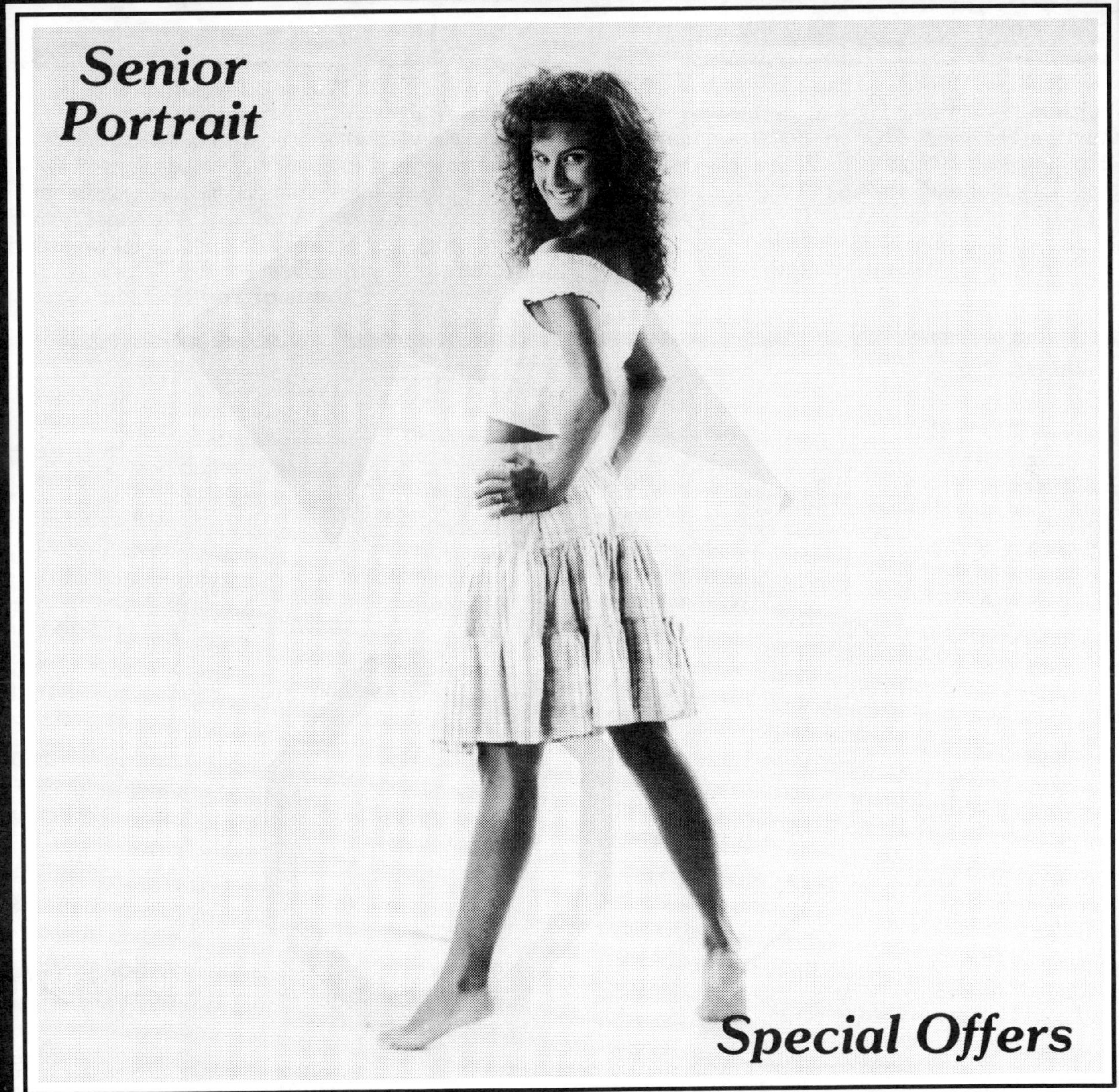

In 1990 we removed the two pages of brags, the two pages on b/w portraits, and some of the testimonials, but added a page for parents' comments, for a total of eight pages. Still a success.

What About The Parents Comments!

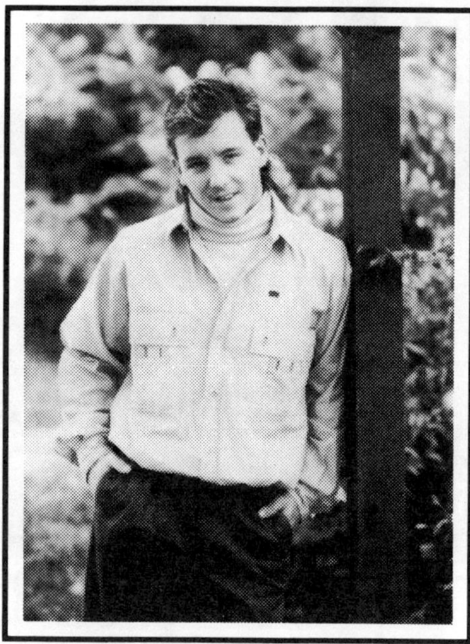

William Whited—Hilliard

We wanted our son photographed by you, because he is very special to us and you also treated him so special, it's more of a person to person thing with your studio. With all the beautiful landscaping you have that really makes the photographs even more special. You are really great people with your very special photography. You will be highly recommended by us!!

Parents Of William Whited

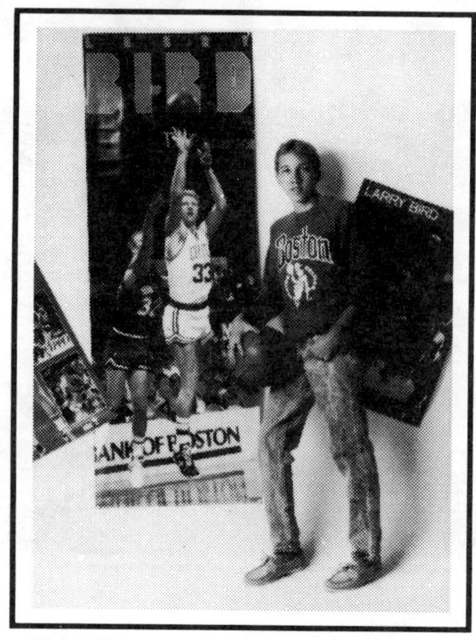

Todd Wilson—Nelsonville-York

We chose Mr. Peters to photograph our son's senior pictures because we were so pleased with our daughter's pictures that he photographed the year before. We were very impressed with the creativeness, friendliness and the amount of props used for so many different sittings. We chose Peters because your photographs are very unique. In fact we are so pleased with your work that we have arranged a family portrait sitting.

Parents of Todd Wilson

Peters

CAMERA CHARGES

Payable at Sitting Time Scheduled

LIFETIME GUARANTEED COLOR PHOTOGRAPHS

I **THE SENIOR** .... **$24.50 + tax**
8-10 poses indoors, including head and shoulder, close-up, ¾ length, 1 additional clothing change (2 total). Time: - ½ hour.

II **THE DELUXE *"Our Most Popular"*** .... **$30.00 + tax**
18-20 poses, including 10 indoor and 10 outdoor. Head & shoulder poses, close-up, ¾ length, environmental in our garden setting, bring your imagination, bring 6 clothing changes (We'll help you pick the best 4 which are included in the sitting). Time: 1½-2 hours.

III **BLACK AND WHITE GLAMOUR**
"Our Newest" .... **$55.00 + tax**
Not intended to replace the color portrait, but to be a unique experience. Make-up session to be a corrective make over, 20 poses, 4 changes of clothing (Black and white prices on separate price list). Time: 2 hours

IV **LOCATION (Color or Black and White)** .... **$75.00 + tax**
24-30 poses, including 10 indoor poses at the studio in color and 20 poses in color at your choice of location within 20 miles of London **or** 20 poses in Black and White (no make-up) within 20 miles London. Great for modeling, urban locations, alleys, beaches or wherever you would like to be photographed - 6 clothing changes. Time: ¾ hour at the studio, and 1½ hour at the chosen location.

V **COMBINATION COLOR AND BLACK & WHITE** .... **$80.00 + tax**
18-20 poses in color to include traditional poses and unusual backgrounds. 10 indoor and 10 outdoor (weather permitting) PLUS 10 poses in a contemporary black and white including a make-over for a real image change. 6 clothing changes - 30 poses. Time: 3 3½ hours

VI **JUST FOR THE FUN OF IT** .... **$2.00 per pose, (minimum 5 poses) + tax**
Add to any 20 pose session. Bring clothing styles that you've always dreamed of, modeling poses or use our hats for ***"Off The Wall Crazy Poses"*** 2 Clothing changes per 5 poses. Time: additional ¼ hr. per 5 poses.

VII **THE 'ELITE' *"Our Very Best"*** .... **$95.00 + tax**
The Senior girl interested in the best we have to offer. First session begins with a color analysis of client to determine the best colors suited for her complexion. Second session is our make-up session in which we apply the correct colors and amounts for a photography session. Last, a photo session to remember, including 10 outdoor poses and 20 indoor poses. Special poses, lighting, fans and props that anyone serious about photography will appreciate. Two appointments required (6 clothing changes) Time: 2½-3 hrs.

Because You're Only A Senior Once!
The Very Best We Have To Offer!!
AN **ELITE** PORTRAIT SESSION - **$95.00**

Includes:

★ A color analysis session as a pre-appointment consultation to determine your best colors and the clothing you should wear.

★ A makeover for color photography.

★ 30 incredible poses, and an unbelievable 6 clothing changes.

If you don't know what's best in make-up and clothing, this ones for you!!

Why Take Chances . . . Do It Right!

Peters Main Street Photography, Inc.
314 North Main Street
London, Ohio 43140
(614) 852-2731

LIFETIME GUARANTEED COLOR PHOTOGRAPHS

Peters

BULK RATE
US Postage Paid
LONDON, OHIO
Permit No. 27

Senior Hot Line - 1-800-446-1922

There are other promotions, of course, but the important thing to remember is to not build yourself up as being a great photographer or as being the offical school photographer. To be honest, seniors don't care. Their question is, "What do I get out of the photography session?" We demonstrate this with outstanding sample photographs and we reinforce it with a money-saving offer on the mailing piece.

Last but not least, you need to stir them to action with your mailing pieces by giving them a deadline. Challenge them to participate and design your literature to reflect the professional image you want to project. Use this as a guideline for the first year, then improve on your ideas the second year by making everything fit your particular marketing situation. I do suggest, unless you are a good writer, that you not change these pieces the first year because the contents can be ruined by what only seems to be a minor change or a better idea. This "better idea" can easily distort the message the mailer was designed to convey.

Much, much more could be said on direct mail, and I strongly suggest a visit to the library or closest book store to get more literature on direct mail marketing. You will be amazed at what is avialable and the ideas you can adapt to use in your studio.

The key points to remember about direct mail advertising are:

1. Do it repetitively. One flyer will do no good.
2. Offer them something to motivate them into action now. You must give them a reason to call you for an appointment.
3. Put a final date on your offer. A deadline suggests urgency and this should get students to call.
4. Each succeeding mailer should vary in size, shape and color from the previous one. Use an envelope this time, a postcard the next, or go from black and white to color.

I suggest a studio spend approximately five percent of its gross business for advertising. The majority of this budget should go into direct mail because it reaches the clients directly and is cheaper than any other form. Direct mail is not the easiest form of advertising because it requires folding, stapling, stuffing, counting and addressing, but the time and effort taken will be directly related to the amount of business produced. Go after what you can afford and the amount you want but also realize that only one and one-half percent (on average) of the people you contact are going to respond to your mailing pieces.

If you are the new photographer in town, start locally but regularly. As your skill as a photographer improves, the number of clients you mail your literature to should grow also.

When you are building a photography business, if you sink all your funds into equipment and facilities and leave little for promotions - especially direct mail - you are designing a business that is sure to fail. I suggest you develop the marketing campaign and then worry about the extra equipment when you have the money to spend on it.

DESIGNING YOUR OWN MAIL PIECES

The mechanics involved in designing your own mail pieces vary, so get a book on layout and paste-up from the art supplies store; it will tell you much that you need to know before you start.

When you are beginning, the cheapest way to prepare your ads is probably the best. I suggest the use of transfer lettering (obtainable at any art store and many stationers), a carbon ribbon typewriter and black and white images. Graph paper makes a good layout sheet if the lines are light blue so they disappear when the printing plate is made.

Colored ink can be effective as an eye catcher. Fine line tape (also from an art store) can be used to outline and enhance your copy. After you finish preparing the layout, take the originals to a quick print shop and you are on your way.

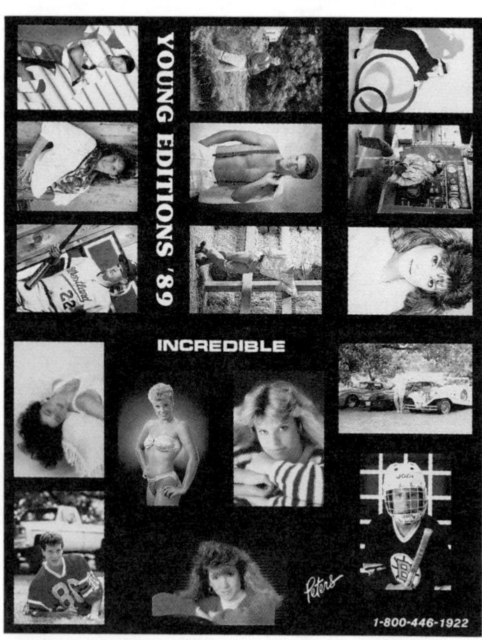

To take advantage of lower printing prices, we often lay out our mailers so several can be printed on one larger sheet. This one was printed on 8½x11 postcard stock, cut into oversize 5½ cards and mailed as two distinct mailings.

After you outgrow this, the next step may be preparing your literature on a word processor. You can control borders and titles and easily correct errors on the screen before you print out a finished copy. A laser printer will print out copy that is indistinguishable from typesetting, but it's an extremely expensive item and I would not recommend its purchase until you can fully justify it, which will probably be never. Many people who use a laser printer, don't own one; they use a friend's or they take their floppy disc to a shop that will print it for a fee. One final way is to take the disc to a commercial typesetter who can work from disc - often receiving it by telephone through the use of a modem. This usually costs about 30% less than typesetting keyed in by an operator, yet it is identical to the hand- typed version.

A simple system I employ for making color layouts is to order selected color yearbook glossy prints and then to arrange them in a pleasing fashion on a piece of clear acetate. This sheet is send out-of-town to a printer such as McGrew Color Graphics in Kansas City, Missouri, which specializes in volume color printing. They gang-print your job with other similar work which greatly reduces the cost and saves you a bundle. We have been printing two or three different offers on a single sheet of 8½x11, then having them cut apart for the individual mailings.

Preparing mailing pieces like this permits you to have several full color mailers at the cost of just one printing job. This method is extremely cost-effective; you can impress your clients with three different color mailings for the price of just one. Most of the color printers, however, have a minimum order of 3000 8½x11" pieces, so be sure you have a need for 3 x 3000 mailers before you design and purchase this many.

Ask around as several color printers have a minimum of 1000; although the per piece price is higher, it's still cheaper than throwing out 2000 at the end of the year.

EXHIBITS

A great place to exhibit your final products is on the walls of your studio, but only those who come into your studio can appreciate them there. Doesn't it make a lot more sense to get those images in front of the people who are potential customers? Here are a couple of exhibit ideas which are very effective for senior photographers; they all should be used at one time or another.

FAIR EXHIBITS

In this country and especially in the Midwest, the County Fair is the place where many students hang out, spending their summer evenings visiting with friends they haven't seen since school was dismissed for the summer. We discovered that fairs are a neat place for promoting our newest ideas in senior or other types of photography. An effective display (background) can be easily assembled, covered with Velcro, and lighted externally to show off your photography.

Of course, any exhibit at a fair must be attended. Someone needs to be there to hand out offers, flyers and business cards, and to answer the questions of potential clients. The people you staff your exhibit with should be both knowledgeable and personable so you get maximum impact from your presence at the Fair.

We frequently include an album full of selected sample portraits on a table for viewing. I believe the album is more effective than a slide display from a rear projection system. Prospective customers will leaf page by page through these albums at their leisure and once they start looking at your samples, they will almost always go through the entire album. Projected slides or a video shown on a TV screen have no definite and foreseeable ending and people walking by your exhibit are less likely to stand and watch because they are not sure how long it will continue. An album, however, has a definite beginning and an equally definite end and passersby can quite accurately figure the time needed to look at all the pictures.

Large prints of your most unusual images are vital for attracting attention. Take care in selecting these portraits because they project your business image. Of course, a drawing for a door prize, or a sign up sheet for information will provide you with names, addresses and phone numbers you can follow up as you seek to book an appointment.

It may be a good idea to pass out cards offering discounts on sitting charges. Complimentary sitting certificates distributed to selected persons will clearly show that you want to do business with them.

Most counties have fairs and you can rent a booth, normally a space ten by ten feet, for your display. The fee is usually nominal. Call the manager of your local fair for further information.

COURTESY CARD

This card entitles

____

to a Deluxe sitting with my compliments.

Offer expires ____________

MALL EXHIBITS

A progressive shopping mall is always on the lookout for high quality exhibitions and if your approach to the management is properly done, an exhibit may cost you nothing at all. Whether or not you can get in free, a mall is a great place to exhibit.

My wife came up with a great idea that has been a valuable asset to our mall exhibits. The reason this idea is so great is that while you display the best of your work in this exhibit, your customers foot the bill.

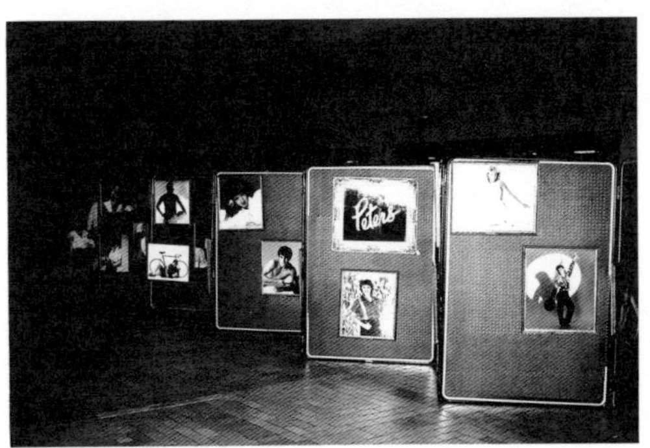

Here is how it works: early each morning before our employees arrive I look at all the preview prints which came from the printer the day before, and I select the images that I believe to be my best work. Then I copy these proofs on our plain paper copier and write the names and addresses of the students and the schools they attend on this sheet of paper.

When we are in the midst of photographing hundreds of seniors, we are too busy to work with these portraits, so I just put them in a file basket until the senior season is over. At that time, we take out these rough proofs, note the names and write a letter to each one. In this letter we enclose the copied proof and a special offer on a twenty by twenty-four sample print at a sharply reduced price. We don't make any money on these because this price is about fifteen dollars over the actual print cost, but we get tremendous advertising mileage out of them. The gimmick is that they get a big, handsome print for very little money, while we get to use them in our mall display first: the kids don't take delivery until the end of the exhibit.

Making a lot on each print is not our aim. The object of all this is to mount a great display of photographs that represent our normal, everyday work which I have selected from my daily creations. This becomes a tremendously effective advertising vehicle, yet the cost to us is nil because the students pay for the prints.

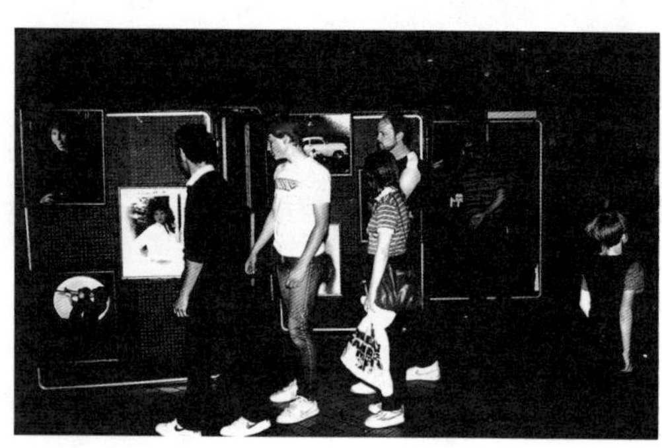

The first year we did this I took a few of the better portraits to a local mall office to see the manager and suggested a display honoring the graduating seniors from the area. He was very impressed with the concept and was completely open and receptive to having the exhibit in his mall. This display lasted for three days, although I would have preferred longer; I would also like to have shown it over the Memorial Day weekend.

Incidentally, all the prints in our exhibits must be pre-paid so we don't have the expense of a lab bill on this many large prints. The last two years we've had a fifty percent response rate to our invitation to be in the show, which works out to approximately seventy- five photographs. An exhibit this size can project a great image for your studio just by sheer numbers, but our senior display keeps growing each year. We are now at the point where the kids ask how they can be included in our exhibition. Now that's a successful promotion! Although we have done this only with our seniors, I believe this kind of exhibit can be worked anywhere with any type of portraiture. Give it a try: I know you'll like what it does for the bottom line.

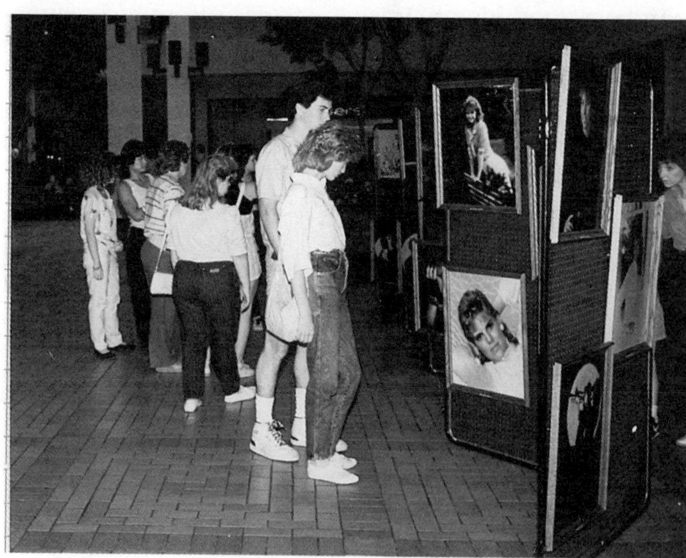

AUDIO-VISUAL PRESENTATIONS

An audio-visual program has got to be one of the best promotional devices available to the professional photographer. Through such a program you can generate enthusiasm, show variety in posing and background and give potential clients information they will remember long after they leave the studio.

This type of presentation is best done with two projectors to show your slides. The show itself should be managed by a programmable dissolve unit and a taped narration backed up by exceptional music of the type you perceive as best for the purpose. You can use the same images in your slide presentation as you used (or would use) in the print exhibit, samples of your best work from your daily proofings. This, just as with the print display, must be a presentation which truly shows your best work.

I recommend you divide the presentation into four areas:

1. INTRODUCTION
   a. Start the musical background with a short song that has a fast beat, preferably a current song of considerable popularity. This should catch and hold the audience's attention long enough so you can tell them in your recorded narration how today's portraits reflect the way people look at themselves, their friends and family. Then, as you switch to softer music, the announcer says, "Now is the time to show them at their best, to create an image that will last a lifetime, one of an exciting person - full of life, ready to grasp the next few years, anxious to snatch all the good things life has to offer."
   b. The images on the screen at this section should be varied to show what lies ahead in the program and the music and narration must be of top quality. If you try to save a few dollars on the recording with a do-it-yourself approach, you may destroy the entire mood you want to create. Here's a suggestion: most radio announcer-deejay types do freelance work, so pick out one who has a good voice and ask what the charge would be to create the excellent music and narrated program you need. You will probably be pleasantly surprised at how inexpensive it can be; most deejays can use the station's equipment and record library to make a high quality product, so the cost need not be excessive.
2. TRADITIONAL PORTRAITS

   This section, of course, will include the poses students might expect to see, poses that are the usual yearbook head and shoulder poses. Keep this section of your presentation short, perhaps ten to fifteen images, because these are not the poses that will motivate the kids to come to you for their senior pictures. After all, these are the things every other photographer does. You should include three-quarter length poses, draped poses, poses with the bookcase background, or any other poses which fit the pattern of a traditional senior portrait in your part of the world. Drop the music to a little more mellow sound, and the commentary might say, "Traditional poses are designed to picture you as a mature adult. Often parents, grandparents, and yearbooks prefer this type of a pose because it presents a dignified senior at the time of graduation. You should know your yearbook deadline, because you do not want to be left out. What good is a class portrait with even one person missing? Enjoy the traditional poses and get even more ideas for your own portrait session."

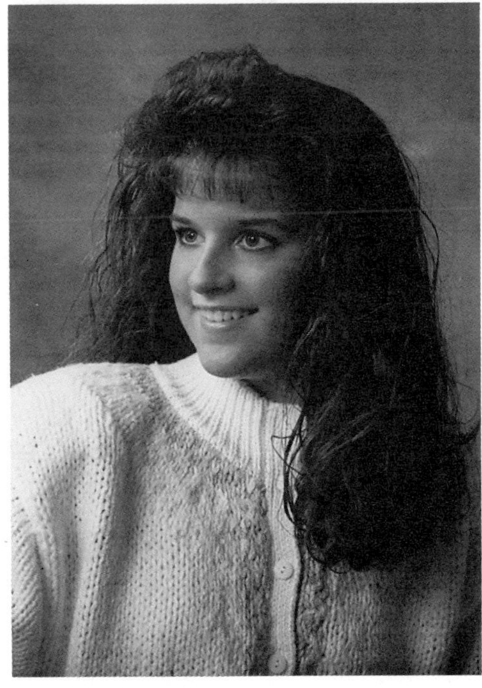

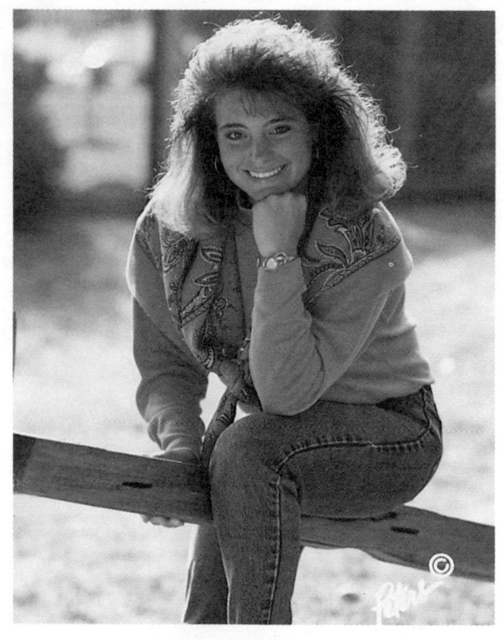

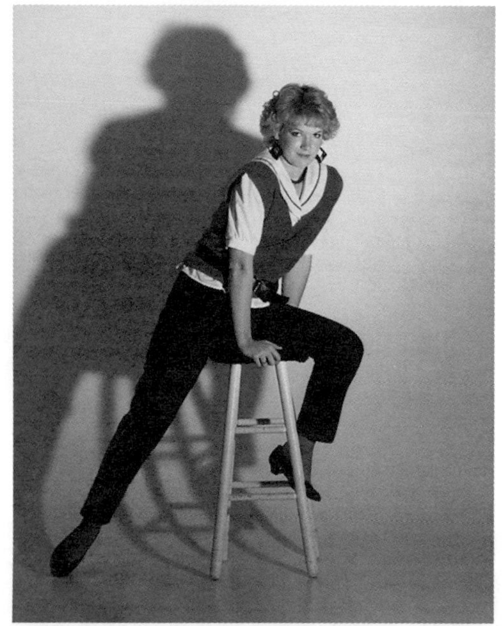

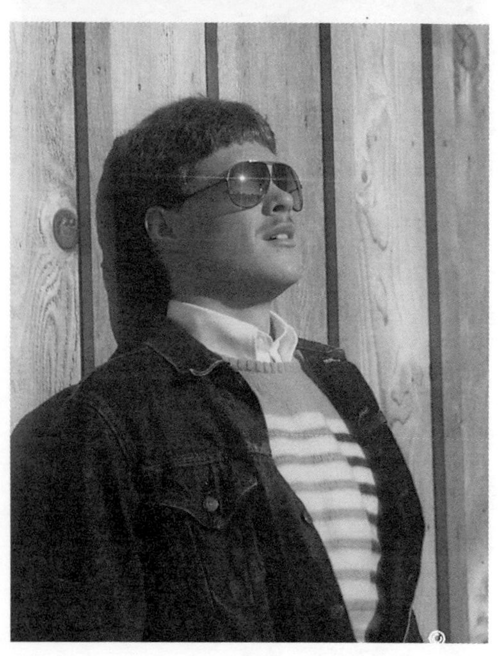

3. OUTDOOR PHOTOGRAPHY

   In the Midwest the idea of being photographed in the outdoors and close to nature has been something high school seniors have embraced with joy. In presenting this part of the program, continue playing the same song as in the traditional section, but lower the sound level as the announcer says: "Yes, the outdoors. For those who want something a little extra, the casual setting of outdoor photography. Let us portray a relaxed you where you can be yourself, so bring props that relate to your likes and hobbies. Just watch as you see what outdoor photography can do for you." This section should be a little longer and include location photos, automobiles, trees, grass, crazy painted walls, swimming pools, or any other shots that depict your studio's attitude toward a contemporary outdoor senior portrait.

4. WHAT IS REALLY HAPPENING?

   This section is where you really start to sizzle. Show your newest, most unusual photography, even the really crazy stuff. The announcer may introduce this section as, "We're still going. We've created more backgrounds, props and poses to show the real you. So just sit back and see what letting go and enjoying a Senior Portrait session is all about. Be yourself or create the image you want to become. Remember it's up to you. Live out your fantasies or create an image that you have always dreamed of becoming." The music is definitely upbeat. I used a J. Geils Band song titled, "Freeze Frame." This song is a good mover, a real toe tapper. This should be the largest section of your show because it will demonstrate your unique style and your creativity to show at their best.

5. THE CLOSING

   We usually stop with the "What Is Happening" section, but have the announcer at the end of the song say something like: "Well, it is up to you to make your decision about the image you want for your senior portrait. Yes, only at Main Street Photography have we got it all, from traditional to bizarre. Call today, don't put it off, this will be the most rewarding photo session that you have ever had."

Here's an example of a good commentary - from start to finish - for your slide show:

"You're fast approaching one of the most memorable years of your life and we're prepared to help you enjoy it! Over the past few years we've been changing the way seniors look at themselves, their school, and their friends. Now, for this reason, we've expanded our senior portraits to include many things in your life that are important to you. Sit back and enjoy our Young Editions, a program with ideas for you. Take special note of how clothing and props make each person truly unique. Now these are the things that will really set your portrait apart from other students'. You are unique, the only one like you, so why shouldn't your portrait sitting be that way, too?

"Let's go with the basics. Traditional head and shoulder portraits represent a formal presentation of your high school days. They're important because parents, grandparents, and yearbooks enjoy traditional views of the graduating senior. Be sure to know your school's deadline so you won't be left out! What good is a class portrait with even one person missing?

"Now, let's go for something extra, the outdoors! Main Street Photography can add another dimension to your image. Many students prefer the casual look of outdoor photography, the relaxed posing, and the fact that you can use any prop you want. Now, don't get caught by bad weather; you should schedule your outdoor portrait in the summer before school takes all your spare time. There's good color until October first, but don't put it off, you may miss out! Let's take a look at what's in store for those who choose outdoor photography.

"Starting to get interested? Well we're still going, we've added more new props and poses to make your portraits look even better. Your class is truly going to benefit from our experience and new additions. Just enjoy for a few minutes what unique backgrounds can do for your portrait. Remember, many students have school-related activities they want to see in a few portraits.

"It's time, people are fun, they enjoy life and all the new things it has to offer, so jump on board, let's create that fantasy world for you and that someone different you've thought of becoming. Have fun with your portrait sitting! Many of you are interested in modeling so we've added clothing consultations, makeup, and hair styling to our best sitting. Just ask, they're available!

"Your possibilities are endless! With our ideas and yours, you'll have the portrait experience of a lifetime. How can you help but be totally excited? There's more in store from traditional to bizarre, and only at Main Street Photography."

Where do you use such a program? We have been able to show this program in the high schools where we have contracts. I have never had a great deal of luck in showing the program in non-contract schools, but if I conducted or lectured in photography classes or even some family living classes, I know the instructors would easily give me permission to show the program to their students.

Another group we show this program to is school representatives and their parents at our ambassador meeting. This is the key that has inspired parents to get behind their children and push them to collect names so the kids will get a free photo session. It also shows the students the different clothing styles that are best for senior portraits, it gives them ideas for props and it makes the Ambassador photo session more rewarding.

Here's another use for such an audio-visual presentation: a photographer friend shuts down his camera room one hour a week and schedules all of the seniors who have appointments for the next two weeks to come to view his ideas about what constitutes senior portraiture. He tells me that most of the students who view his work prior to their photo sessions are better prepared for it. The ideas from the program open their thinking and thus enhance their photo sessions by generating greater excitement. In the end, the result is larger orders and that's not bad, is it?

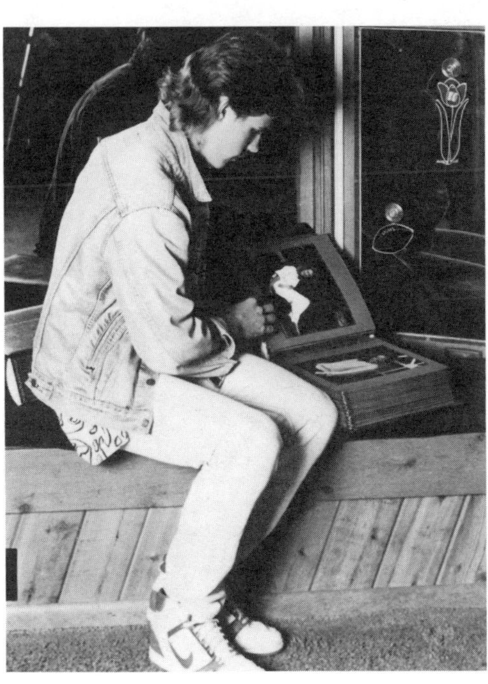

DISPLAY ALBUMS IN YOUR STUDIO

One of the easiest yet most effective ways to promote your photography is to have photographs for clients to look at. A few years ago, when we decided to take the 8x10s off the walls, we put them into albums with SENIOR PORTRAITS stamped on the front. It is hard to say how frequently these albums are looked at, because almost every person who comes to our studio is attracted to them like a magnet. I believe they draw people to look because they want to see if their own photographs are there. I can almost guarantee that once people start to look, each page keeps them right there. I guess they don't want to miss anything.

I have tried showing slides in a carousel at different funtions and find that clients are not sure how long they will have to stand and

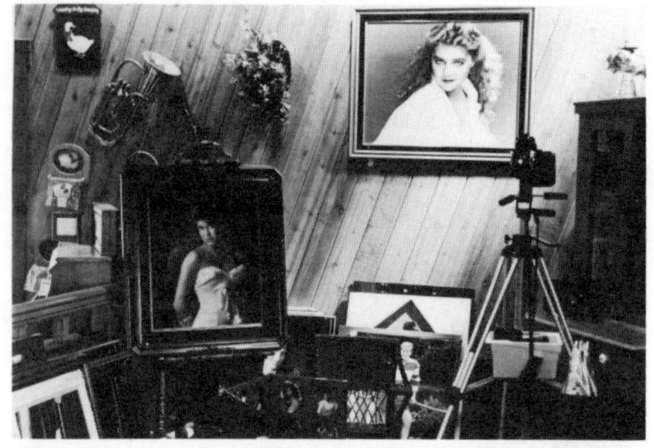

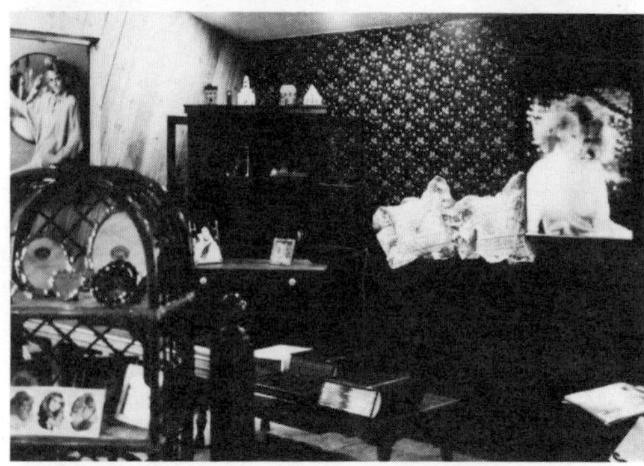

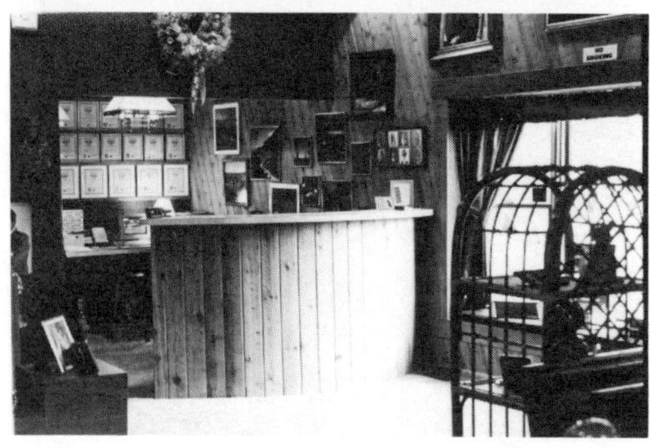

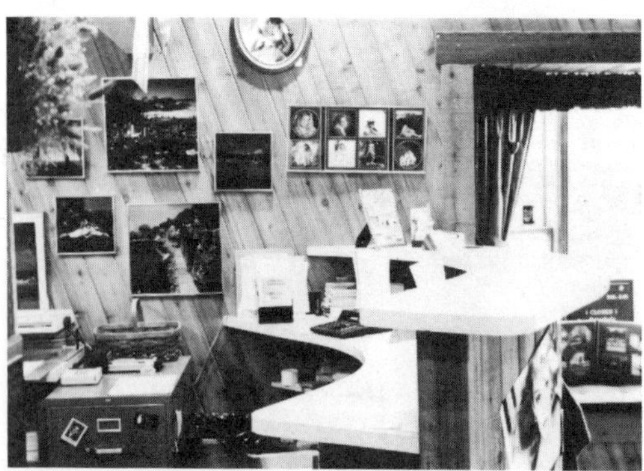

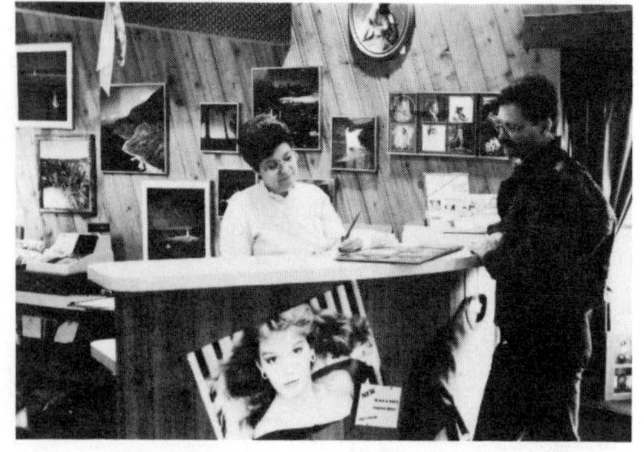

watch a slide presentation. With an album they can see how far it is to the end, look at their own pace and enjoy a great variety of ideas in posing, props, and backgrounds. We are now using four albums that hold eighty 8x10s each.

We have used these albums outside the studio in mall or fair displays and they have the same irresistible attraction. They are fun to change and during the senior season I am constantly changing these images to show what is current and new.

YOUR STUDIO DECOR

Of course, there is much to consider when you select the type and style of decor for your studio. One thing that is rarely mentioned (but which needs to be stressed) is CLEANLINESS. I have visited studios in many different parts of the country, and I find they truly reflect the personalities of the photographer. I mean if you are an organized person, your studio will immediately appear as a neat organized place to those who come through your door. Clutter, unframed pictures, frames stacked everywhere, general lack of neatness and order, however, all erode that critical first impression of your studio.

The types and sizes of photography displayed on your walls will immediately tell people a great deal about the photography available at your studio. Old, faded photographs, photographs that display people in dated clothing, and no print larger than 11x14 all demonstrate that displays are not important to you and that you have no interest in selling any wall portraiture.

If you want to sell large prints, show nothing smaller on your walls than a 20x24, and have most of your prints larger than that. In this way, you demonstrate that your clients need the sizes you display. People will follow your lead, and the larger prints on your walls will recommend and sell wall prints to your clients.

About every four to five years it is essential to redecorate. Replace the carpet, repaint the walls and the exterior, too; do not let your showroom (which is your showcase) cause your image to be degraded: this will drag down the sales.

I realize what we have chosen is not what everyone would want, but it works for us. We have chosen to decorate with a country mood. When you come into the studio, you first enter a room with a fan mounted in the peak of the cathedral ceiling. The colors are navy blue and chestnut brown and there is lots of wood. The furnishings are antiques and they draw plenty of interest and comments from our clients.

This country motif may seem a little odd when you contrast it with a progressive, contemporary and trendy style of photography, but that is probably the reason a country atmosphere works so well. Clients know we are unique and they expect that uniqueness in our images, but a comfortable and very down-to-earth atmosphere makes us seem more approachable. People feel less intimidated when they know they are dealing with people on their own social level, and they often tell us how comfortable they feel when they enter our studio. They see our images and they know we are creative and unusual, that we make images that are different. This can be a little frightening, so we have deliberately made our studio seem very ordinary. Through the studio we develop a very stable, down-home image, yet our walls show how creative we can be. It's a fine line we tread, but it has paid off over the years.

One of the most used areas in our studio is our sales counter. The counter has two tiers, one at chest height where customers place prints for ordering, and a lower level for the employees. This double level lets us keep the paper work below the customers' view and it makes the counter appear much neater to those in the room and those who are just entering.

Having the projection room just off the waiting area makes for greater efficiency. All work areas - order sorting, storage, negative masking and proof sorting areas - should be out of view because they appear as clutter to the customers, causing them to feel you are disorganized. Keep these functions and needs in mind as you design your various work areas.

Frame sales and displays should be handled in your projection area. Having frame displays in the waiting room will only increase the appearance of clutter, so put them where they are needed and where their lack of neatness will seem more natural. Properly arranged displays will make the product easy to pick up and lay over the projected image so the client can see how the portrait will look in a particular frame. And having the frames in one location makes it much easier for your clients to distinguish one display from the other.

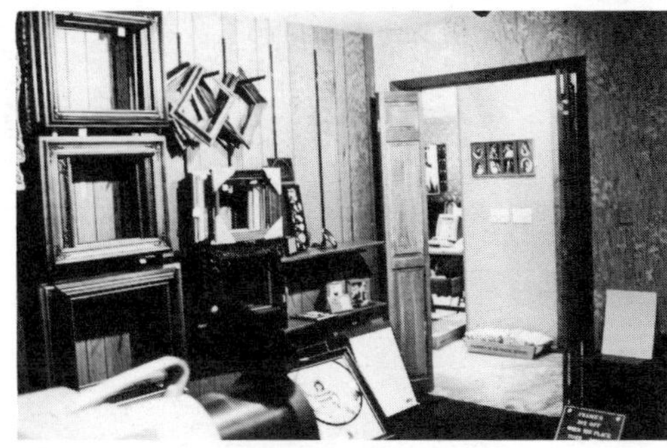

Having the frame sales area right in the projection room has greatly increased our frame turnover.

Visit other studios. See what looks right and what does not. Put all the good points together for your operation. Remember the type of photography you want to sell and choose a decor that complements your style.

Cleanliness is a must.
Neatness means organization.
Clutter is needless and wastes time.
Plan your area to be comfortable and easy to work in.
The better organized you are, the more you will be able to accomplish within a specific day.
If you can do these things and build in efficiency, you have found the secret to studio decor.

This "brag wall" behind the counter is impressive to those who spot it.

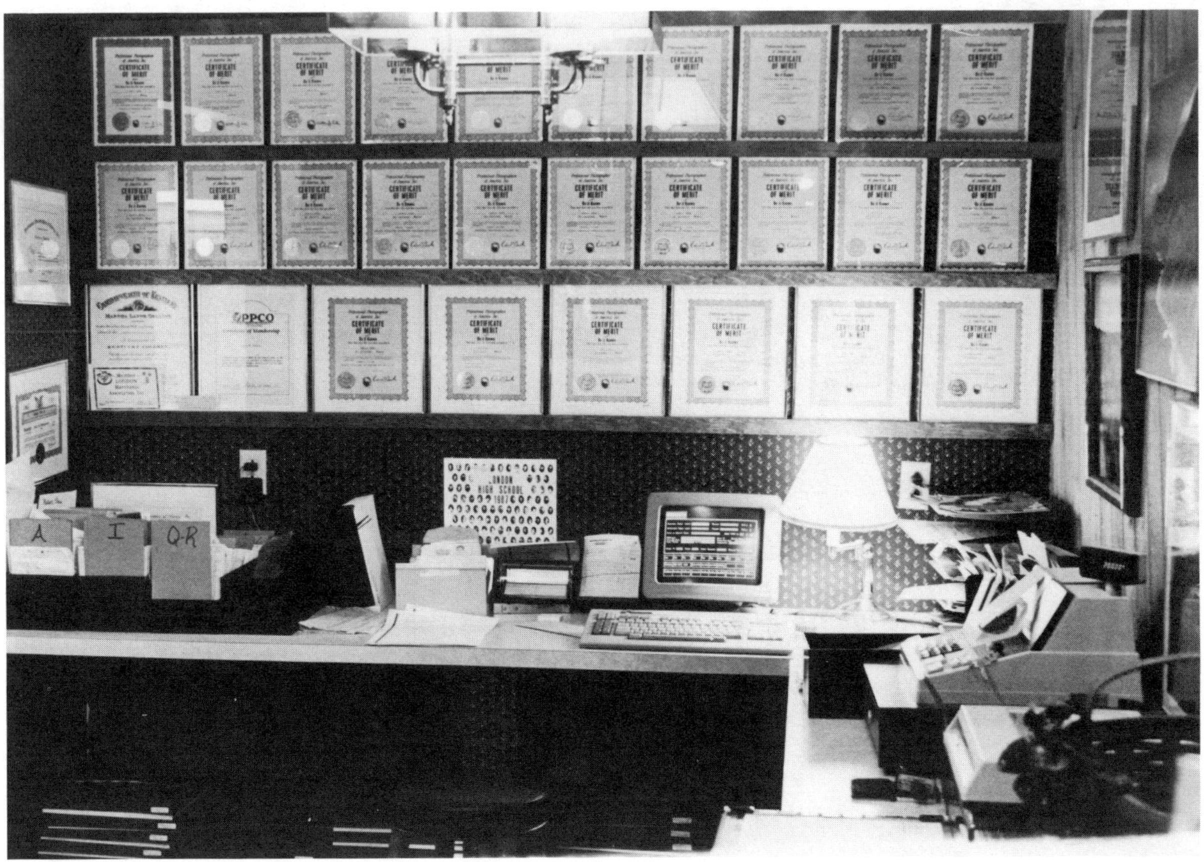

FOR EVERYONE

A color portrait combines art, composition and color to create a beautiful rendition of you, and just like an artist with oils, we must work together to add harmony to the setting, composition and color coordination in order to achieve the mood for your portrait.

When it comes to clothing, make-up and items to personalize your portrait, we need your help. So please read through this brochure before your sitting and use our suggestions. If we haven't covered your question, please call and we will be glad to answer it directly to you. Your preparation will make your portrait even more personable.

Clothing - General Ideas

1. Avoid sleeveless or very short sleeves, because upper arms can be very distracting, especially women.

2. Choose clothing that is neither too tight or too loose so it will hang properly without excessive creases or folds.

3. Plan on bringing one very contemporary outfit.

4. When planning for changes of clothing with a Deluxe Sitting, be sure to bring your favorite clothes. This might include a T-shirt and cutoffs, formal attire, informal clothing outfits as well as any special outfits for individual expression.

5. Often shoes will show so they should compliment your clothing; changes may be necessary with different clothing styles. Many prefer barefoot poses.

6. GLASSES - Please ask your optician to lend you a pair of empty frames in the same style as yours. This is important since glasses often cause reflections and magnifications that cannot be corrected. Photo Gray lenses will be dark and will hide your eyes. If you are unable to have a second set of frames please ask them to remove your lenses before your sitting and replace them afterward.

7. ALL WHITE! is great for a special high key effect. White is a strong color and is great when used properly with a white background. Blonde or light hair looks great with white clothing.

(Continued on Next Page)

PROPS: (Deluxe Sitting and Larger?) BE CREATIVE!

1. Feel free to make arrangements to use a prop of your liking. This could include hats, musical instrument, bicycle, motorcycle, car, pet, tennis racket, or sporting equipment. Use your imagination!

2. Changes of clothing are encouraged.

3. Casual clothing is great for out-of-doors.

4. Clothing that is informal might be: Cheerleading uniform, band uniform, sports clothing, jeans, sweatshirt, swim suit. There is a swimming pool for summer use. Many also use a swim suit as an indoor change.

5. Clothing that is formal might be: Prom dress, tux, for a special idea we could even use formal attire out-of-doors.

GROUP PORTRAITS

1. Plan colors that are compatible.

2. We recommend keeping colors within three colors, that blend together.

3. A family group is held together when each person in the family wears some shade of the same color.

4. Laying clothing out side by side will help in determining colors.

5. Bring additional colors if you have questions.

6. Additional changes are encouraged.

7. Choose a style of clothing (either dressy or casual) that will fit into the room that you plan on displaying the portrait.

8. The person dressed differently will stick out.

MEN

MAKE-UP

1. Be sure to shave within an hour or so of your appointment. 5 o'clock shadow cannot be removed through retouching.

2. If you have facial blemishes use a cover-up stick in your complexion shade and blend it in. Any application will further enhance the finished portrait. Or ask for assistance.

HAIR

1. If you plan a hair cut or perm, try to schedule it one week before your sitting so freshly cut ends won't stand out. DO NOT change your hair style until you have viewed your preview prints.

2. Make sure hair is trimmed out of your eyes, this causes many problems and covers a very important part of your face.

3. Wash your hair one day before, not the same day, unless you have extremely oily hair.

4. Suits, sport coats or sweaters are all good selections for traditional poses.

5. Choose colors that best compliment your hair and skin color.

WOMEN

MAKE-UP

1. To look natural, wear your normal evening makeup.

2. Use eye shadow to bring out eyes.

3. Blemishes can be minimized with cover-up stick.

4. An extra coat of mascara will make your lashes appear larger and fuller.

5. Lip gloss adds a sparkle.

6. Bring make-up for repairs and touch-ups or ask us to help with make up applications available with our best sitting.

7. If you are unsure of the correct colors and amounts to use the Elite Sitting is for you.

HAIR

1. Wear it the way you like it best and DON'T try a new hair style. New styles are great, but make sure it is what you want before the portrait session.

2. Keep your hair smooth because loose ends will pick up light and show prominently.

3. Very light spray will help loose ends.

4. Clean hair makes a healthy appearance, but just washed hair may appear frizzy.

5. DO NOT CHANGE YOUR HAIR STYLE UNTIL AFTER YOU HAVE VIEWED YOUR PREVIEW PRINTS.

6. Please make sure that your bangs don't cover your eyes. Eyes are very important in a girl's portrait.

7. We can arrange for a stylist if you like. NOT TO CUT - just to style.

DRAPES

1. We have several sizes, styles, and colors available for use. These add a nice elegant look when used with soft focus.

SUNTAN

1. Too much sun darkens your skin unnaturally, drys out your hair, makes skin appear shiny and greasy and shows bags under your eyes.

2. Strap marks will show as white marks on draped poses or bare shoulder poses. These cannot be retouched.

3. Don't overdo the sun for a portrait, it looks great, but use in moderation.

4. Keep your tan even.

5. Sunburn is a real problem. Cancel your appointment if burned.

One of these instructional "Guidelines" sheets is given/sent to each senior when the photo session appointment is made.

WORKING BY APPOINTMENT

Information about sittings, styles and prices are mailed out on a regular basis so students know what is available. As a result, oftentimes when the student calls for an appointment, he/she has already selected a sitting style. This is a good time to mention that we installed an 800 number for customers to call and schedule their appointment if they are out of our area. We use this number in many of our advertisements and promote it as our way of making any questions about our studio only a phone call away.

Normally we schedule two sittings of the same style at the same time. In other words, on any given day we would schedule two seniors who both want the Deluxe sitting for a 9:00 appointment. This sitting normally takes an hour if there's only one student to photograph, but with two we allow an hour and a half if I'm the only photographer working. By having one student dressing while I'm working with the other, we save half an hour with our double appointment system. This means we have two seniors arriving at the same time or very close to it.

This system works very well with two appointments of the same length. Needless to say, this calls for several dressing rooms, but it sharply reduces time needed for each student.

The first student to arrive is requested to fill out a form which includes questions about the props, the colors and styles of clothing she brought and whether she was referred to us by someone. These questions help us keep track of the student's identity when the film comes back from the lab.

INFORMATION SHEET

NAME ______________________________

PARENT OR GUARDIAN NAME ______________________________

ADDRESS ______________________________

____

PHONE

Home ______________________________

Office ______________________________

Props you brought ______________________________

____

Total Number of Clothing Changes ______________________________

School ______________________________

Date ______________ Referred By ______________

Please describe at least one of your outfits you are wearing for your portrait sitting today:

____

____

Have you been photographed for your Senior picture prior to today?

YES NO Where ______________________________

Peters Main Street Photography, Inc.
314 N. MAIN
LONDON, OHIO 43140
1-614-852-2731

The original of this is 5½x8½ on a light card stock.

The first person to complete the questionaire is taken by the receptionist to the dressing room where she is asked to put on the traditional clothing. I like to start with this outfit because it gets the students used to me, and to the directions we give during the photo session. Most of the students are photographed in five traditional poses which takes about five minutes.

When that's done, the first student goes to the dressing room to change while I photograph the second student's traditional poses. This works very well as the time I need to take five traditional poses is just about what the other student needs to change clothing and return to the camera room. This keeps appointments moving and I never have to kill time waiting for students to change clothing. In addition, the students change more quickly because they know others are waiting for them.

Depending on the time of the year, the next two appointments may arrive before I am finished with the first two sittings. We recently built another changing area to accommodate early arrivals or slow changers.

When previews are ready we notify the students by postcard their photographs are ready for viewing and that they must call for an appointment to view the originals. The postcard also states that a seventy-five dollar deposit is required if they want to take the photographs out of the studio. Finally, the student is asked to bring a parent for the viewing of the originals.

_____ Your Preview Prints are in. Please call for an appointment to view them and get a complete price explanation. A $75.00 deposit is required if you'd like to take them home.

_____ Your Preview Prints are in. Please call for an appointment to view them and get a complete price explanation. It is a good idea for a parent to accompany you for this appointment. A $75.00 deposit is required to take them home.

_____ Your order is ready for pick-up. Your balance is $_____________

Peters Main Street Photography, Inc.
314 N. MAIN
LONDON, OHIO 43140
1-614-852-2731

Hrs. Monday - Friday 9 a.m. - 5 p.m.
Saturday 9 a.m. - 12 noon

PREVIEW DELIVERY BY PROJECTION

When you add a projection appointment to a senior portrait session, you also add big dollars to that senior's order. We can show pretty conclusively that this one additional step increases each student's order by approximately $100.00.

As studio owners, we place great importance on viewing and pre-selling, so we pay a bonus to each of our sales persons for doing a preview appointment. This way everyone at our studio knows the importance of this appointment.

We believe the preview appointment MUST BE MADE BEFORE THE PHOTOGRAPHS LEAVE THE STUDIO, because it educates our customers about proper photo sizes for different head sizes or full length poses, and about placement in their homes. Often clients think they know sizing, but when they actually see their own photographs in these various sizes they are more likely to purchase larger wall prints.

When students arrive at the studio we escort them and their parents into our projection area. At this time they are presented with their previews. The previews are placed into two to eight print folios, an excellent quality product that further enhances the perceived quality of the portraits. We let the client know this is not a hard-sell session and if they leave a deposit, they can take the previews home in order to make their final selection.

This preview appointment is really designed for educational purposes. Furthermore, we tell them we are going to leave them alone for a few minutes so they can select approximately three poses to be projected. These poses should reflect a close-up, a three-quarters pose, and a full length. You should probably point to these types of poses in their folio so they will better know the type of poses we want them to select. We explain that these poses are not necessarily ones they are going to purchase, but those which represent different types of poses which - when enlarged - will show how different each pose will look as a large print.

Now we leave them for a few moments so they can study the portraits. When we return, the first question we ask is, "Well, how do you like them?" and we immediately know how they feel about the portraits. If there is a problem with anything - hair, clothing, or the photographs in general - now is the time to get it out in the open so you can handle it. We may need to arrange a new sitting or get another opinion, but all too often, clients will make derogatory comments because they want you to tell them how great they look. I suspect it's just insecurity raising its ugly head. Everyone wants to look great, so we go with the flow; we look at their photographs and say honestly which poses we like and why. This reinforces the fact that we are proud of our photography and that we think they really look great.

If a customer is genuinely unhappy, we don't let the photographs leave the studio; we don't need someone displaying our photographs and knocking them down. Fortunately, we only have to retake a little under two percent of all senior sittings. This is important because satisfied customers are what make a business grow and become great.

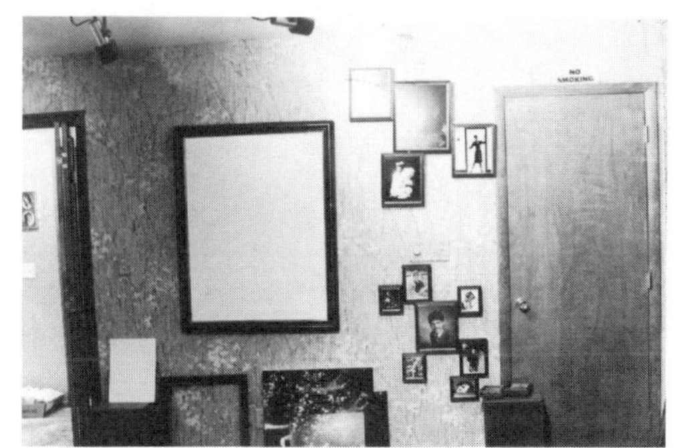

A projection room can be made from spare storage area or the camera room if you are not that busy yet. The room we are using is approximately fifteen feet by fifteen feet although the width is actually greater than we need. A ten foot by eighteen foot room would be ideal, but not all of us have that luxury. On the wall is a thirty by forty inch frame in which we have mounted a Dalite projection screen. The screen was glued to Masonite and then framed. The frame is mounted on the wall with a swivel device that lets us turn the frame from vertical to horizontal, depending on the image being projected.

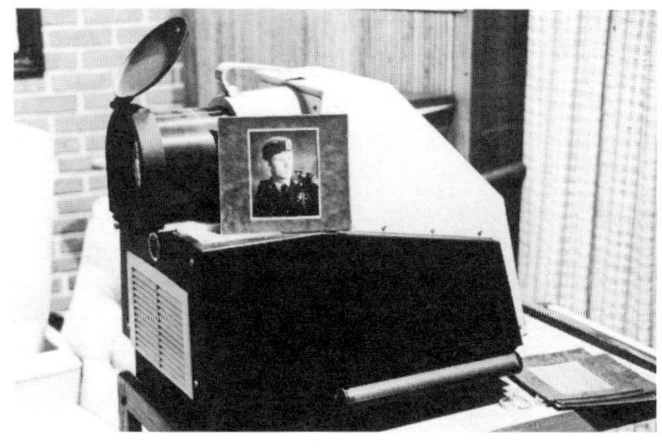

The projector we are using is a Beseler Opaque Vuelite III, the best opaque projector available at this time. It costs a lot of money so if you are on a limited budget it is better to buy a less expensive brand and do the projection appointment than not do it at all. As soon as you see the benefits of this machine you will want to change to the better one.

We have this projector on a microwave oven cart so it can be moved forth and back to change the size of the images.

I know there is a trend for photographers to use slide proofs in viewing wall prints and that may be of great value, but with seniors, paper proofs are the thing that leave our studio. They are a gorgeously packaged selling presentation for all of their friends to see. This is important to me and the growth of my business. If you really feel you have to use slides for projection sessions, my suggestion is that you order paper proofs first, look over the previews when they are returned from the lab, then order slides from just those few images you may want to project. This will be cheaper than purchasing an opaque projector and definitely gives the highest image quality available. The important point to remember is to project for increased sales.

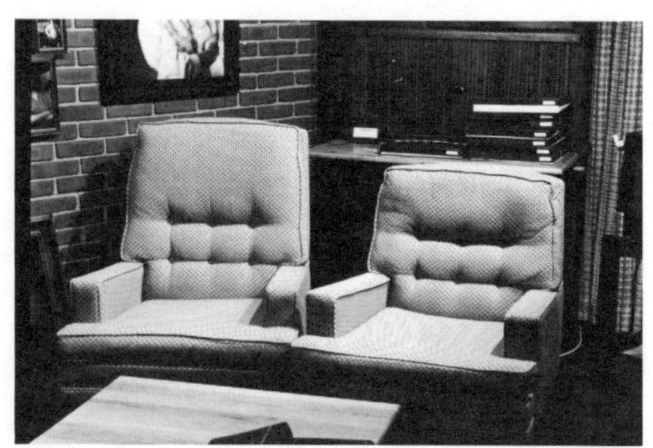

In the projection room we have two comfortable chairs, a coffee table, portrait packages displayed on the wall and on the opposite wall a display of frames suitable for wall portraits. Spotlights on track units point to the package displays, the frame display, and into the customer's lap where they will be viewing the previews. The room is decorated with wood paneling on one wall, bricks on another, the third is a sliding glass door, which we cover with a blackout curtain to make the room dark, and the floor is a dark blue carpet. We wanted a friendly, easy to work in room that would be non-threatening, so our aim was to make it more like a family room than a sales area.

A client is given a week in which to return the previews and place an order. It is totally up to your discretion whether or not you want to schedule an appointed time for them to place their order. We do not. Everything was pre-sold, so when they return to place an order, we find that our salespeople are just taking orders. Pre-selling has made it easy for our clients to form their major buying decision quickly and easily and we just reap the reward.

WHAT TO DO DURING THE PROJECTION APPOINTMENT

The actual appointment takes approximately twenty to twenty-five minutes. After leaving a client alone to view his prints, (approximately five to ten minutes), we return to the room, take the three previews they have selected, place them in the projector one at a time, then show them a twenty-four by thirty, a twenty by twenty-four, and a sixteen by twenty of each photo they have selected.

During this time we also give the customer information about the poses we feel make the best wall size portraits. For example: we suggest full length poses be used for larger wall prints and also wallet size photographs, while a three-quarters pose would be good for "smaller" wall prints and eight by tens. The close up pose will probably be good in almost any size, but if they enlarge it too much it can easily become larger than life. This may appeal to some, but we always suggest that a print this size may need to be displayed in a fairly large area. It will definitely be overpowering in a small room.

It's my aim to treat my customers exactly as I'd want to be treated if I were buying portraits, so it's not uncommon for us to suggest down-sizing a particular print if the photograph selected would suffer from the larger size. We always take pains to explain why we recommend the smaller size. Honesty wins respect and shows that you are just not shoving a certain size at them.

One feature of the Beseler Projector is that it can't be adjusted to give a smaller image than 16x20. So after displaying the three larger sizes of prints, the last thing we do before turning the lights up is to hold an 11x14 mat board in the corner of the 16x20 projected image. This comparison shows how small an 11x14 is for a wall print, and it gives them a visual idea as to size.

Next we turn the lights up and immediately go to our wall display. On the wall are two senior packages. These packages are fairly large and include many photographs. For example, our most successful package contains one 16x20, two 8x10s, six 5x7s and ninety-six wallets.

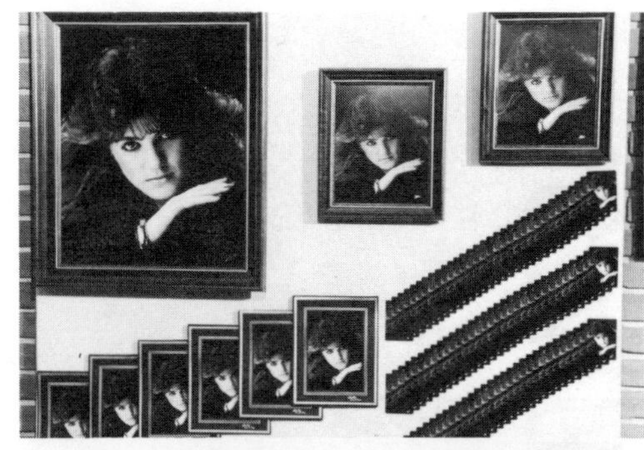

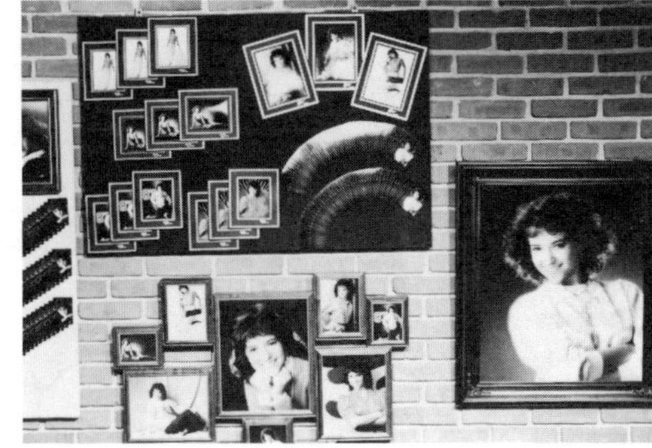

You can design packages any way you want, but it is extremely important to display them in your studio where you can refer to them during the projection time. A discount of twenty to twenty-five per cent under your regular pricing makes it an attractive package.

Also on the wall we have a larger package from several different poses with one 20x24 canvas print, a cluster arrangement consisting of one 11x14, two 8x10s, three 5x7s and four 4x5s all in frames that are fastened together. We also include three 5x7 and twelve 4x5 gift prints in cardboard easel frames, plus ninety-six wallets. This display has brought many dollars into our studio because it is our largest, most expensive package and there are always clients who want the best. One other benefit from this large package is the way it makes the smaller packages seem less expensive.

Approximately fifty percent of the clients we have for senior portraits purchase one of these packages. Last year we sold over 450 16x20 packages, and more than seventy-five 20x24 packages. We feel strongly about this display. These items can add literally thousands of dollars to your income every year and they should definitely be considered in your sales effort.

We have adopted a very simple plan for selling folios and proofs which increases the amount of money seniors spend for their photographs. You decide how much you want a senior to spend and the average for his total order. I believe this amount should be approximately twenty-five to thirty dollars higher than your 16x20 special senior package. Using this figure, tell your clients if their total portrait order goes to this amount, they will receive at no charge all the photographs which were taken for their photo session.

Note: This plan will work only if you have offered eight to ten background changes, close-ups, and full lengths, many props, poses in and out of doors, casual and dressy, flashy and conservative posing, and only if you photograph each senior differently than all the other seniors. Because we shoot poses for incredible variety, we can spin off heavy proof sales to increase our orders. If you do this you can name the amount - $350, $400, $500 - and your client will spend it to get those free previews.

It is incredible to watch them add pose changes, additional prints and anything else to build the order so they get the previews free. I suggest you put a high value on each proof, just a little below the price of your 4x5s which may mean fifteen to twenty dollars each for an outright purchase. This shows what a great deal it is to spend a little more to get the free proofs and folios. Those who choose not to spend $30 more for extra prints will almost always buy some of the proofs, so you can't lose. You either get a larger order that includes free previews or they buy previews at an excellent profit to you. But let me repeat, unless you are photographing for variety, this system will not work.

Our goal is to sell each senior a $500 order and in 1989 we got close with $466. I know displaying the large packages and showing proofs by projection, coupled with a high value placed upon each preview, will get us to this goal in 1991.

DON'T BUY ORDINARY SENIOR PICTURES!

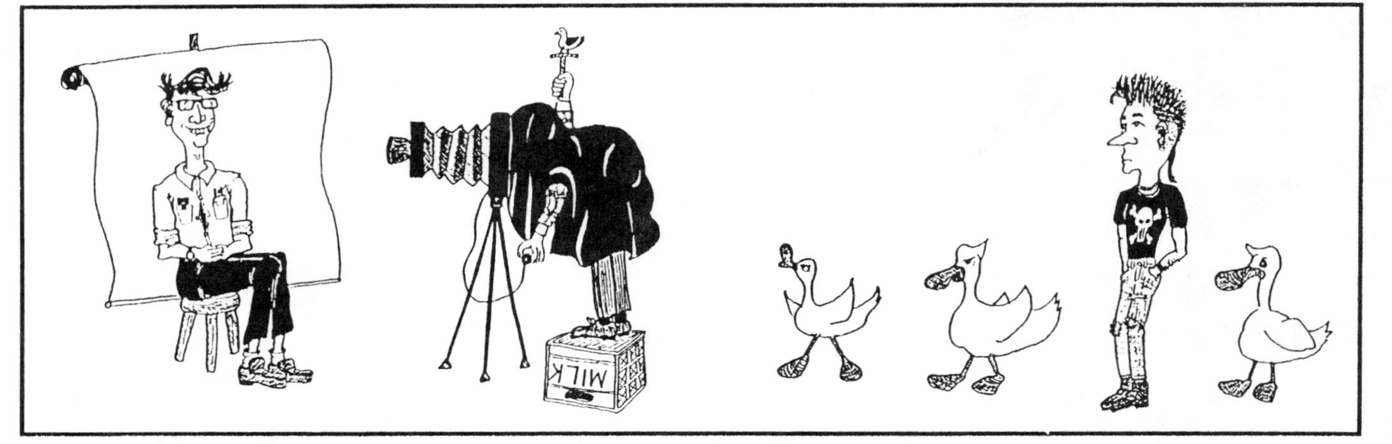

Are YOU like a duck in line to get your senior pictures?

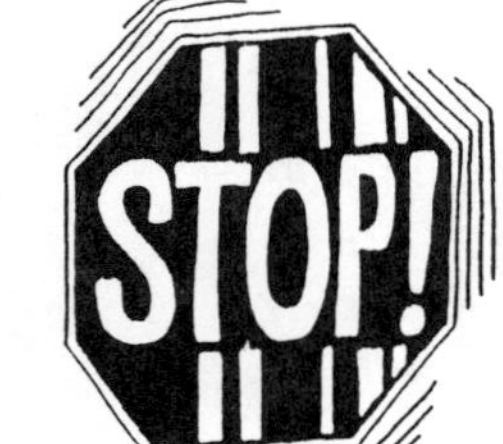

YOU DESERVE MORE!

Has your school TOLD you where to go to get your senior pictures?

***Go Ahead, Do It,* BUT** don't buy anything until you've checked out what's available!

Keep your school happy but only buy when you're sure you've received the **BEST** photography. ***After all, this is only once in a lifetime.***

This is another inexpensive brochure. It is 11x17, on twenty pound bond, with blue text ink and red headlines. It could have been totally ordinary, but four things made it work: the "kid look" drawings, the catchy "Rotten Picture Reward", the free gas offer, and the 800 toll-free number.

★ A Rotten Picture Reward ★

Have you paid for one photo session already?

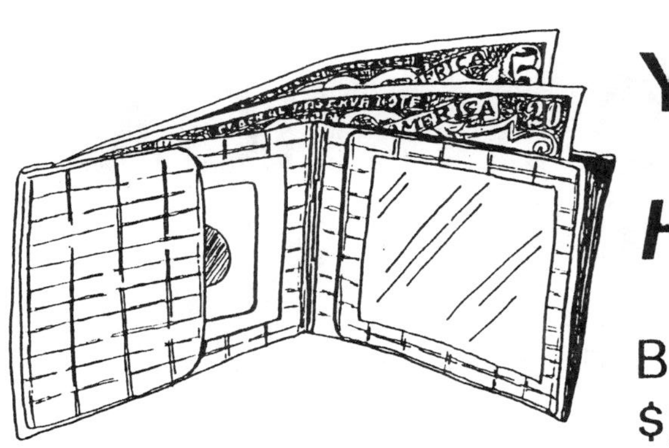

YOU HAVEN'T LOST ANYTHING!

Here's How:

Bring us your receipt and we'll deduct that amount up to $25.00 from your photo session at Peters!

Do You Feel London Is Too Far To Go For A Senior Portrait? - SAVE AGAIN!!

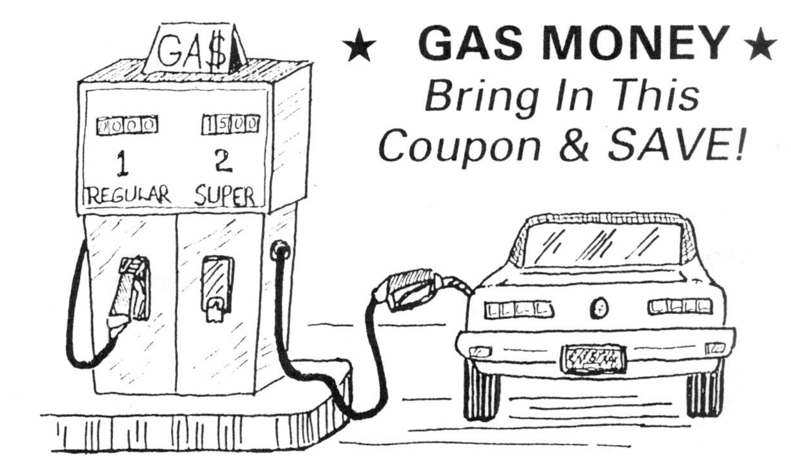

★ GAS MONEY ★
Bring In This Coupon & SAVE!

I've driven 35 miles - **Save $10 on order**
(One Way - Appointment Only)

I've driven 36-50 miles - **Save $15 on order**
(One Way - Appointment Only)

I've driven 51-75 miles - **Save $20 on order**
(One Way - Appointment Only)

I've driven 76-100 miles - **Save $25 on order**
(One Way - Appointment Only)

Bring this coupon with you - we'll help you figure the distance!
—One Coupon Per Customer—

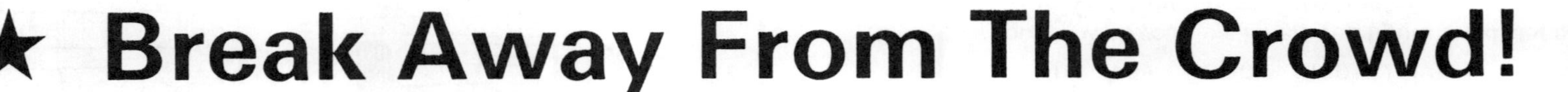

★ Break Away From The Crowd! ★

Be unique and have something different
for your senior portrait

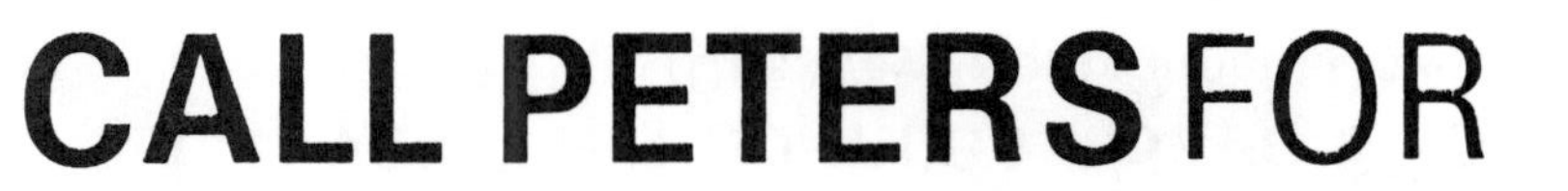

CALL PETERS FOR
YOUR APPOINTMENT
(614) 852-2731

or the

SENIOR HOT LINE
1-800-446-1922

YOU'RE ONLY A SENIOR ONCE!

Peters **MAIN STREET PHOTOGRAPHY, INC.**
314 North Main Street • London, Ohio 43140
PRESENTLY CONSTRUCTING A SECOND STUDIO IN CENTERVILLE, OHIO

Chapter IV

Follow-Up Dollars

Many avenues of promotion are available for those who choose to build a senior business.

MALL EXHIBITS

Mall Exhibits are definitely a follow-up dollar; they have generated good will with our customers and given us a great promotional opportunity for very little time and money invested. Here is how we work it:

Every day I check the proofs as they come from the lab to see if the camera is working right, and to see if new props and poses are doing what I want them to do. As I am going through the photographs, if I find one I particularly like, I pull it out of the folio and make a copy of it on a plain paper copy machine. On the copy I write the student's name, and the name of her school. (We want to include kids from as many schools as we can so I try to see that all are represented in this selection.)

At the end of the senior season, I take this group of papers, look up the addresses and mail out a very tempting offer, one that is hard to refuse. It says that we are preparing a mall exhibit and, as a part of this display, we chose this pose from all of the photographs taken this year. The size of the photograph we would like to use is a 20x24. This photograph (which normally sells for $X) will be available to you after the display for just $50. (This figure may vary a little depending on our price for the print, but we add about $10 to our cost. We are not out to get rich off the prints, but it's nice to be able to use the print in an effective display and have her foot the bill for it.)

The letter goes on to give them two options.

1. ________Please use my photograph for the display. I am honored you have selected a photograph of me. Enclosed is a check for $__ to cover expenses. I understand that I can pick up this portrait after June first.
2. ________Do not use my photograph for your display.

The second option, of course, is blunt and harsh sounding and many people will not want to offend us by checking this option. Our past experience shows that from thirty to fifty percent of the people solicited to participate in this promotion will do so and pre-pay the full amount.

The first year we did this I was hoping only to get samples for a program I was doing about senior portraits. We took several 20x24 photographs to a mall office to explain the idea of honoring graduating seniors with a exhibit. Of course these photos were of students from that area and several were even employed at the mall. The management loved the idea and we have been there for two years. Now, as each year rolls around, about all we have to do is call and set the date. Not all malls will let you have space for a display at no charge. Some of them have a set fee for this and other will make up one just for you.

We had a lattice print holder made especially for this.

The good will from this exhibit has never been immediate, but we hear comments all year long from people who have seen it. Last year ninety customers - the most ever - responded to our letter and the display was a tremendous success.

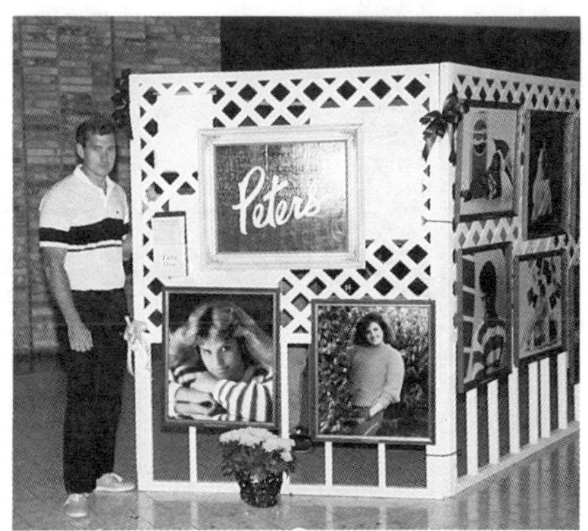

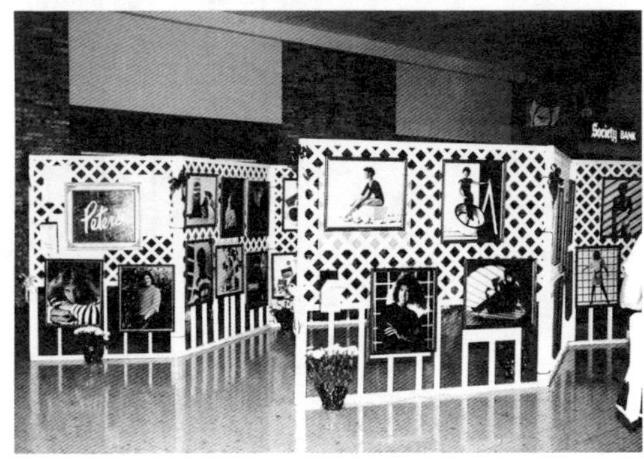

Name________
Address________

City________ Zip________
Phone________
Amt. Collected________
C.O.D.________
Agent________
Date________

Larry Peters

1 8 x 10

FAMILY GROUP PORTRAIT — NATURAL COLOR

REGULAR PRICE
Sitting $15.00
8 x 10 $38.00

Special Offer $15.95

SAVE $37.05

PAY THIS REPRESENTATIVE $5.00 ONLY. Pay $10.95 plus tax, at studio at time of appointment.
This certificate is good for 1-8 x 10 Natural Color family group portrait, unmounted, of no more than 8 persons. Additional persons may be included in same portrait at $2 each.
This portrait is to be photographed at Main Street Photography by appointment only. It is not good for home portrait sittings. No refunds.
Main Street Photography will not be bound by any agreement and representation, either verbal or in writing, except as contained in this certificate.

Please call for your appointment.
THIS CERTIFICATE IS VOID
12 MONTHS FROM DATE SOLD

Amount Paid________
Date________
Agent________

Main Street Photography, Inc.
314 N. Main • London, OH 43140
1-614-852-2731

Yes, our specialty is senior portraits, but we welcome any kind of portraiture. We really want to expand our family sittings, so we promote them year around. A very good time to push family groups is when you do a senior portrait because the family may never be together again.

It has never been my idea to set up a booth in the mall in order to hand out sales literature or talk to people. We keep the advertising simple, just our name prominently displayed in several places on the exhibit, plus some promotional literature which can be picked up by potential clients as they walk by. This promotional piece takes the form of a testimonial flyer with a number of customers explaining why they chose Main Street Photography for their senior portraits. (We get these from customers when they order.) There is a coupon on the flyer with a special offer and it is surprising how many of these little coupons drift in over the year.

FAMILY CERTIFICATES

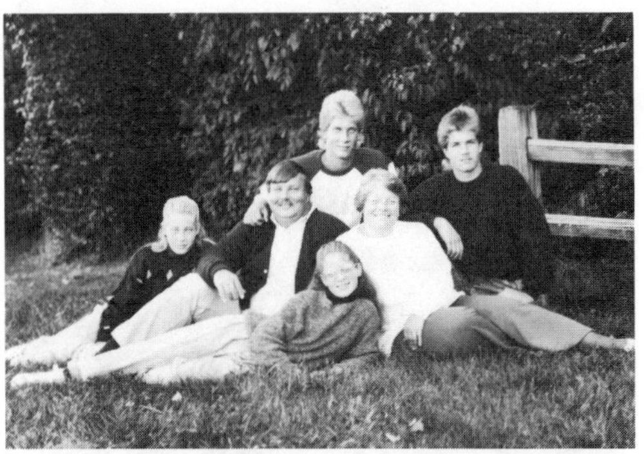

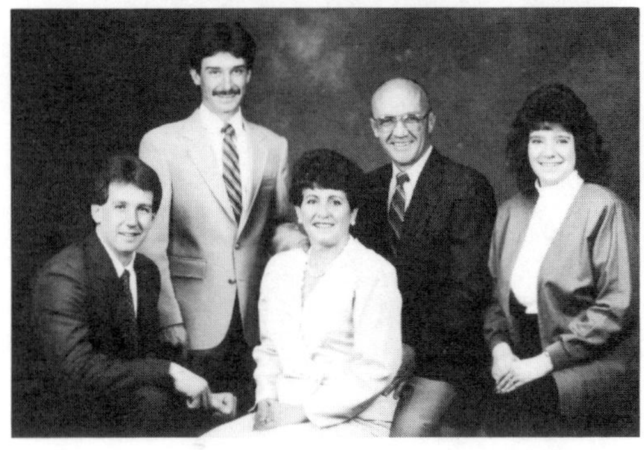

Any photographer can become his own best promotional device by talking to clients about his services. During a photo session with a senior it's so easy for you, your receptionist or salesperson to talk to the parent who accompanies the senior to the photo session. Questions that can open the conversational door are:

"Is your son/daughter going off to college?"

"Do you realize this summer may the last time your family will be all together in one place?"

"Have you thought about having a family portrait made before your son/daughter graduates from high school?"

Many times you can schedule them right on the spot. I feel this is best, but there are many different ways to promote family portrait sittings. Gift certificates given out with finished portrait orders are great for follow-ups. Add a follow-up phone call about the gift certificate and you'll double the response to the certificate. We know we have to work at scheduling families of seniors, but there's so much business right there for the asking.

Some photographers offer families a special price for the senior's family. For example: "If we schedule your family for a portrait session during the first month after you pick up the senior's portraits you can order family portraits at senior prices, just our way of saying 'thank you' for letting us do your senior's graduation portrait."

A letter thanking them for their order is one of the best ways to promote good will. This should be mailed to the senior's home within two weeks after their order is delivered. If we have received a very good order from a senior, we often write a special letter to the parents offering a free family sitting and complimentary 8x10. We know we'll make it back on the reprint order. We make this offer with a one month expiration date. As with any offer, it pulls better when it is dated with a relatively short time for fulfillment.

Working to book family portraits from senior sittings requires persistence and promotional creativity, but there is so much money to be made from senior's families, it's very worth while.

TEEN MODELING

In February, March and April, our business dips very sharply as yours probably does, too, so I use those months to build other types of sittings, to develop new props and to generate business from students other than seniors.

One of the ideas we have developed is a Teen Modeling promotion. Every year many of the teenage magazines offer "modeling contests" for young girls to enter. The photo requirements vary, of course, but usually they ask for close-up and full length photographs to be submitted, normally by the first of June. You can get the exact rules and deadlines from the different magazines.

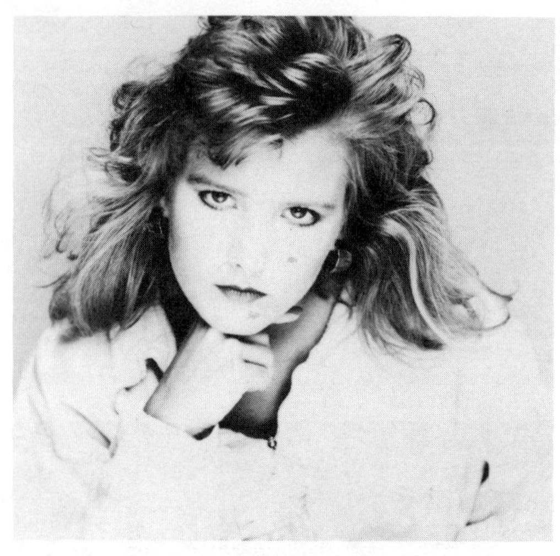

This timing works great with our slow time. We simply design a package that includes the sitting charge, the previews and the photos they need in order to enter these contests. These photographs may be any size from 4x5s to 8x10s, so our minimum package is to sell previews and a folio when the contest calls for 4x5s. The client can send in previews for the contest entry. If the contest calls for larger prints, they can be included in a larger package. One of our sales points is to design custom-made albums in various sizes with the price including six to ten photographs and a monogrammed album.

This promotion is great for those girls in your area or from your mailing list who are interested in modeling or just want photos that look like modeling shots. This offer will not make you rich but it helps keep your staff sharp and alert at the slowest times of the year. If you can offer make-up applications or other options, they also help boost sittings and orders. Make these girls look gorgeous and you will win their trust. If you do a great job for them on this work, guess who gets to do their high school senior portrait?

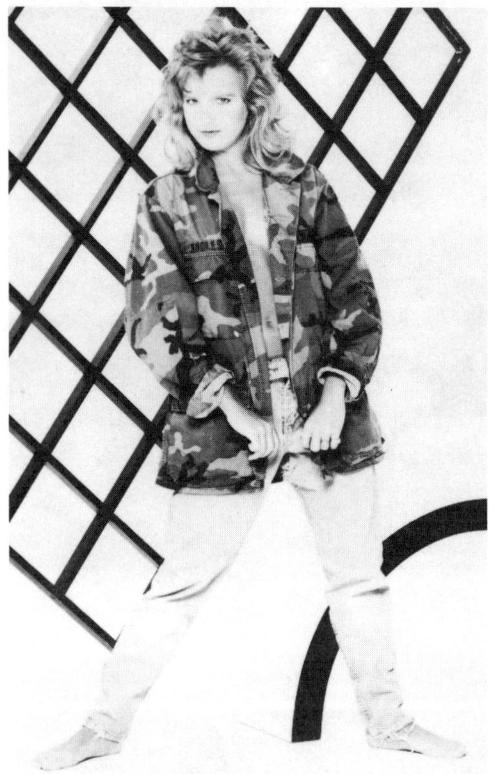

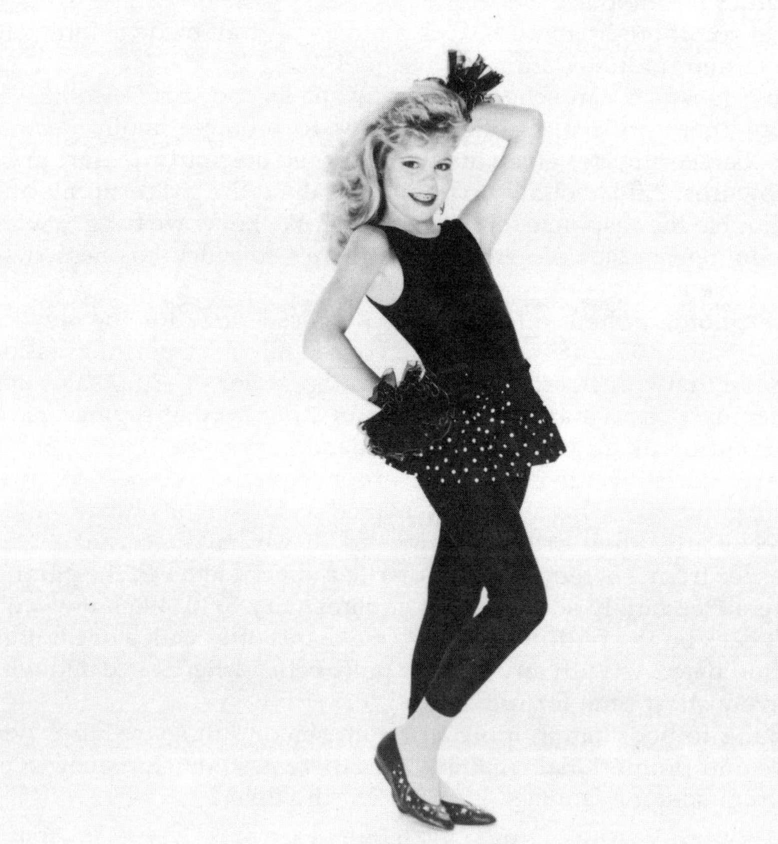

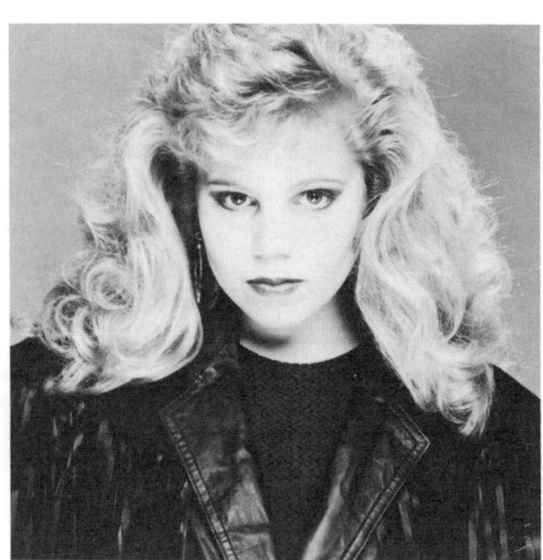

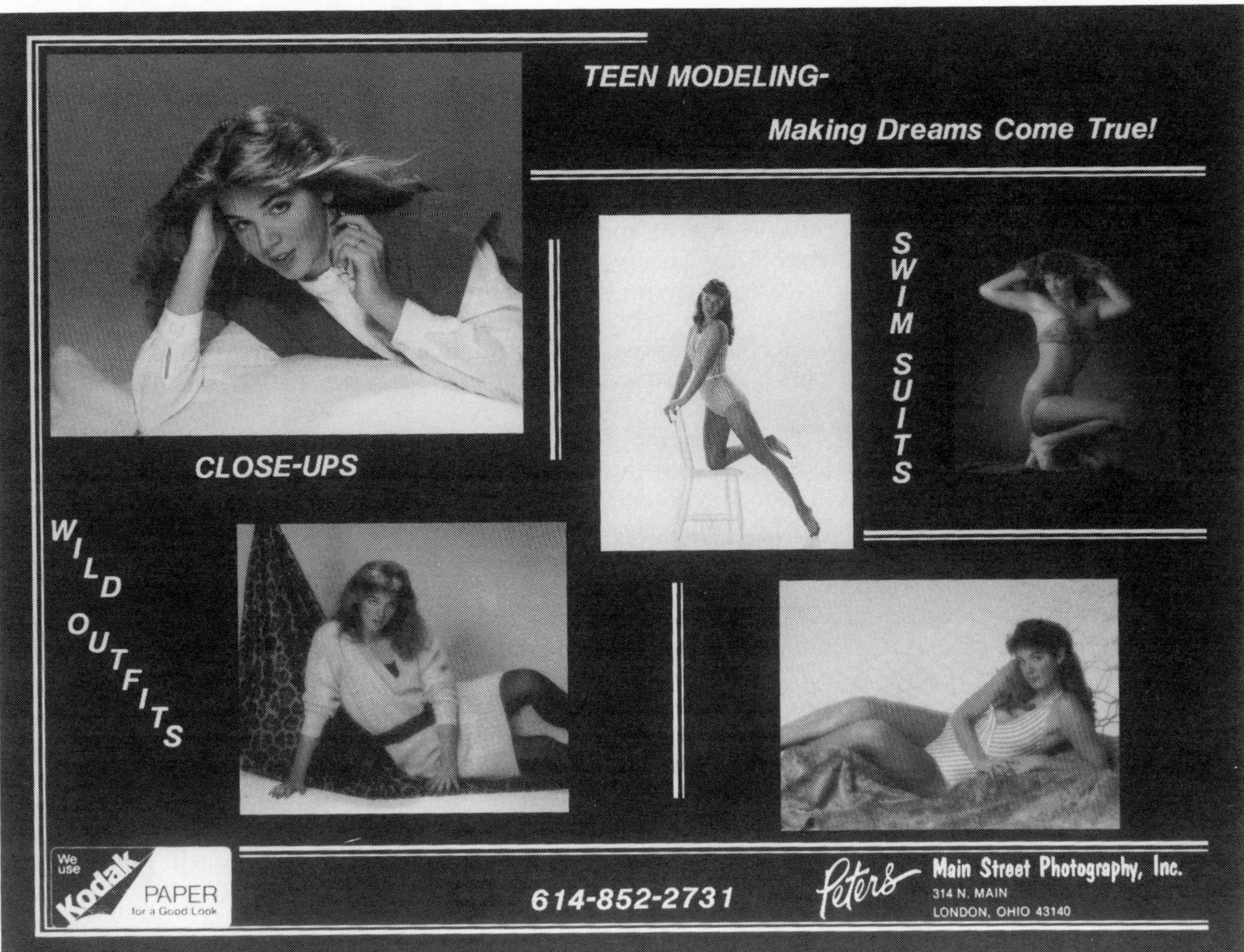

DON'T MISS YOUR CHANCE FOR A PHOTO SESSION JUST FOR TEENAGERS

"BE LIKE A MODEL"

For just $20.00 enjoy a photo session like you've never experienced before.

★★ **Why Should I:** Use these photos to enter the many cover contests now in progress. Example: "TEEN" and "YOUNG MISS" magazines

Start a Modeling Portfolio

Just for Fun! Keep to show your friends and family the way you looked at this time in your life.

★★ **What's It Cost:** BRING A FRIEND AND SAVE ½ OF THE SESSION FEE!
Yes, two people for only $10.00 each. (Appts. must be at same time)
What's it cost? $20.00 for 18 poses and a make-up session.
(Bring a friend and save!!)
Minimum package purchase of only $89.95 includes 8 prints, album and 16 wallets.
OTHER GREAT PACKAGES AVAILABLE!!

★★ **What's Included:** An 18 pose sitting
Complete make-up session
Be "Color Seasoned" for a small fee. "Gives you the extra edge"
UP-TO-DATE hair styling available to complete the session.

THIS IS A SPECIAL SEASONAL OFFER!! Good only until May 15.

CALL NOW!! 614-852-2731 BRING A FRIEND AND SAVE!!

614-852-2731 Peters Main Street Photography, Inc.
314 N. MAIN
LONDON, OHIO 43140

Our Teen Model brochure is 8½x11, full color on the picture side, on 8 pt. coated stock.

FRIENDS PROMOTION

After noticing a trend for more and more seniors to bring friends to their photo session, I thought we might capitalize on a Friends Photo Session. March and April are the months for this. Example: Bring in your classmates (up to ten people) and we will do a group sitting for half the price of our regular photo session. The advertisment shows girls dressed alike, perhaps in cheerleader's or similar garb. Once we even photographed a group of girls in swimsuits in the middle of winter! These ideas seemed the most appealing to the students we have photographed.

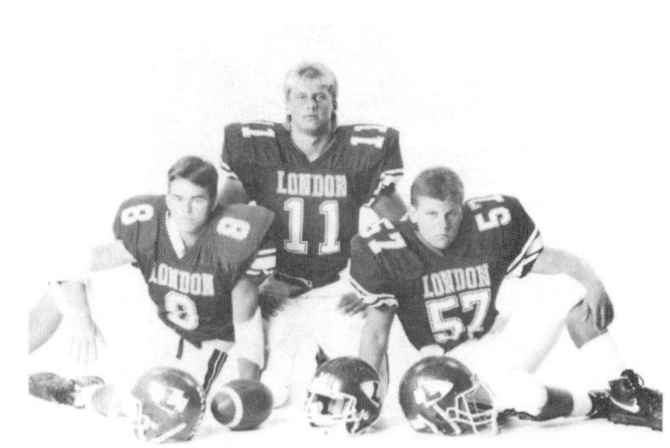

The photographs we sell are priced directly from the senior price list, except for one special. We promote a 20x30 poster print for approximately $40. This print is processed by the local one hour photo-finisher and costs about $17. We expect to sell one to each person in the group, but, if in a group of ten students, six of them buy a poster, we have had a good (money-making) photo session.

This Friends Promotion will bring those seniors you have already photographed back into your studio, plus some that you haven't. Have fun, crank up the music for the crazy poses and backgrounds. Do something different with them, they are gonna love you for it!

Photographs may also be purchased for gifts to club advisors, as well as for the kids to keep for memories: this promotion will definitely help your cash flow.

We like to make things happen, not sit and let the business come to us. This way you can be sure something will happen. Direct mail advertising is the method of promotion, and word of mouth will help to make it work.

Many friendships are cultivated through high school and your studio can help them keep these memories alive. In the process you will plant forever in their young minds the services your studio offers. In later years whenever they need a photographer, they will be more apt to think of you.

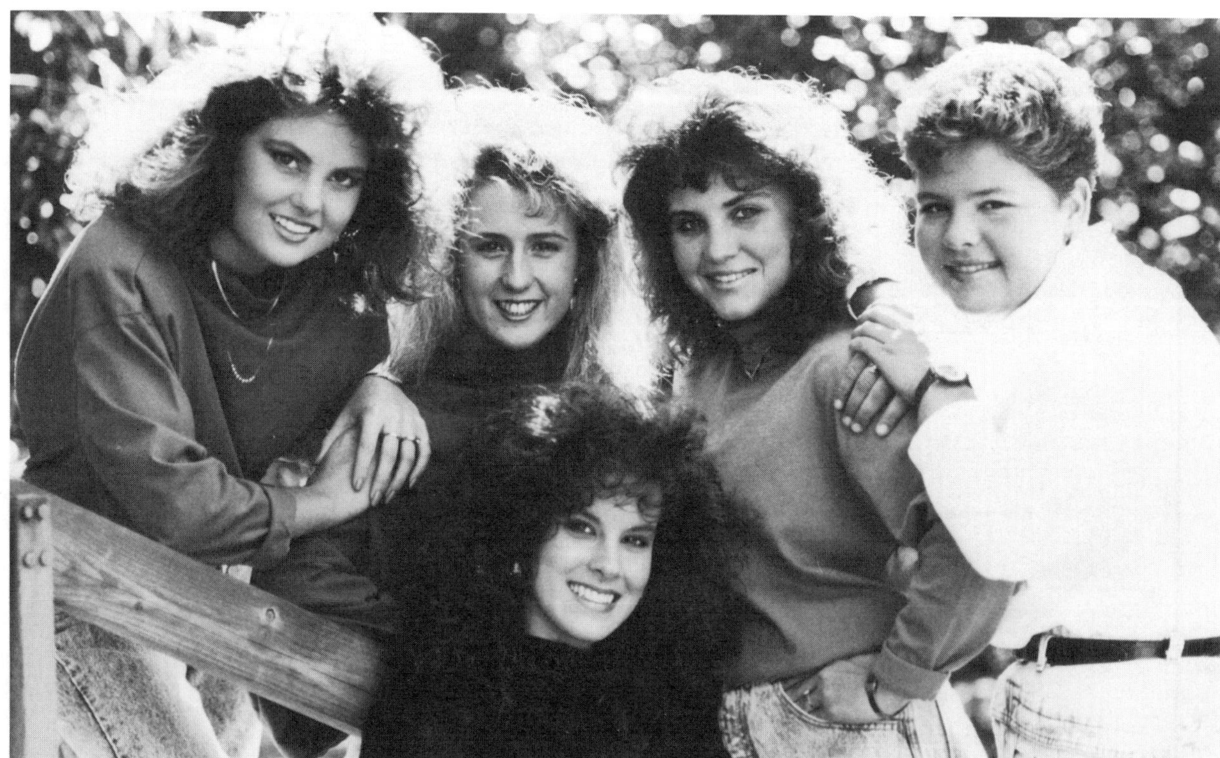

WALLET SPECIAL

In the winter months our studio business almost comes to a halt. Sometimes we think it might be better to shut the doors for a couple of months and head south for the winter, but those dreams pass and we go back to work. It is during this time that we do special promotions to get the clients to come in again.

One promotion that has worked for us during this time has been a wallet sale. Call this a thank-you gesture or whatever you wish, but just before graduation students do need additional photographs to include with their graduation announcements. The color lab we normally work with provides a three month special price for wallets. This pricing applies to any previously ordered and masked negative so the process is easy. Go to your file, pull the negatives, group them together and ship them off to the lab for package printing.

You will have to prepare a catchy flyer about this wallet sale. A friend of mine gave me this ad idea:

"Are your friends threatening to tie you up unless you give them the wallet photo you promised? Save Big, Order Today. Offer expires (date)."

We also advertise this by telling anyone who reorders wallets for about a month before the special to wait for the discount before placing the order. I have always believed this was good business practice because the customers appreciate my saving them money.

Everthing goes back to promotion because the profit margin on an offer like this is so minimal. I believe if you over-advertise something like this it can easily turn into a money loser, not a money maker. Choose your method of advertising with care and offer it only to customers who placed orders with your studio that were large enough to merit receiving the special.

★★ WALLET SPECIAL ★★

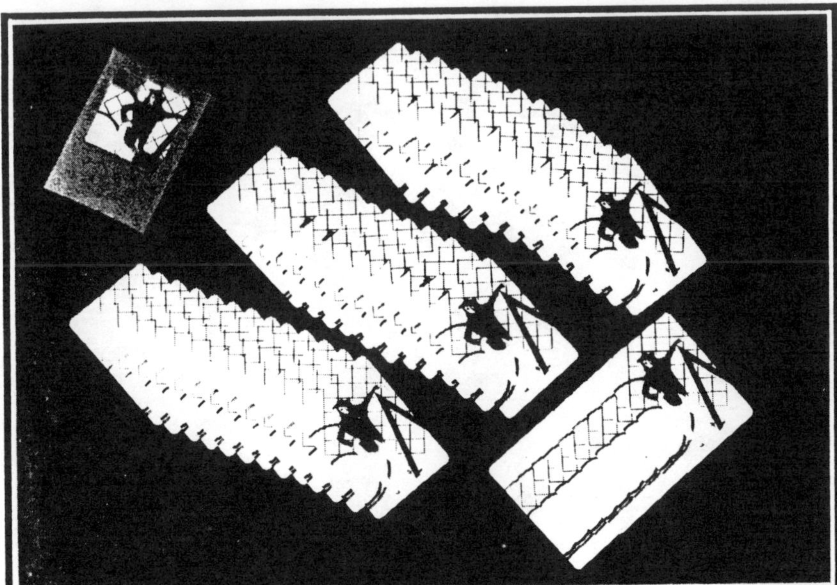

48 Color Wallets* **$35.80
plus tax &
$3.00 Re-Order Charge

(Sorry, No B&W Wallet Special)

*All 48 wallets must be from the same previously ordered pose.

OFFER GOOD THROUGH MARCH 30, 1990

Regular Prices Go Into Effect May 1, 1990

Rush charges will be added to any orders placed after May 1, 1990 for graduation deadlines.

—ORDER FORM—

Name: ______________ Photo No. (From Proof or send sample of picture)

Street Address: ______________

City/State/Zip: ______________

______ WALLET SPECIALS AT $35.80 ea. ______

Re-Order Charge $3.00

6% Tax ______

Total Enclosed ______

Peters Main Street Photography, Inc.
314 North Main Street
London, Ohio 43140
(614) 852-2731 or 1-800-446-1922

PAYMENT POLICY: PAYMENT MUST BE IN FULL. Phone orders must be paid by Credit Card in full. All others must be made by mail or in person.

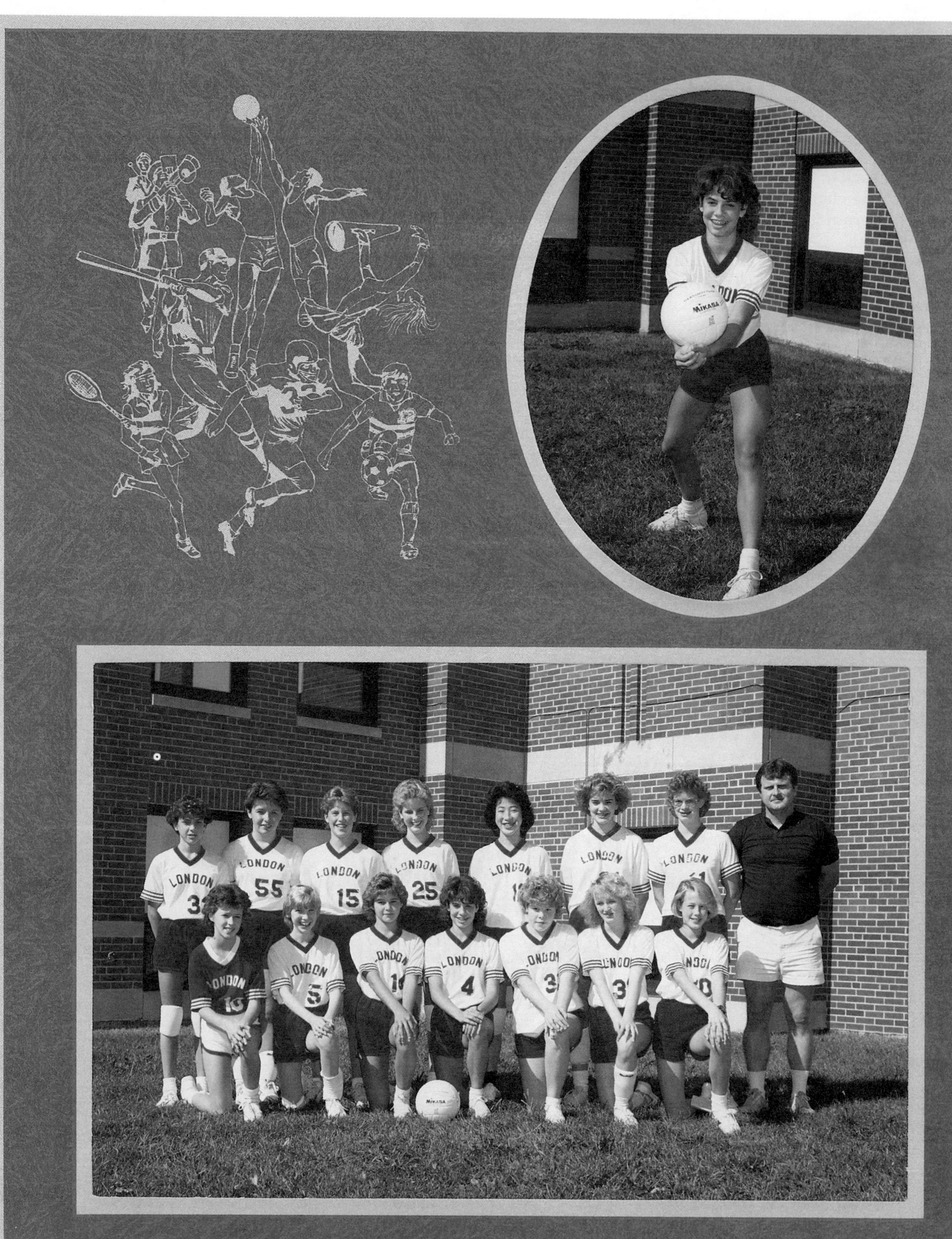

LONDON
55
LONDON
15
LONDON
25
LONDON
LONDON
LONDON
LONDON
5
4

Chapter V

Spin-Off Business Available to the School Contract Photographer

Additional profits come to the senior photographer that are rarely discussed. If you choose, you can add hundreds of dollars to your annual income. It seems that choosing to make money in a certain way determines what your income will be, and if you choose to make something happen, the chances of its happening are greatly enhanced.

SPORTS PHOTOS

Most sports, especially those that take place in the fall and winter, attract both participants and viewers in great numbers. Many schools print up programs for these events, which opens a window of opportunity for you. The programs are often prepared and the ads in them marketed by para-school organizations - usually parents groups, sometimes allied with athletics directors and teachers, or volunteer groups such as the Boosters Club. Whatever the group, these are the ones to contact about providing the photography for the program.

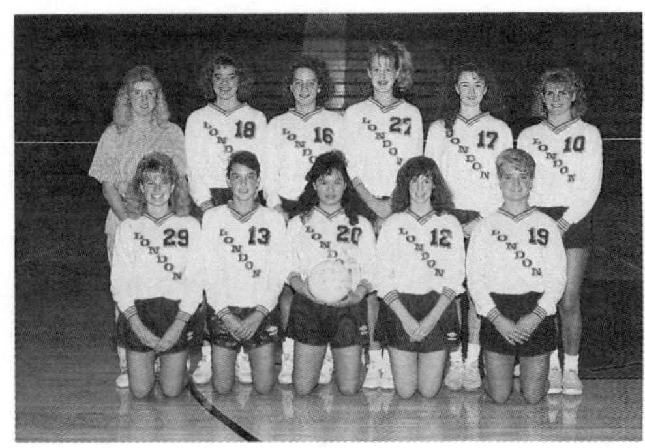

You should arrange a trade-off with them in which you provide b/w photographs for the program in exchange for a list of names and addresses of the kids, cooperation in taking orders for the photographs and help with distribution, scheduling the times for photography, perhaps an assistant at the photography session, plus anything else you can get to make your job easier. You may not get all you want, but you should get most of it.

Usually you can arrange the photography sessions for the evening or late afternoons after school, which means you don't have to interrupt you normal studio hours and activities for sports photography. In this way, team photography becomes a total bonus.

It is a good idea to use a nearby lab that will give you a quick turn-around on b/w photographs and can provide a wide variety of items to be sold to the students. Some of the most popular items are:

1) The Memory Mate, a photograph of the individual team member, plus a team photo, all in the same cardboard photo mount.
2) The Statuette, a photograph of the player mounted on a stiff board and cut out around the figure with a scroll saw and affixed to a base as a free-standing photograph.
3) The ever-popular button, which may be a group but is usually just an individual. These are extremely popular with parents. The parents will wear them to show their support for their child and team.
4) Wallets are another good sale item for sports photos. They are normally sold in groups of eight or nine, but you can package them any way that's good for you.

Many other items such as posters, key chain photos, trading cards and mirrors, can also be sold to increase your profits. Choose the items that you know will sell well in your area.

You can sell any or all of these from a single exposure if you work with a lab that provides a log sheet. By this I mean that you keep track of each frame you shoot by the client's name and so can order exactly what each person wants frame by frame, which gives you the luxury of shooting just one pose of each person. Sales can be tremendous if each player knows in advance exactly what each item is and how much it costs. This usually means that you have to make up a price sheet that carefully explains each photographic item you are offering. Yes, sports can be fun and very rewarding if you work them properly.

Amt. Ordered **ACTIVITY & SPORTS PICTURES**

Amt. Ordered	Item	Price	
____	**5 X 7 Team Picture in Frame**	**$ 7.00**	________
____	**8 X 10 Team Picture in Frame**	**$ 9.00**	________
____	**Memory Mate** 1 - 5 X 7 Team or Group and 1 - 4 X 5 Individual in One Frame	**$ 9.00**	________
____	**Wallets (8)**	**$ 8.00**	________
____	**8" Statue on Wooden Base**	**$15.00**	________
____	Buttons	**$ 4.00**	________
		Grand Total	________

Name ________________

Address ________________

City ________________

State ________ **Zip Code** ________

Phone No. ________________

Sport (Varsity Basketball, Reserve Basketball, etc.) or Team Name

____

Uniform Number ________________

—Payable In Advance—

Peters **Main Street Photography, Inc.**
314 N. MAIN
LONDON, OHIO 43140
1-614-852-2731

PLEASE ALLOW 4 WEEKS FOR DELIVERY

We use this 4½x6½ envelope for all activity photo transactions. Notice that we ask for payment in advance and we recommend that you do the same.

DANCE PACKAGES

Most school photographers keep very quiet about dance packages and that they are often part of a school agreement, but if you cover the various dances and proms held throughout the school year, you will make enough profit to pay for most of the free services you give to the school. In other words, dances are so profitable that they can more than pay for the expense of the freebies you have to give. This means the portraits don't have to pay for them, so the portraits produce a normal profit.

School photographers complain about losing students to non-contract photographers and how they will never be able to make it without the contract students' business, but the truth is they can lose as much as thirty per cent before there is a serious loss of income. They may need to decide whether to continue with a deteriorating contract, but before things get that bad, they should work to turn this situation around by improving their marketing, photography, or personal attitudes. This is something that has to be personally evaluated.

Design the dance packages to allow the students to make choices. We have usually use three packages with the package we really want to sell in the middle. The packages we have used for the past couple of years are:

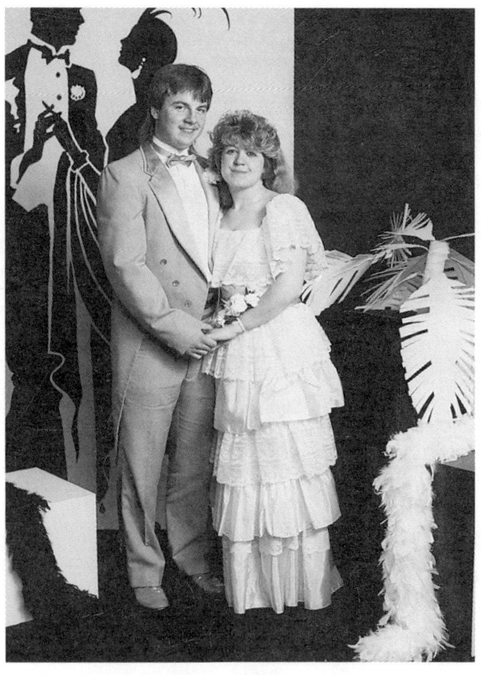

I. 2-5x7
   4-Wallets
   ALL PHOTOS ARE OF THE COUPLE
II. 2-8x10
   8-Wallets
   ALL OF THE COUPLE
III. A DANCE SPECIAL IN ONE TRIPLE STYLE CARDBOARD MOUNT
   2-8x10
   8-Wallets
   ALL OF THE COUPLE

   2-5x7
   4-Wallets
   OF BOY ALONE

   2-5x7
   4-Wallets
   OF GIRL ALONE

Package III is one the students and parents particularly like because there are individual photographs included in the price. Many parents want professional photographs of their child alone to carry in their wallet along with the couple shot. It's also nice to have the single poses if the couple breaks up (which most of them do).

"NO LINE" SCHEDULING

For years, one of the things that bothered me the most about dances were the lines students had to stand in to get their photographs taken. These lines made me feel tense and pressured and the students became angry because they had to wait to have their photograph taken. My wife, Karen, designed a simple scheduling system that eliminated both the line and the pressures we all felt.

Now, when the students enter the dance they are asked if they plan to purchase photographs. If so, they are given a sheet of paper that has our packages listed, a place for the name and address and the schedule. Here is how it works:

We have written a number in the upper corner of each form, starting with one through however many couples have purchased tickets to the dance. Because we know in advance how many students will be there, we can take the hours the dance will last and divide by the number of couples who will attend, which tells how many couples we should plan to photograph in an hour. Then we break it down to quarter hours by dividing by four. So in advance we know exactly how many couples we need to photograph in each fifteen minute period.

On the sheet the students are given, there is a schedule that tells couples, say, one through fifteen to be photographed at 9:00-9:15, couples sixteen through thirty to be photographed at 9:15-9:30 and so on. This schedule has made the wait for these students very minimal, and has made it easy for me to crank them out. Sometimes there is even a lull just before the next group comes. It is hard to believe that you can pace yourself, get more done, and actually have a few minutes to relax between groups, but it's true: this system works extremely well.

GROUP COMPOSITES

Many photographers in the area thrive on being able to go into school systems and photograph some of the larger groups such as the chorus or band. If you can schedule the time there is quite a bit of money to

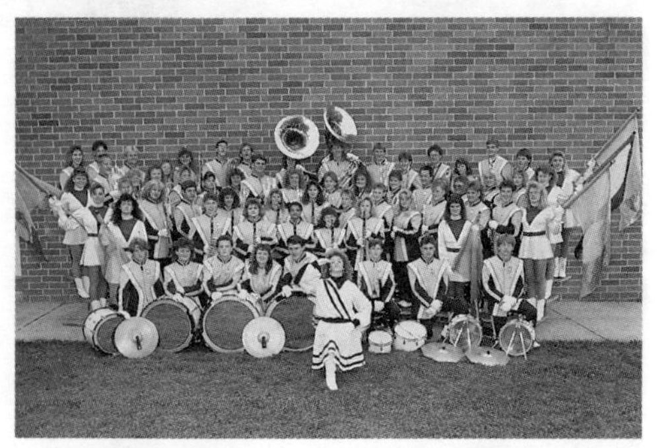
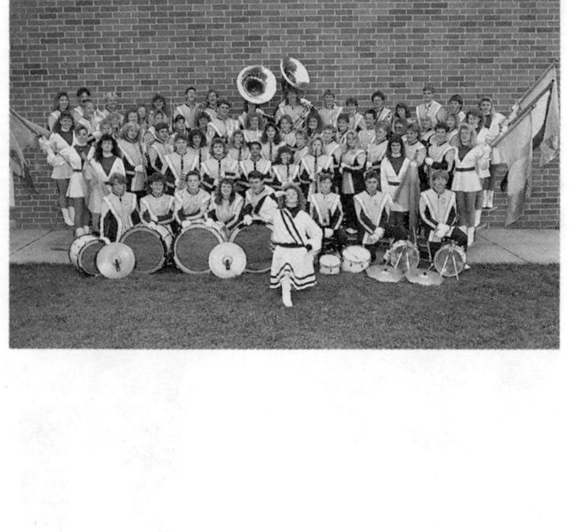

be made from these big groups. The system we adopted for doing composite photography is very simple, requires no sales staff and is very effective, even though some of the students who want to be included in the composite photo will not buy anything.

I tell the people in charge of the group that in order to make this work, they must handle all distribution of photographs and collection of money and that we must be allowed to set up equipment at the school. I usually take an assistant to keep track of records.

Our lighting usually consists of a large forty-two inch soft box, a silver reflector for a fill, and a hair light. Black seamless paper is used as the background, and we use a background light that will take colored gels and we will probably use the school colors in it.

Posing consists of head and shoulders and during the approximately one to one and a half minutes we need to photograph each student, we do a straight-forward pose, one in soft focus and one with a musical instrument, and they can choose whichever pose they desire for the composite.

I have the film processed and wallet size photographs made of each student which we place in an envelope with an order form. We let the students know the photograph they choose from this group of three is the actual one that will appear on the composite and they have to handle it carefully. They can purchase the other two proofs.

We make low cost packages available which include no retouching, spraying, or framing, and they can order from any of their proofs, but only one proof can be used for their composite. The photographs are given to the director to identify and to pass out for a two-day examination at home. If the proofs are not returned, it is the director's responsibility to follow up on them. Any student not returning the photographs will automatically be omitted from the composite.

The order form enclosed with the proofs states that payment must be made before the order will be accepted and processed. This eliminates trying to collect afterwards.

This is not a great money maker: but it does keep you busy, and it gets your name to students before they reach their senior year. Orders will vary in size from fifteen to thirty-five dollars with a certain number not ordering anything.

The system for taking these photographs is very uncomplicated, it does not require much time and it provides a great fill-in at a time when senior business is slow.

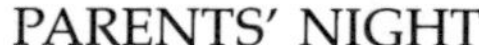

PARENTS' NIGHT

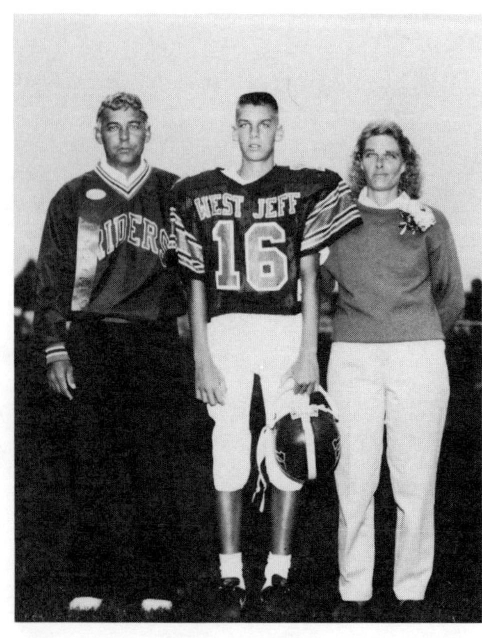

Many school systems have adopted a night in the fall or winter to publicly recognize senior students with their parents. Many parents look forward with great anticipation to this recognition because of their pride in their child, and we are there with camera to photograph those who have previously signed up. The yearbook advisor is a good person to assist you in setting up this type of a photograph by advising the students that photos will be taken, by passing out sign-up sheets, and by collecting the money which should be prepaid before the actual date.

Usually the offer we make is the same to all students, two 5x7s and four wallets. Again, having an assistant is important to keep track of orders and tell you when to photograph the right person.

There are literally dozens, perhaps hundreds, of ways the contract photographer can find to profitably serve his clientele. We are just touching on a few.

As with any business there is a risk involved and most of the problems occur because equipment is not working properly, so we always carry back-up equipment to our out-of-studio assignments. Another problem is nervous blinking by someone who is a little twitchy. If you're taking pictures where you expose a single frame, watch for blinks and cover yourself with a second exposure when you even suspect someone has blinked.

GRADUATION

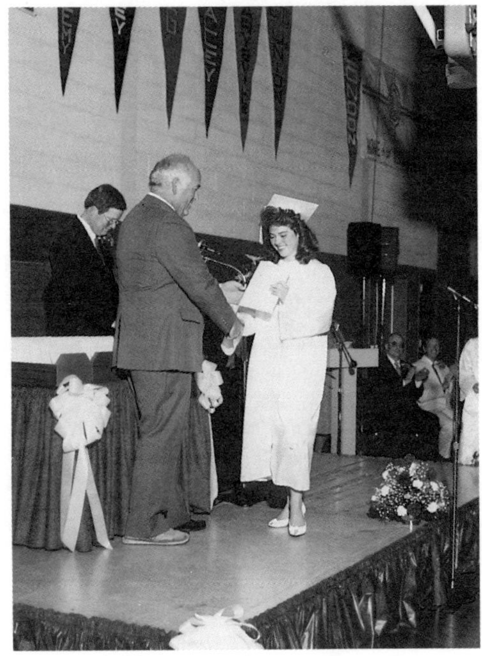

We have planned the year so we will be photographing students all year long in a variety of activities. Some of these activities are easy to record, while others are much tougher. One of the toughest is the last one of the year when we photograph students receiving their diplomas at graduation ceremonies. It was too difficult to do every person, so we went to a pre-pay system. Now those students who want to be photographed as they receive the sheepskin can sign up in advance and prepay for the picture. Traditionally about one-third of the students in a class are interested in this service.

We have found it easiest to use a long-roll film adapter if there are many students to photograph. When we have fewer, we use interchangeable, pre-loaded backs, but be prepared for anything and everything to happen. Because this is a one time shot, have spare equipment at your finger tips in case something goes wrong with your first outfit. And bring someone who can tell you who to photograph, since you don't photograph every member of the class.

We always treat the graduation photograph as a service to these students and their families: this is an important photograph to many of them, one that can add to their memories of their high school years.

Questions & Answers

Payment:

1. Camera charges payable at time of sitting.
2. A $75.00 deposit will be applied to your order when previews leave the studio.
3. One-half deposit is due before orders will be processed.
4. Balance is due in full within 30 days of notification of completion of finished order. If not picked up in 30 days, service charges will be added.
5. Visa or MasterCard welcome.
6. A charge of $10.00 will be made for all checks returned.
7. Finance charges — All complete orders are to be picked up within 30 days notice of its completion or charges of 1½% per month will be added at an annual percentage rate of 18%.
8. **SAVINGS!** Receive a 5% Cash Discount for full pre-payment of an original complete portrait order. Of course, your satisfaction is guaranteed on all finished portrait orders.

Can I Order Later?
Yes, but prices can change and in order to insure current rates, you should order what you need at one time. A $3.00 handling charge will be applied to all re-orders.

When Do I Return Previews?
Previews are loaned to you in order to help you decide but they must be returned within 7 days or you will be billed at a rate of $15.00 per photograph, plus folios. $2.00 per day is charged if previews are not returned by due date.

Copying —
All photographs taken by Peters Main Street Photography are subject to Copyright Laws. Any individual who so violates the law by unlawfully duplicating any preview, wallet or part of an order will be subject to Prosecution! Don't Take A Costly Chance. **Purchase Originals!**

Complexion Retouching —
Complexion retouching is included. However, corrections on hair or clothing will be made by quotation only at a rate of $30.00 per hour. Minimum charge is $15.00.

-ALL PRICES SUBJECT TO CHANGE WITHOUT NOTICE-

Save 20% on all frames when you order them at the time you place your portrait order.

LIFETIME GUARANTEED COLOR PHOTOGRAPHS

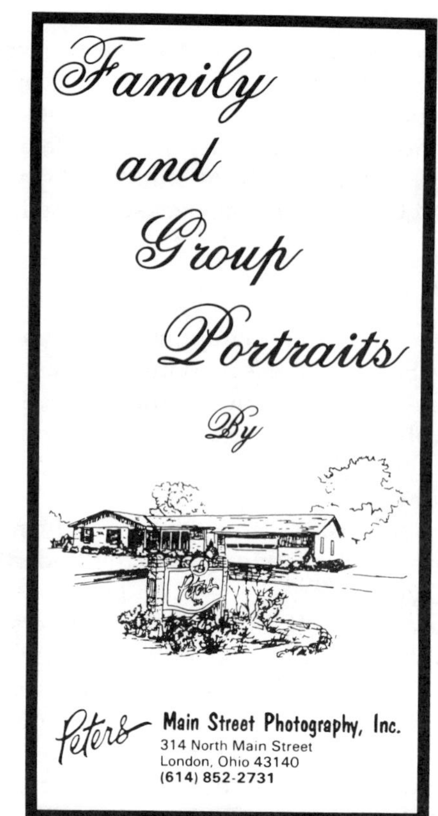

Purchasing Previews

Todays technology allows us to offer customers original portraits that are more permanent than proofs of the past. The photography variety with the many different sittings create cherished memories for years to come.

1. Previews are not available for sale without a minimum order of $75.00.
2. Individual prices after the minimum order of $75.00 is $15.00 each.
3. As your order size increases, the cost of the previews goes down.

ORDER SIZE	NUMBER OF POSES	COST
$75.00-$225.00	10	$65.00
	12	79.00
	20	130.00
$226.00-$374.00	10	60.00
	12	72.00
	20	120.00

OVER $450.00, all previews are free, plus a bonus of the folio(s) for prints. This does not include sitting fee or tax.

Camera Charges

Payable At Sitting Time Scheduled

—SELECT THE PROPER ONE FOR YOU—

I STUDIO SESSION **$15.00** + tax
8-10 poses indoors, including head and shoulder, close-up, ¾ length, 1 additional clothing change (2 total) Time: - ½ hour.

II THE DELUXE *"Our Most Popular"* **$30.00** + tax
18-20 poses, including 10 indoor and 10 outdoor or 20 indoor. Head and shoulder poses, close-up, ¾ length, environmental in our garden setting, bring your imagination, several clothing changes (no more than 4). Time - 1-1¼ hour.

III LOCATION **$60.00** + tax
24-30 poses, including 10 indoor and 20 at your choice of location within 20 miles of London, 2 appointments required. Time: ½ hour studio, 1½ hour location.

IV THE "ELITE" - *Our Very Best* **$95.00** + tax
The girl interested in the best we have to offer. First session begins with a color analysis of client to determine the best colors suited for her complexion. Second session is our make-up session in which we apply the correct colors and amounts for a photography session. You will have a photo session to remember, including 10 out-of-doors poses and 20 indoor poses. Special poses, lighting, fans and props that anyone serious about photography will appreciate. Two appointments required (6 clothing changes) Time 2½-3 hours.

Finish Explanation

I CUSTOM PORTRAIT - Custom portraits are the best photographs that you can purchase. For print corrections, its necessary for a trained person to carefully study your portrait in order to decide what corrections need to be done in order to get the best results. All such corrections are included when you purchase our best photograph. Choose from two finishes:

A. *Old Master Finish* - Our very best finish. Portraits are bonded permanently to canvas and then mounted on a stretcher frame. Brush strokes are added to give the photograph a real painted appearance.

B. *Embassy* - Portraits include retouching and corrective artwork to create the best presentation available.

II DELUXE PORTRAIT - Deluxe portraits contain retouching and a smooth lacquer finish. Wall prints are mounted and ready for framing.

Portraits To Fit Your Needs

SIZES	QUANTITY	CUSTOM PORTRAITS		DELUXE
		Old Master	*Embassy*	
30x40	1		1,080.00	
30x30	1	1,500.00	865.00	
24x30	1	1,075.00	645.00	
24x24	1	925.00	535.00	
20x24	1	775.00	425.00	
20x20	1	525.00	285.00	
16x20	1	430.00	220.00	
8x10 In Folders	1		75.00	46.00
	2*		125.00	88.00
	3*		175.00	126.00
	Additional*		47.00	40.00
5x7 In Folders	2*			48.00
	4*			92.00
	6*			132.00
	2 additional*			42.00
Wallets	16*			26.40
	24*			39.00
	32*			52.80
	8 additional*			6.00

**Additional copies of the same pose.*

Package

30x40 — 2-8x10
16 wallets

Regular-$1,198.40 **SALE-$998.00**

(This package includes all previews and folio at no charge.)

Chapter VI

What to do About Photocopying

Have you ever seen a senior portrait that you recognize as one of yours but the colors were distorted, the highlights and shadows were misrepresented and the sharpness was off? The chances are that it was copied from one of your previews and the prints you saw were made from this "interneg". The copyist made a little money from those prints and you got nothing.

This problem has plagued the portraitist for years as unscrupulous copyists have profited from our work and talent by ripping off both us and our customers. What can we do about it? Let me say first that I am not a attorney and I don't give legal advice, but the PP of A has engaged top lawyers to fight our battles and they have been singularly successful in beating off the copyists. The current copyright laws give us complete protection from this theft of our work if we will take just one simple step and put on our photographs our name, the date and the copyright symbol (a c in a circle). The usual arrangement is © 1990, Larry Peters.

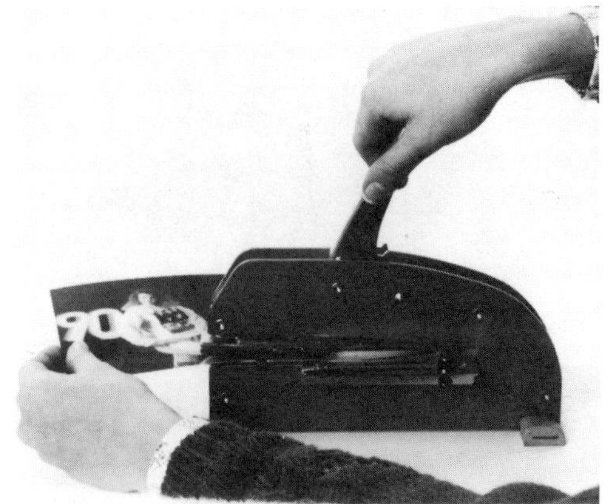

We do several things beyond this to protect ourselves, especially with the previews/proofs because they are so vulnerable. Customers used to place a minimum portrait order to purchase the proofs, then went elsewhere to have the prints they wanted made from copy negs. I am also sure that some people never even ordered, but took the proofs directly to the copy person to have the negs made, then brought the proofs back to us without placing an order.

Our program for protection against copying is this:

We emboss each proof with our name, the copyright symbol and the year using an embossing device like that used by a notary public. You can order one at any stationery store and have it read just the way you want. This embosser puts our name on the face of the photo in a non-demanding way that does not seem to bother anyone. Perhaps it does not bother anyone because it has no color, just a texture, and no one objects even when we put them in a folio and sell them. Incidentally, before we arrived at the embosser, we tried to gold-stamp the same information on the photos, but it did not look as professional.

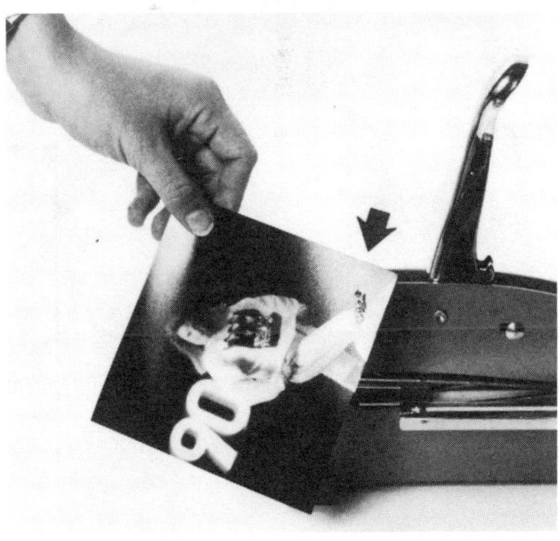

What does the embossing do that makes it work? First of all, it is relatively invisible when you look at it, but under the copy lights the texture stands out and spoils the copy job. It's almost impossible to eliminate the words and numbers that stand out on every copy print.

This one step cut down tremendously on the copying of our work, but we didn't stop there. On the back of every proof we also put self-adhesive labels that say the photograph is the property of Main Street Photography and it cannot be duplicated in any manner. It also has the copyright symbol, date and our name and address. It also mentions a $10,000 penalty for illegal copying. A label goes on the back of every original photograph created in our studio and it's very hard to remove without ruining the preview. None of this is easy, but we are gradually educating our clients on how much better it is to order prints from the original rather than a copy negative. We are also educating the pirates not to fool with Main Street Photography or it may prove to be very expensive.

Reproduction of this photo without written permission of the maker is a violation of Federal law punishable by a $10,000 fine. Photo-copying is not worth the risk!
COPYRIGHT 1990
MAIN STREET PHOTOGRAPHY

There is a third step we take to protect our copyright and that's a "preview receipt" which each customer signs before the proofs leave the studio. This form tells the client several things:

1. How many proofs are taken from the studio;
2. How much they will have to pay for the previews if they are not returned.
3. It gives them a date when they must return the photographs.
4. By signing the receipt they agree not to copy the photographs by any means at any time.
5. They date it and sign the receipt. We give them the NCR copy of the form and retain the original for our files.

If they do not return their previews on time, we call to inquire why they are late. If they still do not return the previews, we make a photo copy of their signed preview receipt and mail it to them showing they have agreed to pay a certain amount for their photos if they are not returned. This usually does the trick and they come flying in with the photographs; they don't want a bill for just the previews. Occasionally we use a collection agency to chase past due accounts, but rarely do these include people who have failed to return previews: they usually represent orders that have not been picked up and are just sitting on the shelf.

We recently heard of one Colorado photographer who also does all the above, but added another step that worked very well for him. He had his attorney draft a letter stating that the studio owner would prosecute anyone who violated his copyright; a copy of this letter was mailed to every photo shop advertising copy services and to all the one hour labs in Denver Metro. The result was that every such business in the area knew what the penalties for violation of copyright were and that this photographer would take them to court. At last report the copy shops were calling him to ask permission to copy which was routinely refused. Of course. This man states that his orders - especially for wallets - jumped quite noticeably after that.

TO: PETERS MAIN STREET PHOTOGRAPHY

I hereby acknowledge receipt of a portfolio consisting of ____________ previews for home examination. I have paid $_________ as a deposit to insure safe return of the previews. In further consideration, I hereby acknowledge that the previews are the sole property of ***Peters Main Street Photography*** until paid for and that I will not copy, by any means whatsoever, at any time, the previews. I agree to return the previews to you on or before ________________ 19 _____ If not returned by that date, I will be billed for $__________ plus $21.00 for each folio.

Date: ______________________________ ______________________________

Chapter VII

Traditional Poses and Yearbook Deadlines

In the past some contract photographers have made it part of their deal with the school that only their portraits can be used in the yearbook. There seems to be less of that now, but it's well to check with each school before you commit to getting your photographs in the annual. What you have to be absolutely aware of is the date for turning in the portraits to the school. Most schools set a deadline to push the students to have their portraits made as early as possible. Even so, many of them put it off to the last moment and then try to squeeze in a sitting, so being aware of these deadlines is a definite advantage to the photographer. It can also be your neck if you don't know the date and you miss the deadline. There will be kids who will never forgive you and advisors who will bad-mouth you forever if you don't get those photos in on time.

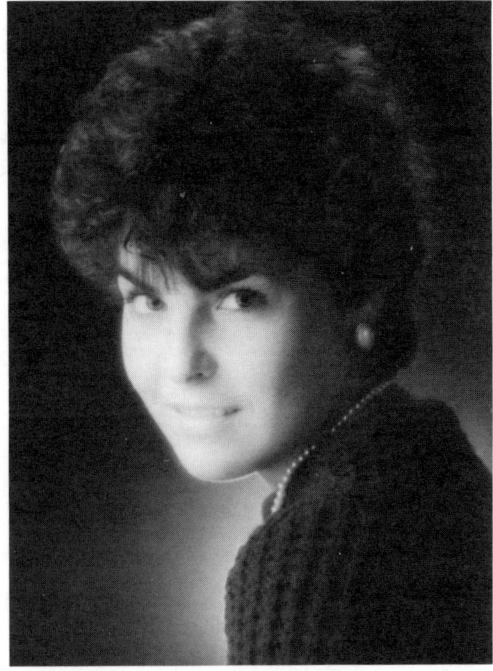

You can nail it all down tight by sending a letter of inquiry to each school in the Spring of the year to learn their deadlines long before they occur. At the same time you should also ask:

1. Does your school require a special size photograph for the yearbook?
2. Do you need all traditional poses or can the students use any photograph they want?
3. Will the yearbook photos be in b/w or in color?
4. Do you require a special head size for each student?

All this information makes you better prepared to handle the needs of your senior students and will earn the respect of the yearbook advisors. It shows you care about them and what they are trying to do.

RUSH TIME

In our area, the rush occurs from Thanksgiving to Christmas because this is the time most yearbook photos are to be turned in. Because we have our own small lab. we can deliver a color or b/w yearbook photograph in a matter of minutes. I do not promote having a large lab and printing everything you do, but it is nice to be able to turn out a quick image to meet these deadlines.

We use a Beseler tabletop processor for color prints and an Agfa-Gaevert stabilization processor for black and white prints. We are not experienced lab people, but one of my employees does an acceptable job of printing these small photographs for yearbook use.

Every year we have students who say, "My yearbook deadline is today (or tomorrow) and I don't suppose you can do anything for me, can you?" They are really desperate but they have pretty much given up on getting their photograph in the annual. I always try to help these students however I can.

We pull out the RB67 with 180mm lens and a Polaroid film back and do a quick instant image which can be used for a yearbook photo. We provide this service at no charge, but the kids never forget it and their appreciation produces for us long after the incident. They always seem to remember it was their fault for waiting too long, and you helped them when there was no way for them to be included in the yearbook. We have made many, many friends for our studio with this service. Of course, we also book a regular sitting at this time.

Because You're Only A Senior Once!

The Very Best We Have To Offer!!

AN **ELITE** PORTRAIT SESSION - **$95.00**

Includes:

★ A color analysis session as a pre-appointment consultation to determine your best colors and the clothing you should wear.

★ A makeover for color photography.

★ 30 incredible poses, and an unbelievable 6 clothing changes.

If you don't know what's best in make-up and clothing, *this ones for you!!*

Why Take Chances . . . Do It Right!

Peters **Main Street Photography, Inc.**
314 North Main Street
London, Ohio 43140
(614) 852-2731

LIFETIME GUARANTEED COLOR PHOTOGRAPHS

Peters

BULK RATE
US Postage Paid
LONDON, OHIO
Permit No. 27

Senior Hot Line - 1-800-446-1922

"Everyone Should Look Great In Their Senior Portrait"

"Everyday we photograph great looking people who have worn the wrong clothing and used the incorrect colors of make-up. They feel they are at their best. But we know they have great potential and don't even realize it. **DON'T BE ONE OF THOSE!!** Choose our Elite Portrait Session or Black and White Image Changing session and **DO IT RIGHT!"**

Our Elite Sitting

Pre-appointment consultation with color analysis, clothing suggestions, a make-up session for photography and a great 30 pose 6-outfit sitting with extra time spent with you.
ALL FOR ONLY . . . $95.00

Black & White Image Changing Sittings

A choice of 2 black and white image changing portrait sessions. Call for more information. Sitting fees range from $49.50 to $65.00.

At Peters, We Suit Your Portrait Needs!!

CALL NOW!

Peters **Main Street Photography, Inc.**
314 N. MAIN
LONDON, OHIO 43140

Peters

BULK RATE
US Postage Paid
LONDON, OHIO
Permit No. 27

Senior Hotline
1-800-446-1922
All Questions Answered

LIFETIME GUARANTEED COLOR PHOTOGRAPHS

Lets Make This A Portrait You'll Be Proud Of For Years To Come!!

We also use full color cards to offer our Elite sittings. We know they are working as we do more and more Elites every year.

Chapter VIII

The Yearbook Pose

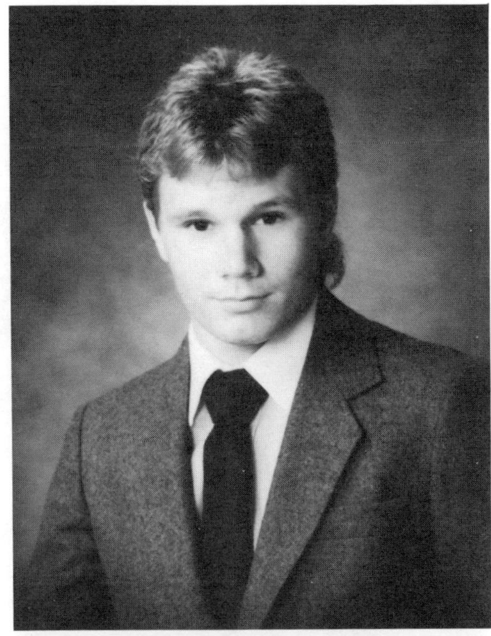

Fortunately, the yearbook is strong in the Mid-Western States. Man, I love those yearbook companies because their promotion of memories is my livelihood. Probably few seniors would even bother to have their portrait made if it wasn't going to be in the yearbook. This photograph is normally a very basic head and shoulder pose and is thought of as one that rarely changes over the decades. The basic principles of lighting and posing are common in these poses.

I personally believe a good traditional type portrait is important to the total overall senior package. This photograph is the one parents, grandparents, and seniors usually expect to receive from their portrait sitting. The secret is doing it right, posing it well, lighting it properly, and - most important - catching the proper expression. There are as many ideas as as there are photographers as to what works best in lighting and posing and I, like everyone else, have my own way of doing things. Let me share the reasoning behind why I do things the way I do.

LIGHTING THE TRADITIONAL POSE

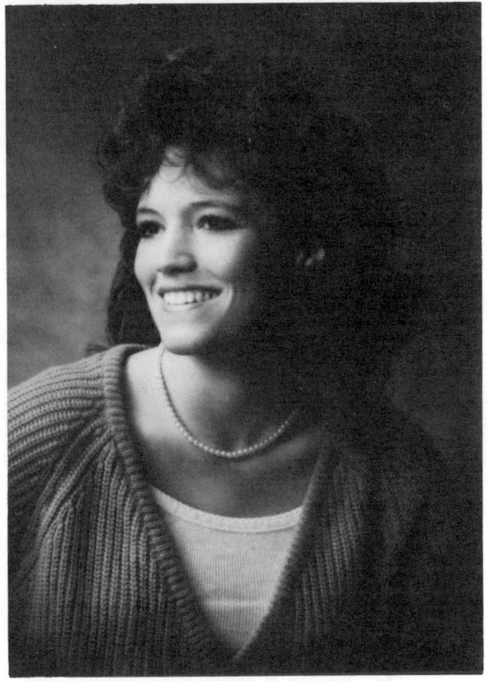

We use basic lighting equipment to create this portrait which consists of:

1. FILL LIGHT, a forty-two inch umbrella with a 400 WS power supply approximately nine feet from the subject metering at F8. We are using Kodak Vericolor III film with a Minolta Flash meter set at ASA 125.
2. MAIN LIGHT, a twenty-four inch pan light with approximately 100 WS of power metering when fired simultaneously with the fill light at F11. The light distance from the subject is approximately forty-five inches.
3. HAIR LIGHT. For hair light I use a twenty-four inch silver umbrella on a boom. I prefer a broad source hair light because it not only shows the texture of the hair, it also gives nice separation between the shoulders and the background. This light meters at F:56 and is approximately thirty inches above and slightly to the rear of the subject.
4. BACKGROUND LIGHT. For backgrounds we use a small five to six inch reflector on a very short stand directly behind the subject's back and about thirty-six inches from the background. The light has 100 WS of power and when you hold the light meter directly behind the subject's head, it meters at F8 the same as the fill light. This is a good way to be sure that "what you see is what you get." Of course, if the modeling lamps are proportional to the light output, it is easier to see the lighting results.

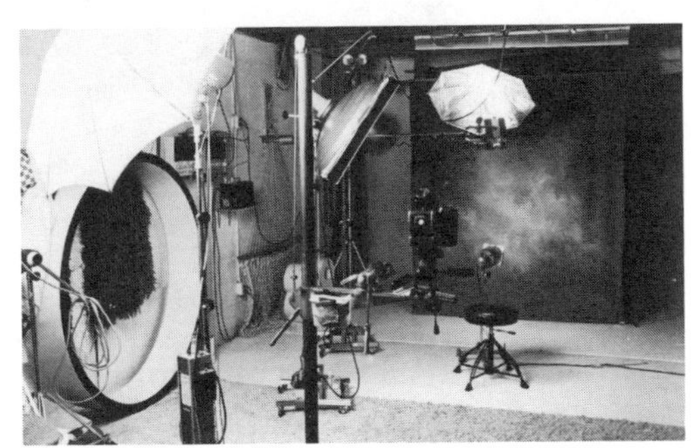

BACKGROUNDS

With a traditional portrait the background is important to the overall view of the portrait. Care should be taken not to choose one that is too dark or over-powering. My primary background for traditional posing is one by LaMar Williamson of Greenville, South Carolina. The colors in it include blue, grey, tan, and a touch of green and they go well with many clothing colors. We formerly used a brown-toned background and received many complaints that it was too dark. We have eliminated this complaint with this lighter background.

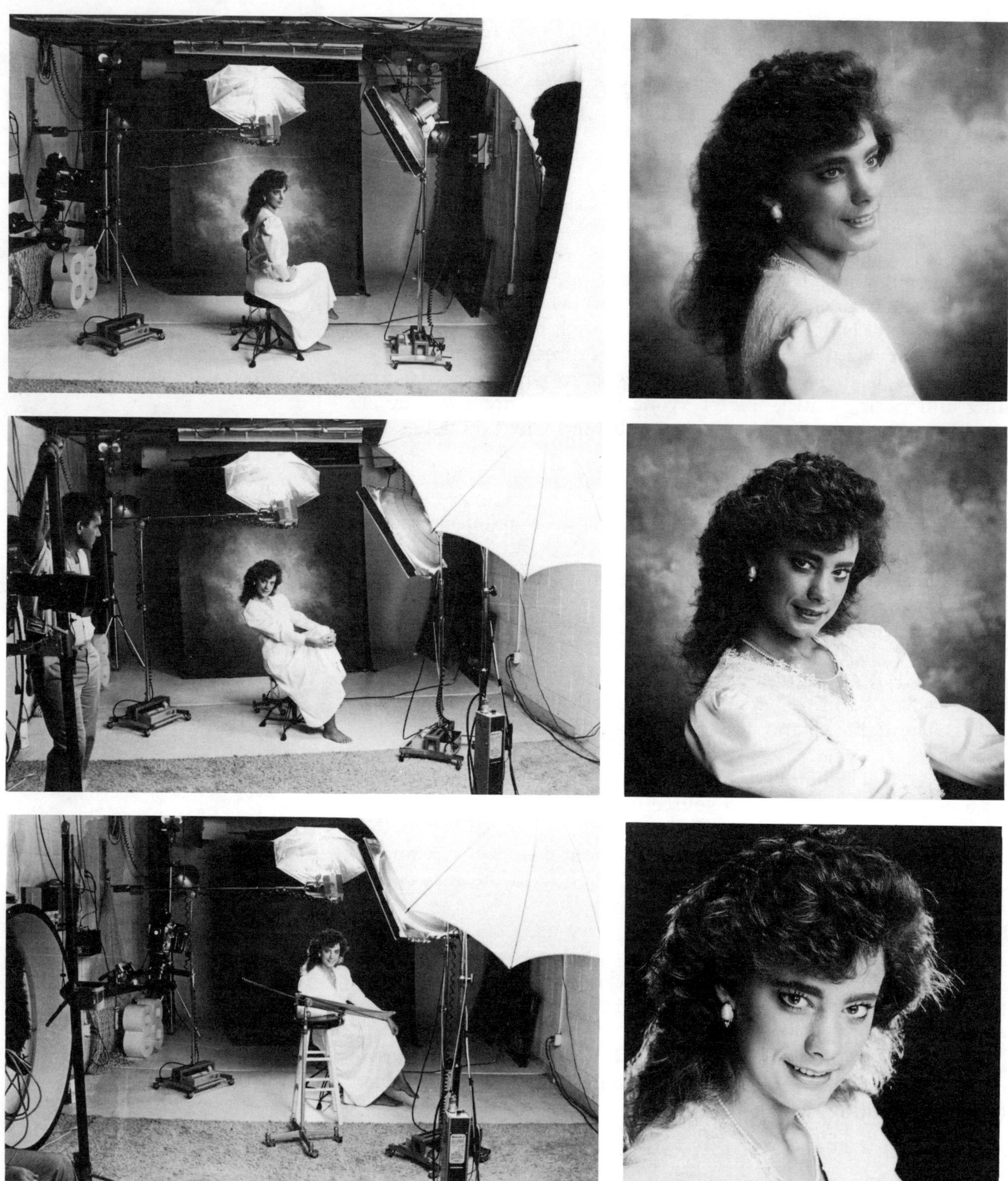

The top pair of photos shows our typical set-up with a parabolic main, umbrella fill and hair lights, background light and a little diffusion. The second pair is very similar, but without diffusion. The third set adds a silver reflector just below the frame, plus diffusion, for a very up to date and glamourous effect.

CAMERA

I use a Hasselblad camera with a 150MM lens. For the traditional shots, the camera lens is set half-way between f:8 and f:11. The lens is protected with a Lindall Pro Lens shade that permits filters to be inserted in a slot close to the lens and vignettes in two other slots further out. A home made vignetter is placed in the middle slot to add a finished look to the bottom of the traditional portrait. We use a Hasselblad Softar II for soft focus photography. I believe you can judge a soft focus filter only after making a twenty by twenty-four enlargement of a close up portrait. Many soft filters look great on previews but not on finished portraits. As a matter of personal preference, I usually open up one-half stop when doing soft focus photography.

Another filter we incorporate in different situations is the Singh Ray UV. The SRUV filter greatly enhances color by removing ultraviolet light from the image. We use this filter for outdoor photography and whenever we switch to high key backgrounds.

Most of our sitting choices are based around five poses with each particular clothing change, so two changes of clothing uses ten shots. But the Hasselblad gives twelve exposures per roll, so we always have two extra shots on each roll of film which is a nice safety factor in case of blinks or whatever. For example, if someone orders a twenty pose portrait session, I have a cushion of four frames.

With the Hasselblad, I always pre-release the mirror before each photograph because I find that mirror-up photography makes for sharper negatives and better prints.

Another reason for pre-releasing the mirror on a professional camera is to foil the blinkers. There really are students who can blink at the precise moment the lens is released, resulting in portraits with closed eyes. No one buys portraits with the "windows of the soul" closed for the winter, so I trip the mirror, then release the shutter when the eyes open again. This seems like a little thing but it guarantees more saleable proofs.

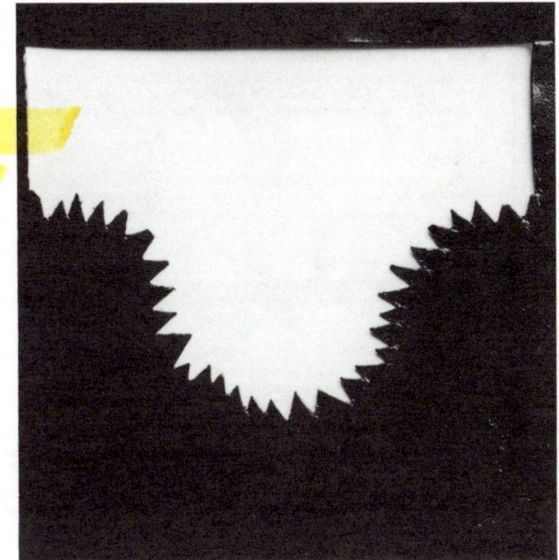

This is my home-made vignetter snipped from aluminum sheet and sprayed with matte black paint.

The Hasselblad with 150mm lens and Lindahl shade. It is rigged with a flash for outdoor use.

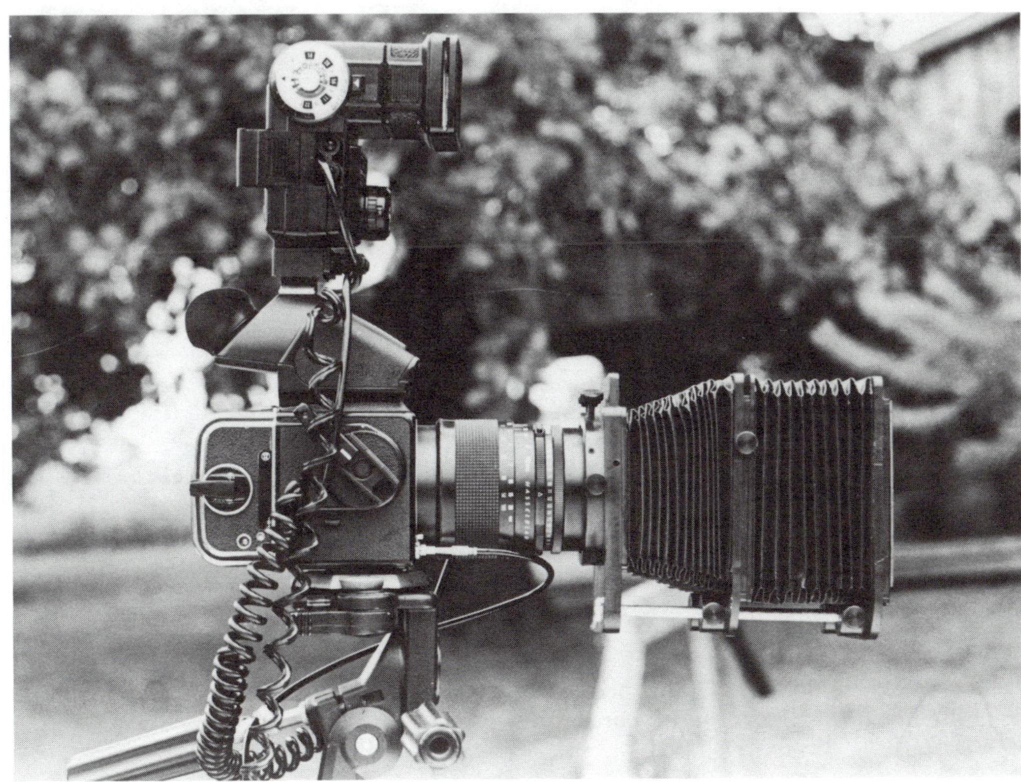

Questions & Answers

Payment:

1. Camera charges payable at time of sitting.
2. A $75.00 deposit will be applied to your order when previews leave the studio.
3. One-half deposit is due before orders will be processed.
4. Balance is due in full within 30 days of notification of completion of finished order. If not picked up in 30 days, service charges will be added.
5. Visa or Master Card welcome.
6. A charge of $10.00 will be made for all checks returned.
7. Finance Charges — All complete orders are to be picked up within 30 days notice of its completion or charges of 1½% per month will be added at an annual percentage rate of 18%.
8. **SAVINGS.** Receive a 5% Cash Discount for full pre-payment of an original complete portrait order. Of course your satisfaction is guaranteed on all finished portrait orders.

Can I Order Later?

Yes, but prices can change and in order to insure current rates, you should order what you need at one time. A $3.00 handling charge will be applied to all re-orders.

When Do I Return Previews?

Previews are loaned to you in order to help you decide but they must be returned within 7 days or you will be billed at a rate of $15.00 per photograph, plus folios. $2.00 per day is charged if previews are not returned by due date.

Copying —

All photographs taken by Main Street Photography are subject to Copyright Laws. Any individual who so violates the law by unlawfully duplicating any preview, wallet or part of an order will be subject to Prosecution. Don't Take A Costly Chance. Purchase Originals.

Complexion Retouching —

Complexion retouching included. However corrections on hair or clothing will be made by quotation only at a rate of $30.00 per hour. Minimum charge $15.00.

What About Yearbook?

We like unusual portraits but we've found that traditional head & shoulder poses still are best for your yearbook. One will be included at no charge if ordered from a pose chosen for your portrait order, if another pose is chosen, add $9.00 for pose change.

All Prices Subject To Change Without Notice.

What About Purchasing Previews?

Todays technology allows us to offer customers original portraits that are more permanent than proofs of the past. The photography variety with the many different sittings create cherished memories for years to come.

1. Previews are not available for sale without a minimum order of $75.00.

2. Individual prices after the minimum order of $75.00 is $15.00 each.

3. As your order size increases the cost of the previews goes down.

ORDER SIZE	NUMBER OF POSES	COST
$75.00 - $225.00	10	$65.00
	12	79.00
	20	130.00
$226.00 - $374.00	10	60.00
	12	72.00
	20	120.00

OVER $450.00, all previews free, plus a bonus of the folio(s) for prints. Does not include sitting fee and tax.

4. Protective lacquer spray is available at a cost of $.75 per preview.

5. Presentation folios (many styles available)
   12 print, triple - $29.75
   8 print w/ wings - 21.00
   1 - 8x10 w/4 - 4x5 on wings - $21.00

6. FOLIO FRAME - (Now you can hang your folio) (Gold or Wood)
   8 opening - $30.00
   12 opening - $40.00

7. **Want a Folio for a Friend?**
   8 - 4x5's in a Folio $70.00
   (This may be purchased only after purchase of the first set of previews)

8. Locker Poster - 8"x16" - $35.00
   unretouched, unsprayed, unmounted

LIFETIME GUARANTEED
COLOR PHOTOGRAPHS

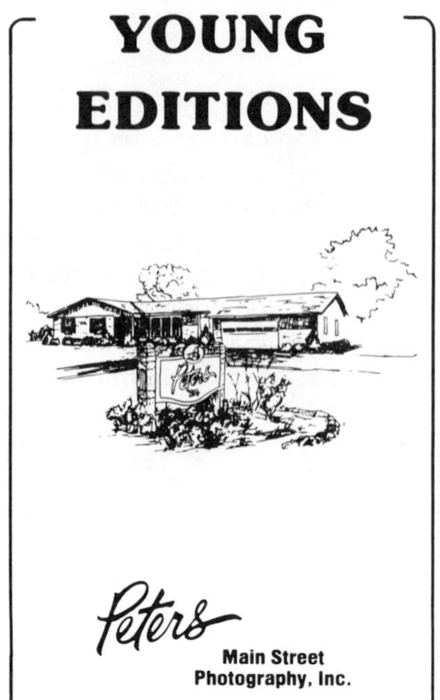

Effective February 1988

Camera Charges

Payable At Sitting Time Scheduled

SELECT PROPER ONE FOR YOU

I THE SENIOR — **$15.00 + tax**
8-10 poses indoors, including head & shoulder, close-up, ¾ length, 1 additional clothing changes (2 total) Time: - ½ hour

II THE DELUXE "OUR MOST POPULAR" — **$30.00 + tax**
18-20 poses, including 10 indoor and 10 outdoor. Head & shoulder poses, close-up, ¾ length, environmental in our garden setting, bring your imagination, up to 6 clothing changes (We'll help you pick the best 4 which are included in the sitting) Time - 1-1¼ hour

III BLACK AND WHITE GLAMOUR "OUR NEWEST" — **$49.50 + tax**
Not intended to replace the color portrait, but to be a unique experience. Make-up session to be a corrective make over, 20 poses presented on contact sheets, 4 changes of clothing. (Black and white prices on separate price list) Time: 2 hours

IV COMBINATION BLACK AND WHITE AND COLOR — **$65.00 + tax**
10 poses in color to include traditional poses and unusual backgrounds PLUS 10 poses in black and white including a make-over for contemporary Black and White. 4 Clothing changes. Time: 2½ hours

V LOCATION — **$60.00 + tax**
24-30 poses, including 10 indoor and 20 at your choice of location within 20 miles of London, 2 appointments required. Time: ½ hour studio, 1½ hour at location

VI JUST FOR THE FUN OF IT OR "OFF THE WALL" POSES — **$2.00 per pose (minimum 5 poses) + tax**
Add to any 20 pose session. Bring the clothing that you've always dreamed of, modeling poses or use our hats for "Off the Wall Crazy Poses" 2 Clothing changes per 5 poses. Time: ½ hour per 5 poses

VII THE "ELITE" - OUR VERY BEST — **$110.00 + tax**
The Senior girl interested in the best we have to offer. First session begins with a color analysis of client to determine the best colors suited for her complexion. Second session is our make-up session in which we apply the correct colors and amounts for a photography session. Next, a hair stylist will enhance your present hair style or design a new look for your photo session. Last, a photo session to remember, including 10 out-doors poses and 20 indoor poses. Special poses, lighting, fans and props that anyone serious about photography will appreciate. Two appointments required (6 clothing changes) Time 2½-3 hours

PACKAGES AVAILABLE

CLUSTER
4 - 4x5 prints
2 - 5x7 prints
1 - 8x10 print
4 - 4x5 wooden frames w/glass
2 - 5x7 wooden frames w/glass
1 - 8x10 wooden frame w/glass
2 - 5x7 prints (loose)
$176.00 using Previews
$220.00 using Reprints

BUDGET
8 - Wallets
1 - 8x10
- Less Spray
- No Pose Change
$52.50

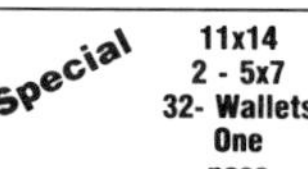

11x14 Wood Frame
5x7 Folders
$193.60

FINISHING TOUCHES

Gallery - Portraits are mounted on canvas and then enhanced with hand applied brush strokes that add depth to a fine photograph.

Deluxe - Includes a slight textured finish with photograph mounted (on 11x14 and larger) to heavy mounting board. Protective spray available in lustre or clear. Unless specified, finishes will be lustre. Clear enhances colors but some glare is noticeable with this finish.

FOR YOUR WALLET
See B & W prices for B & W wallets
(quantity prices based on one pose)
Add $9.00 per pose for dividing wallets.

32 - $52.80
48 - 70.40
64 - 82.50
80 - 95.70
96 - 108.90
112 - 122.10
144 - 148.50
160 - 161.70
200 - 194.70
$6.00 per 8 additional after 200 purchased

Wallet album for your friends' photographs
20 print - $4.50 50 print - $8.00

OUR LARGEST PACKAGE

1 20x24 Gallery Print w/walnut frame
1 11x14 in cluster frame
1 8x10 in cluster frame
1 8x10 in cluster frame
2 5x7 (1 in cluster frame and 1 loose)
2 5x7 (1 in cluster frame and 1 loose)
2 5x7 (1 in cluster frame and 1 loose)
4 4x5 (1 in cluster frame and 3 loose)
4 4x5 (1 in cluster frame and 3 loose)
4 4x5 (1 in cluster frame and 3 loose)
4 4x5 (1 in cluster frame and 3 loose)
96 wallets (all same pose)
* loose prints are framed in easel frames

Regular . . . $930.77
Sale Price . . . $650.89

Bonus:
1 - 8" x 16" locker poster
1 - 5x5 Deluxe album w/ 20 previews
GREAT GIFT!!!

Design A Package

(Less Frames)

SIZE	QTY.	GALLERY	DELUXE
30x30 or 30x40	1	$700.00	$376.00
24x24 or 24x30	1	450.00	272.00
20x20 or 20x24	1	290.00	205.00
16x20	1	200.00	156.00
11x14	1	130.00	96.00
10x10 or 8x10	1	Gallery Not Recommended for 8x10 or Smaller:	42.00
	2*		79.00
	3*		112.00
2 - 5x7	2*		44.00
same pose	4*	"	84.00
	6*	"	116.00
1 - 5x7			33.00 ea.
4 - 4x5	4*	"	46.00
same pose	8*	"	86.00
	12*	"	124.00

*** All portraits from the same pose.**

EASEL FOLDERS — 4x5 - $2.00 ea.
5x7 - $2.50 ea.
8x10 - $4.00 ea.

"20% off wooden frames if purchased at time of order."

Our senior price list is 9x15, folded to 5x9 and printed in two colors on coated white stock. Notice that one panel answers the questions the come up constantly.

Chapter IX

Other Lighting Techniques for Special Poses

I believe if you want to show versatility, you have to use more than a basic lighting set-up, so this section is a guide to some lighting set-ups which demonstrate creativity in photography.

SOFT BOX

Soft lighting from a broad source has been around since the beginning of photography, but in recent years the portrait photographer has been rediscovering how easy it is to work with a broad light and how flattering it is almost any subject. We prefer to use a forty-two inch soft box and a Photogenic Silfoil four by six foot reflector for lighting a subject, especially with colored backgrounds. Dean Collins popularized this type of lighting some years ago. I have found that if you position your subject somewhat farther than normal from the background and use a soft box at the side plus a reflector fill, you will get darker, more vibrant background colors. I treat the seamless paper background like a front projection screen in that I keep the light from striking it, knowing that I will get better and purer colors.

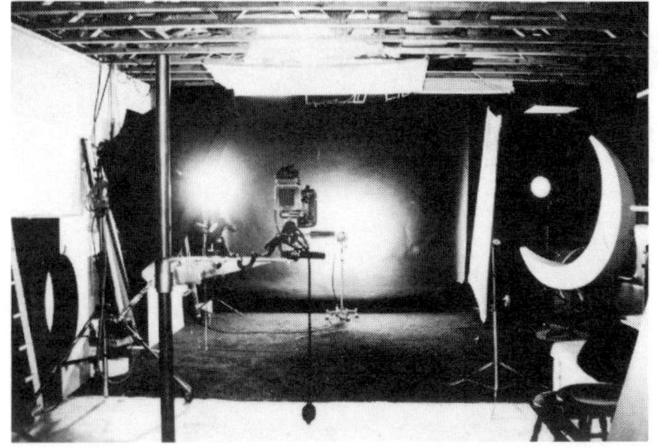

When working with soft lighting, the big box and reflector are not the only light sources. We also have a four by six foot soft box permanently mounted on the ceiling which acts as a hairlight and also separates the subject from the background by adding a soft glow around the shoulders.

We also add separation lights which are twelve inch square softboxes. These are used as edge lights to further separate the subject from the background. We frequently use colored gels on them to add one more dimension. We position these lights behind the subject, pointed in at approximately forty-five degrees on each side. The meter reading we use is approximately F:4.

The final light with this particular set-up is the background light and for this we use a Photogenic Studiomaster, one of the best lights ever made. I like it because it can be used with a five inch reflector and a holder for the colored gets. It can also be used as a bare bulb light source with the gel wrapped around the tube; the bare bulb lights not only the background, but also throws color on the subject's hair from underneath for a radically different look.

The power of this light source is determined by the color of the gel used. Our experience is that when we use warm colors such as red or amber, we need only 100 watts-seconds, but when we switch to cool colors like blue, aqua, purple, or green, we usually have to boost the power setting to 200 watts. That's our experience, but you need to check this out for yourself by making tests with your own equipment.

Incidentally, the use of colored backgrounds has opened new looks in contemporary senior photography with the result that many students now bring in brighter, more colorful outfits that show their personality. If you can accommodate yourself to this trend, you can reap extra monetary benefits.

After determining the exposure of the big soft box main light, we use that number as a guide in determining how bright to make the hair light. I believe you can add light to any photograph from many directions, as long as these lights are not brighter than your main light. If the main calls for an exposure of f:8, the hair light should meter out at f:5.6 or a little less. Don't let this light be any brighter than this or it becomes directional and may cast shadows on the subject's face.

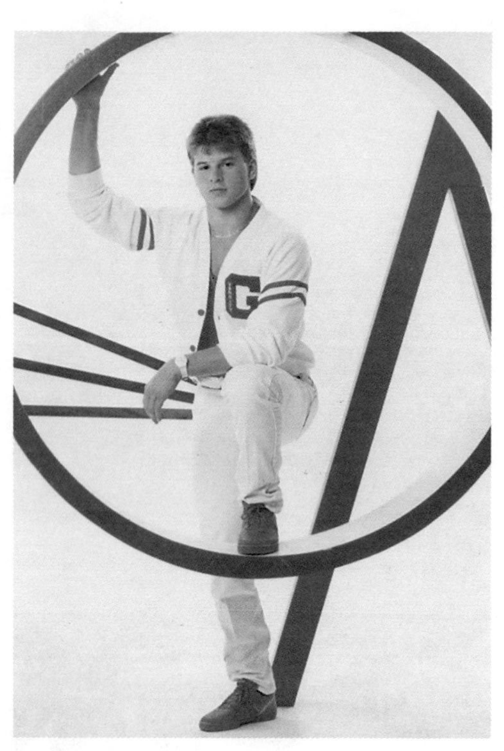

HIGH KEY

A very popular lighting today is high key which is usually interpreted as a flatly lighted portrait against a pure white background. In practice it often means you have to shoot in a totally white room. In one of our camera rooms we have a permanent white sweep that we built expressly to do all-white backgrounds with as many students as we can.

The construction of this sweep is simple and straight forward. First, we nailed 2x4" studs to the wall; then we cut 3/4" thick plywood cut in a two foot radius and nailed one to the side of each 2x4 and feathered them into the floor. (See illustration.)

Next we attached drywall material (you may know it as plasterboard, wallboard or gypsum board) to the back wall above the curved section. The curve and the floor are made from several pieces of 1/4" thick mahogany plywood (also called "Lauan") We had to soak the plywood in water to make it flexible enough to bend. The panel was then placed into the curve and glued to the floor with construction adhesive.

We built up the floor with several panels of the same plywood glued to the floor. This new floor extends about ten feet from the wall.

The seams in the wall board were covered with tape and spackled, then painted with flat white. The floor should be done with a good porch and deck paint for maximum wear. Even so, it gets a lot of use and we find we have to touch up the paint about once a month during the senior rush. Of course, if you can find some pure white linoleum, that would make an impervious floor that would never need touching up.

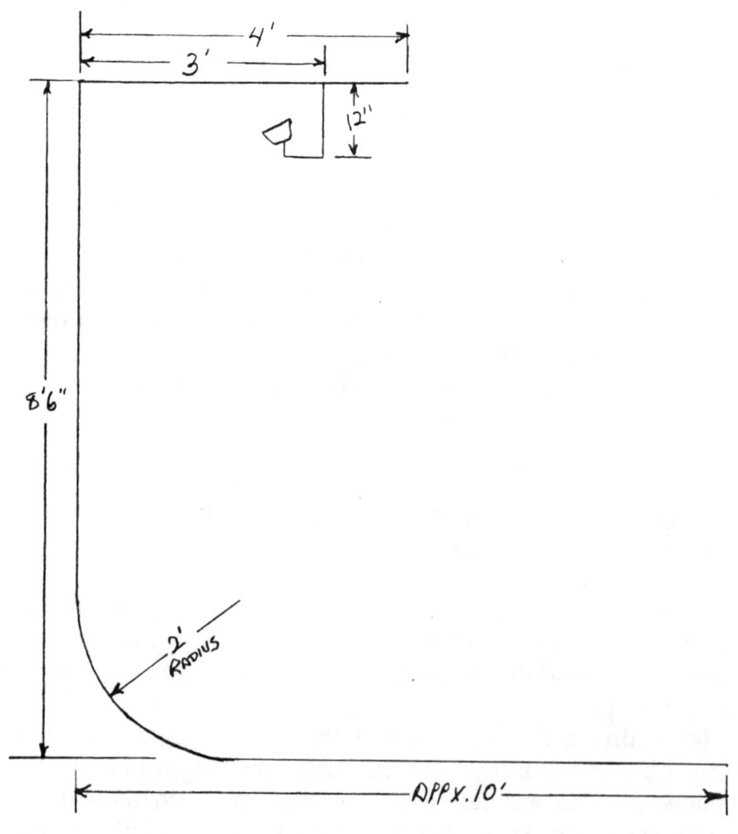

LIGHTING A WHITE ROOM

We are presently lighting the white room with a technique I acquired from Ron Ahrens in Fond du Lac, Wisconsin. The lighting consists of two lampheads, one on each side of the background, which are pointed up into the ceiling. We tip them slightly toward the back wall and slightly toward the center of the room.

We don't have to use a lot of power with this set-up, just 240 w/s in each head. This gives a consistent reading in the center of the background of between f:16 and f:22 while the floor reads f:16 as far out from the wall as six feet.

We fill this arrangement with a forty-two inch umbrella at f:8 and use a twenty-four inch soft box as a main light. This light also meters about f:8 and provides drection and modeling.

The good points of this lighting are:

1. A pure white background and floor, even in the foreground because the umbrella and soft box spill on the floor in front. There are no gray areas.
2. Because the lighting on the wall is indirect, you can hang things on it and not be troubled by heavy shadows nor are they ever washed out because the light is bounced and soft. Since the back wall is dry wall, push points are great for pinning objects to the wall. Sure, the points make tiny holes in the wall, but we spackle them in when we do our monthly floor painting and touch up with a little paint and it's brand new again.

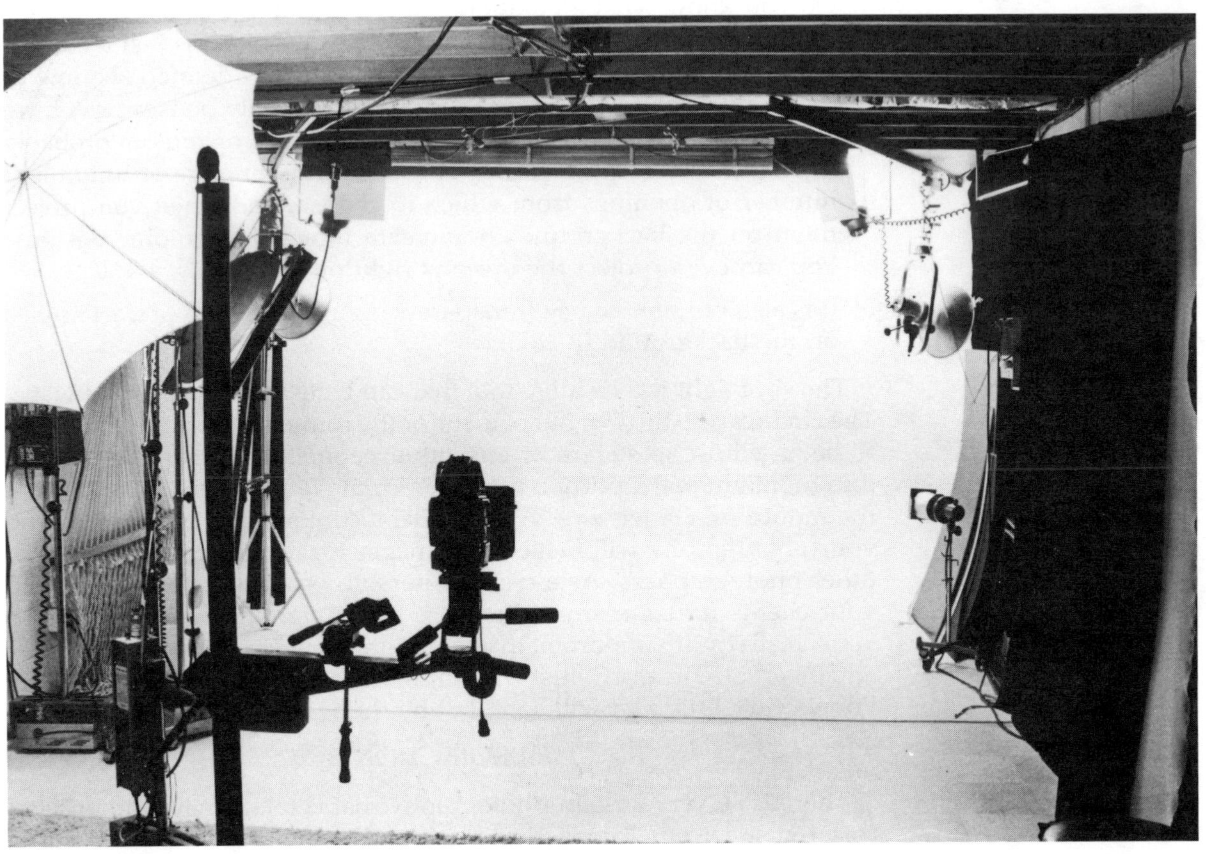

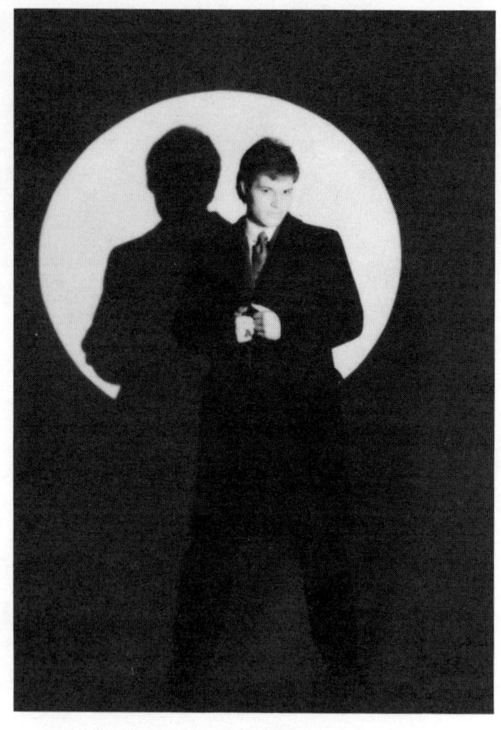

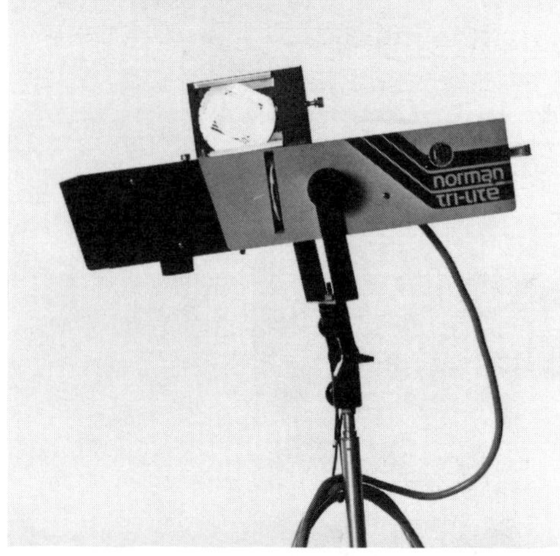

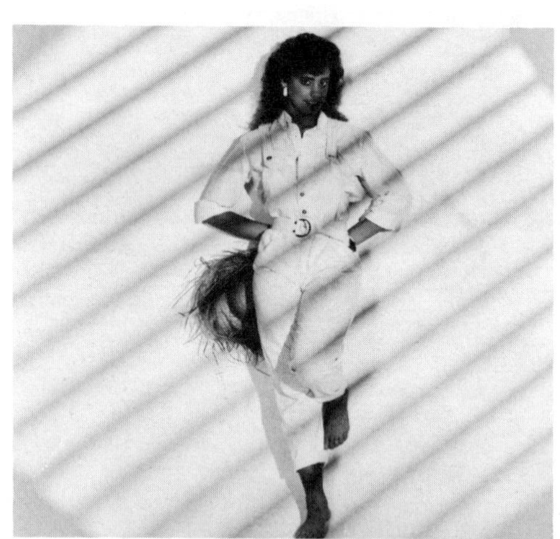

SPOTLIGHT

Most of us younger photographers have never used any studio lighting other than electronic flash in open reflectors, umbrellas or soft boxes. That's the way we learned to do it and it has been very successful for us. But some of the old-timers among us can remember when much portraiture - and virtually all of it that came from Hollywood - was done with a spotlight as the main source. I suspect the reason the spots fell into disuse is that until quite recently no one made a spot with a flash tube inside and there's no easy way to do portraits with both electronic flash and hot lights combined.

Now several of the manufacturers of electronic lighting equipment have re-introduced the spotlight which has opened a whole new area for the creative professional. Some of the techniques I have adopted for use with the spot light are:

1. Using it as the only light source, creating a circle of light on a white or even a colored wall.
2. Using the spot light in combination with a fill covered with a colored gel. This colored fill, when metered two stops under the main, adds a deep, rich hue of the gel's color on the background, but adds virtually no color to the subject. This gives an totally different look that will perk up sales.
3. For a special effect shot, we incorporate a Cokin #209 multi-image parallel filter in front of the camera lens to create a stroboscopic movement effect.
4. Do you know what a cukuloris is? It's commonly called a "cookie" by the movie people who use it extensively, and it is just a cut-out that fits in a slot in the spot and casts a sharply defined shadow of itself on the background. Many theatrical supply houses now have them available for different brands of spotlights, or you can probably make your own quite easily. These cut-outs provide an unlimited number of openings from which to choose, and when you project them on the background they create interesting graphic designs. You can even project the designs right on a person.
5. It is also possible to use transparencies in the spot to project scenes on the background in color.

The spot light is a creative tool that can be used in a variety of ways. The circle can be thrown out of focus or the round shape can be modified to be an ellipse, a square or any other geometric shape. You can use it to highlight just a portion of a person, the face, for instance, or even the mouth or a single eye. Any special technique you incorporate into your photography will make your images look different from those of other photographers. As a creative person, you owe it to yourself and your clients to use many different types of lighting so as to increase your creativity. It's important that you continue to grow as a photographer and an artist. The portraitist who thinks he already knows it all actually knows very little and will soon fall by the wayside.

THE PROJECTION BOX

There is so very little in photography that is totally new and original that I suspect our "projection box" probably has a twin in a studio somewhere in the country. It's quite simple, just a box with a lens on one end and a light on the other and an adjustable stage in the middle. The lens can be from a magnifier or a fresnel lens from an old spotlight, but the light should be a fairly powerful electronic flash. (We use a 1000 w/s unit.) The sliding stage inside the box uses magnetic tape to hold a cookie, strips of Rosco gel material or a negative with the class year numbers. You can put anything in it and project its image on the background or splash it across the student and the BG. It works like a spot, but we feel it is more versatile because it makes possible a great variety of BG colors and shapes. We are just beginning to learn how to exploit this inexpensive gadget to get effects we could only imagine before.

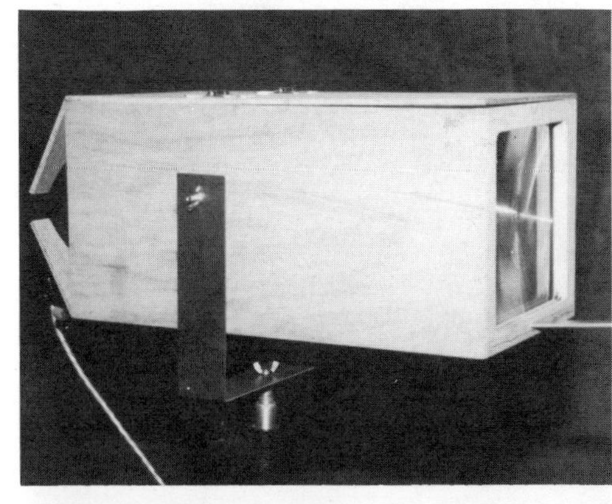

FASHION LIGHTING

Many photographers refer to this type of lighting as a flat lighting, meaning it comes from a light source located quite close to the camera lens and pointed straight on toward the sitter's face. It is virtually shadowless. This lighting is used a lot in fashion magazine photography, probably because it shows off clothing very well. But it also can be extremely flattering to a narrow face or to someone who is wearing a very creative make-up. Because a lighting like this is so straight-on and revealing and because it adds no shadows to the face, you must rely on make-up for facial contouring. A good make-up artist can correct faulty facial structure - narrow a fat face, shorten a long nose, create the appearance of bigger eyes and so on. It is very rewarding to enhance the appearance of a person with make-up, but even if you don't have a makeup artist, flat lighting techniques can add variety to your photography.

We use a very simple set-up for flat lighting: the main light is a thirty inch Halo on a boom. When I properly placed this light right at the camera, its stand got in the way, so I mounted the lighting unit on a home-made, counter-weighted boom. The boom arm is six feet of electrical conduit pipe which provides adequate strength and will not bend, but weighs very little.

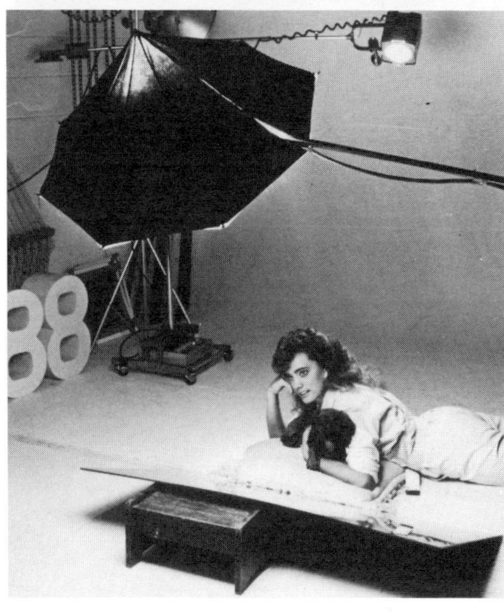

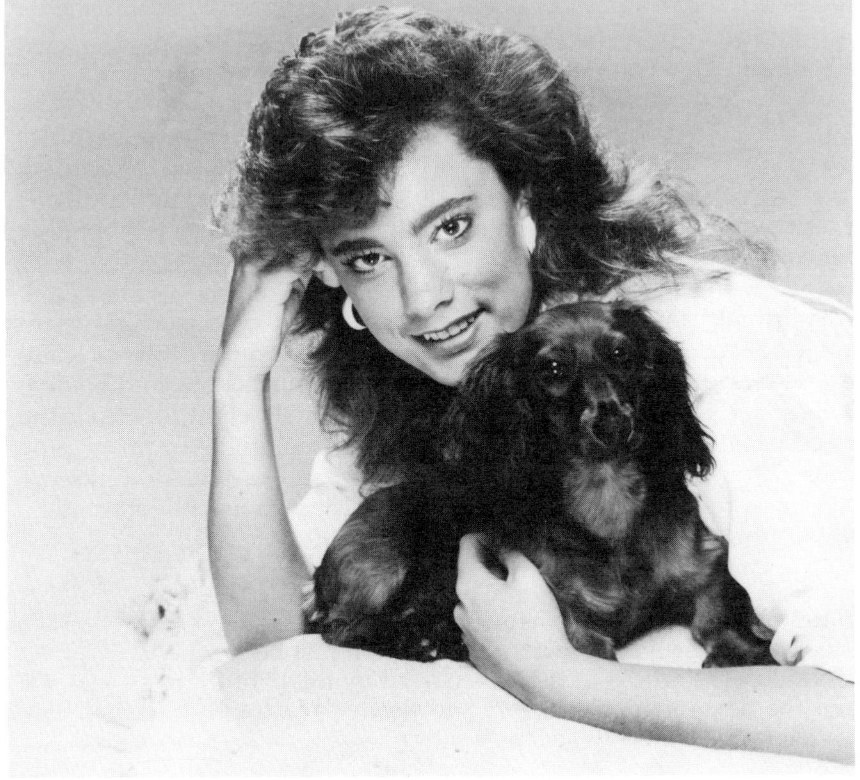

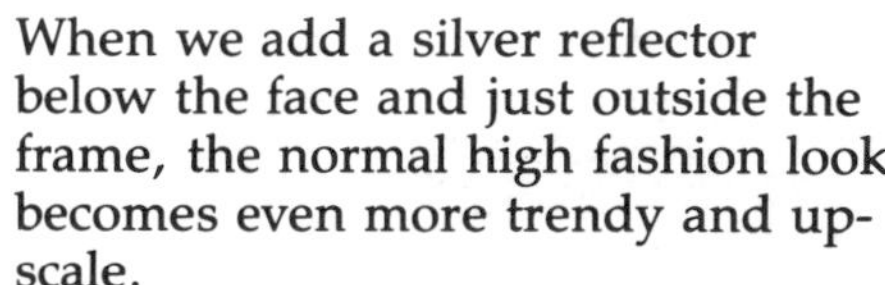

When we add a silver reflector below the face and just outside the frame, the normal high fashion look becomes even more trendy and upscale.

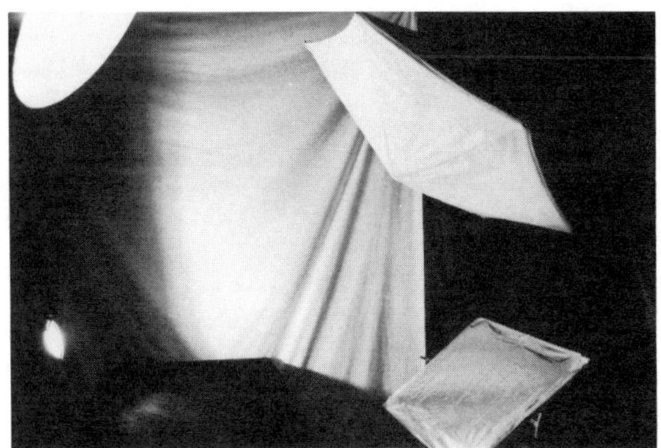

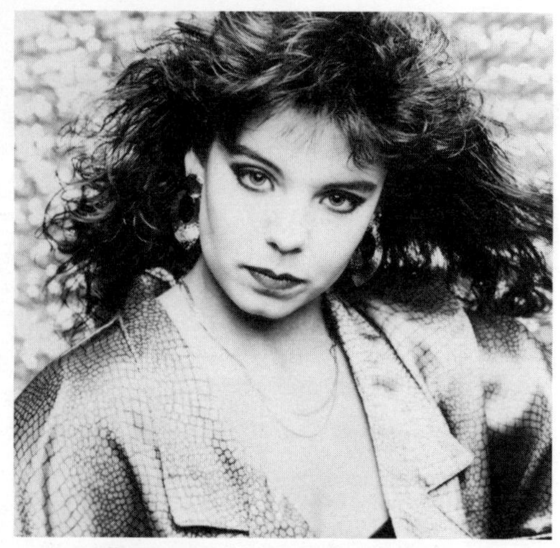

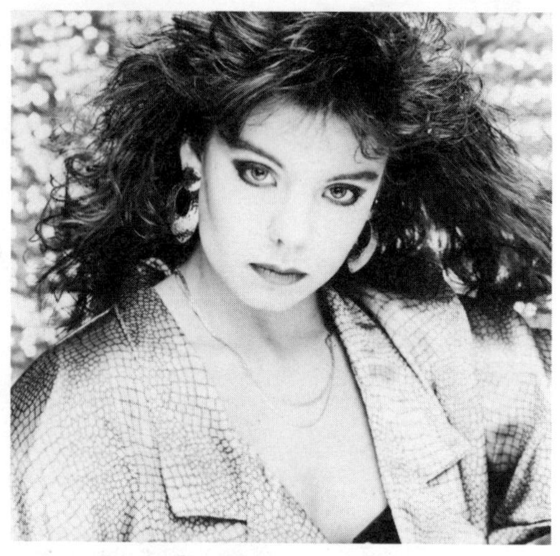

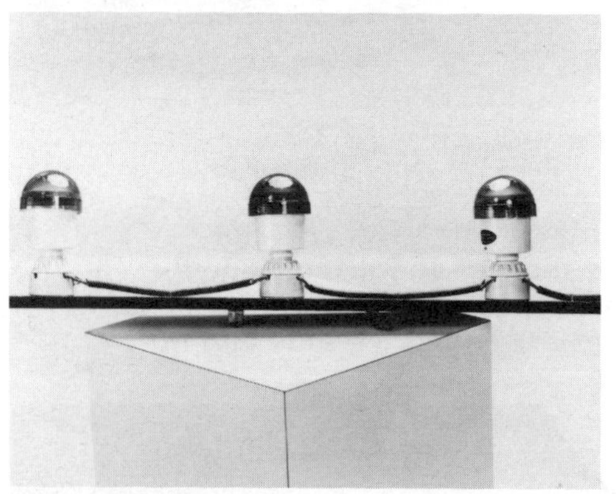

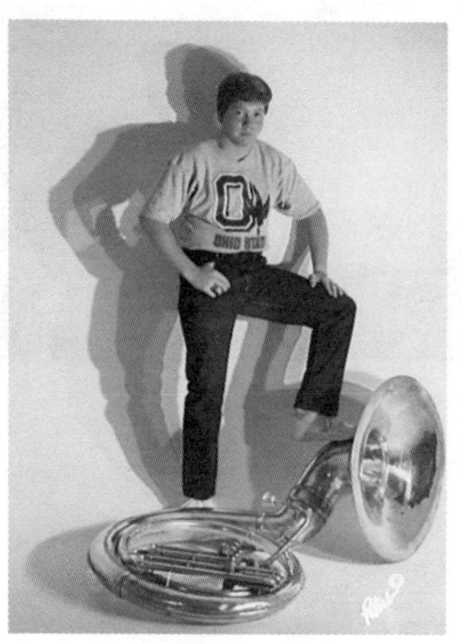

Most of the posing with this lighting set-up is done with people either sitting or lying on the floor. This casual position is very relaxing for the subject and it allows for many different poses. We have incorporated a plastic mirror on the floor as a reflector. The mirrored surface is two by four feet, and the back edge is propped up approximately six inches. This bounces the reflected light into the subject's face filling in the small shadow areas the Halo creates and adding an interesting catch-light in the eyes at 6:00 o'clock. These catch-lights are very trendy and they add a high fashion look. As you can imagine, senior girls love it!

For a hair light, I use a regular Photogenic Hair light on a boom arm also directly from above and slightly behind the subject. The metering of the lights are F:8 front and F:11 or one stop brighter for hair. We normally use the all white area for taking these photographs, but leave the background lights off so the white photographs as light gray. Because we rarely work with professional models or people who do extremely good jobs with their makeup we soften the camera lens for a more saleable product.

STROBOSCOPIC EFFECT

This is a lighting effect I found quite by accident. With three inexpensive AC flash units you can create an image that appears to move or vibrate. A real plus is that it also produces three shadows in three different colors. Here is how you do it:

Using a piece of 1x4″ or 1x6″ wood three feet long, mount three sockets on it about a foot apart. Use standard Edison-base porcelain sockets, the kind that accept a standard light bulb. Wire them all together in parallel (NOT series) and add enough wire to reach the socket. Attach a standard two-prong plug on the wire so the lights can be plugged into any electrical wall outlet. In the sockets screw three small AC flash units, the kind that are available from a number of sources. (If you can't find them locally, you can order from JL Originals, address below).

You can order an accessory set of five colored domes with these lights which just snap over the dome to color the emitted light. We use the red, blue and green domes on them which - when combined - illuminate the subject with white light. But wherever there are shadows cast by one of the units but filled by one or two of the others, the shadows will be colored. There will be colors in the nose shadows and the shadow cast by the chin, but those are negligible. The shadows that really draw the comments are those cast on the wall behind the subject, where the three colors can be seen quite clearly and sharply, creating a true wild look.

We normally position the subject quite close to the background, even leaning against it, with no light on it except for the tri-colored spill. The effect is of one heck of a lot of movement, action, and color. I usually place this light on the floor approximately eight feet from the subject, but it can be mounted on a stand or boom with ordinary pipe clamps obtainable at any hardware store. Because the AC units are small, low-powered and covered with light-absorbing colored domes, you will find that exposure will be on the order of f:5.6.

The two top photos show what happens to the normal high fashion look when a silver reflector is positioned just below the camera's vision. The whole look is is changed by the light from below and the new catch light is very provocative and trendy.

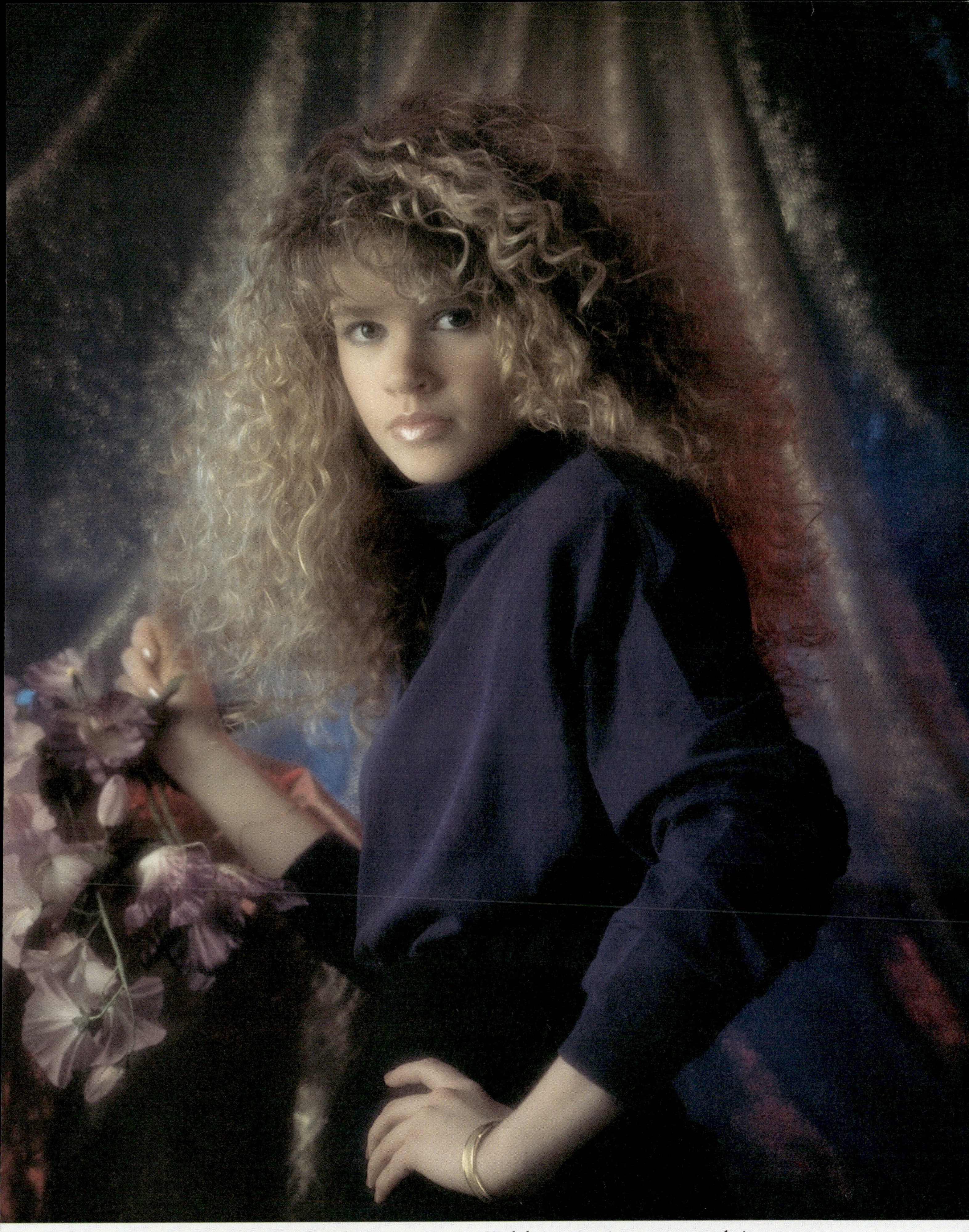

This is one of Larry's best-known portraits: Kodak is using it to promote their newest color paper and it will be featured in all their trade show booths in 1990.

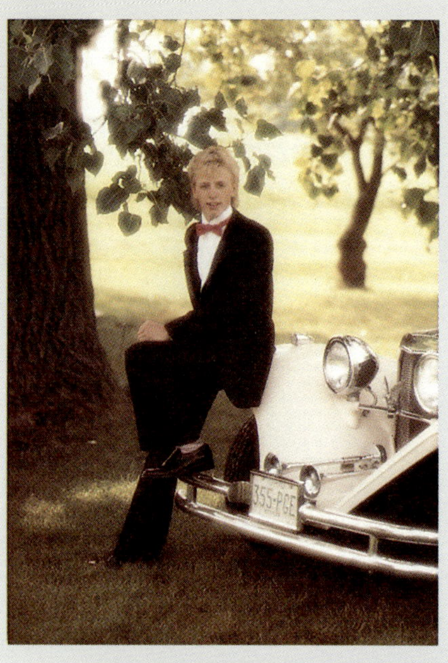

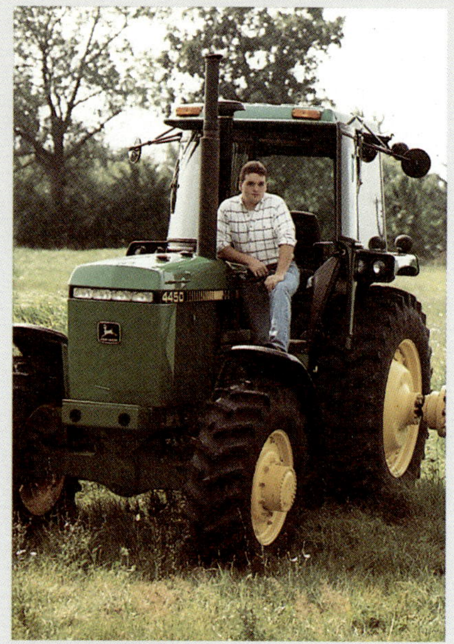

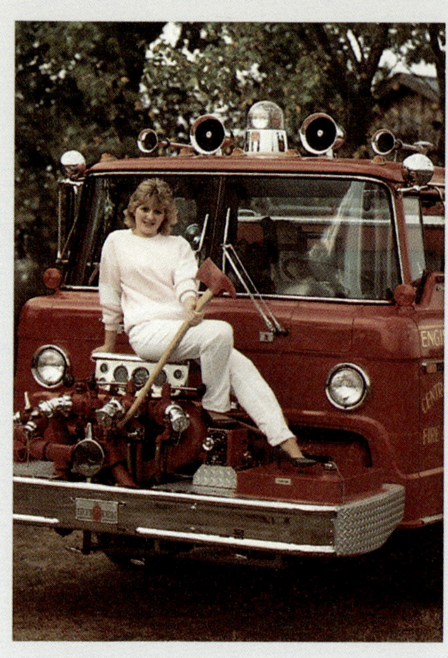

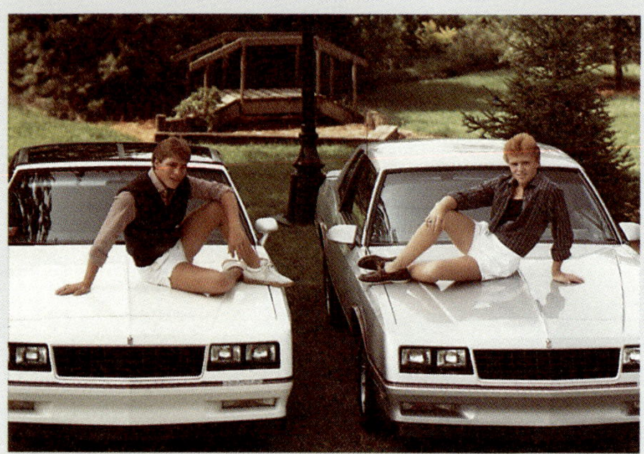

Wheels, wheels, wheels

Sure-fire sales are portraits taken with the kids' favorite vehicles. No longer limited to the guys only, more and more girls are bringing cars, motorbikes and, yes, even fire engines to their sessions.

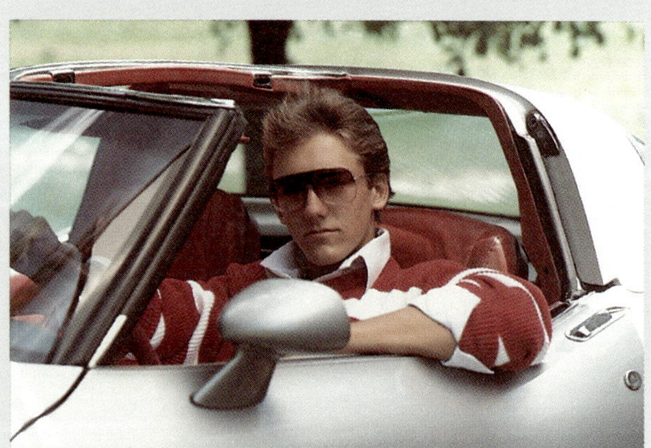

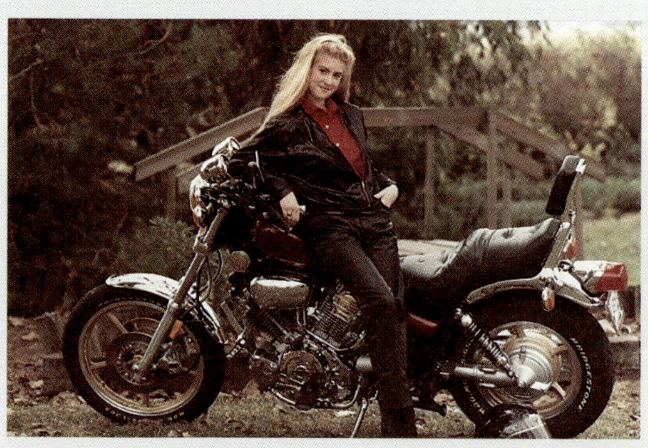

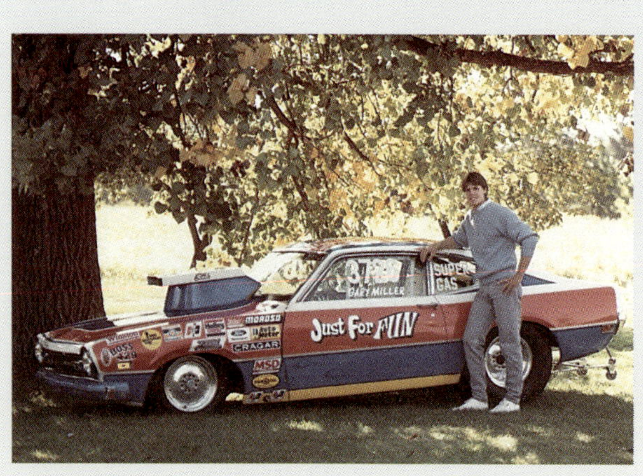

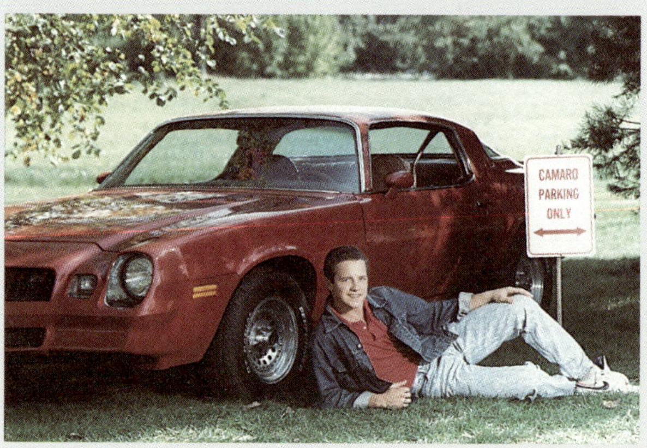

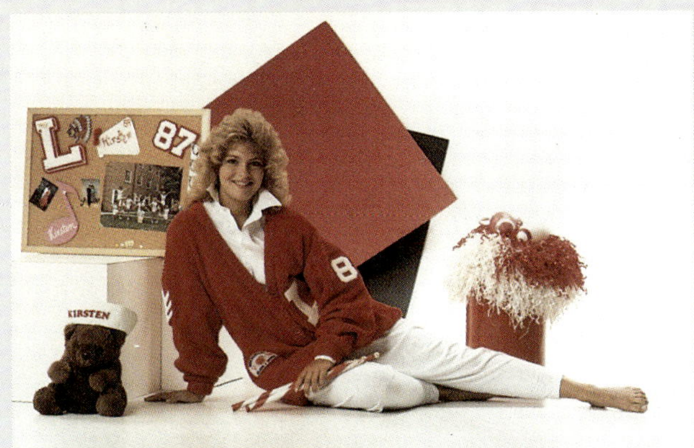

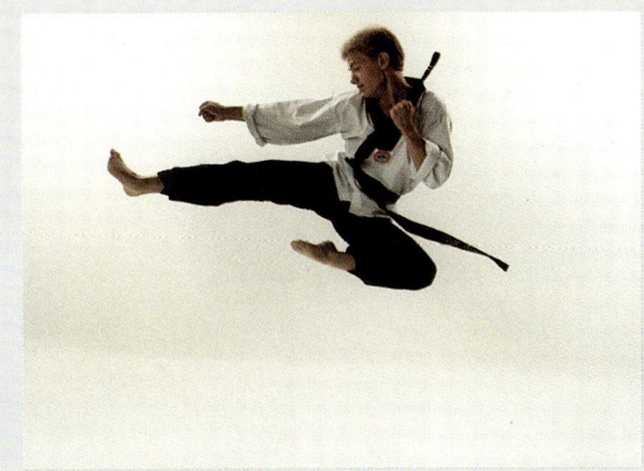

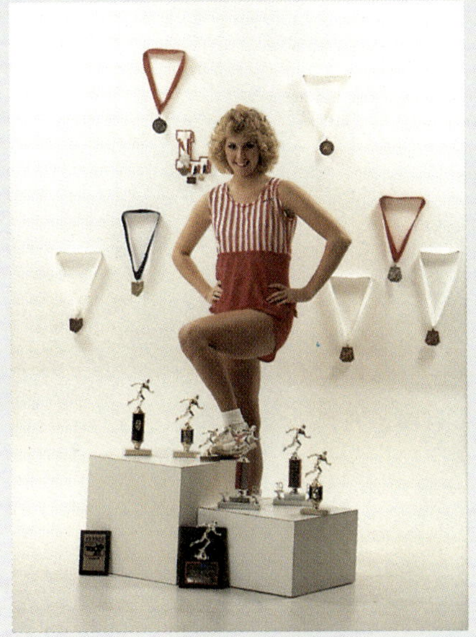

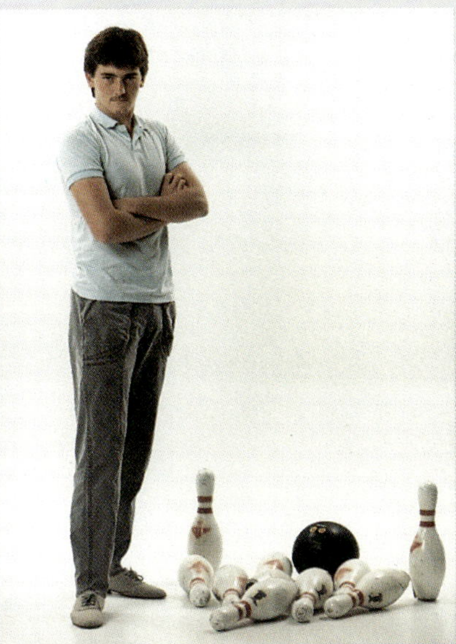

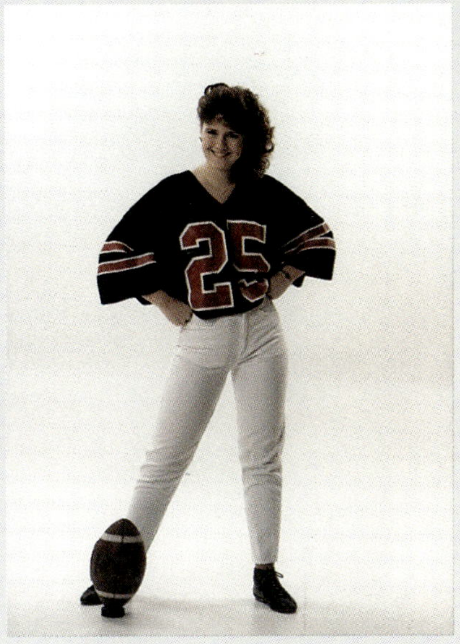

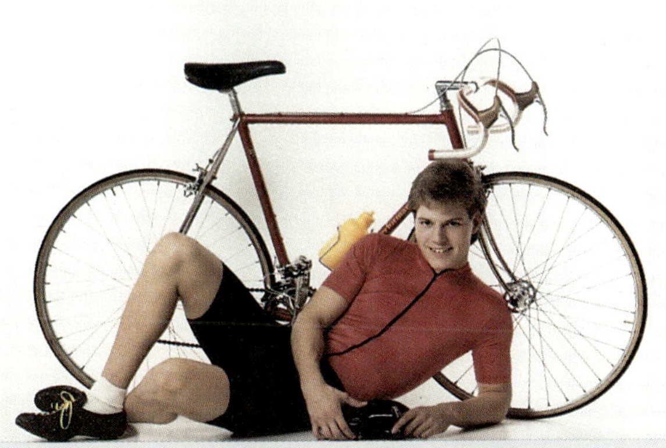

Hobbies

Hobbies and sports are very big with young people, so we are always happy to photograph seniors with the accoutrements of their outside interests. These portraits always sell.

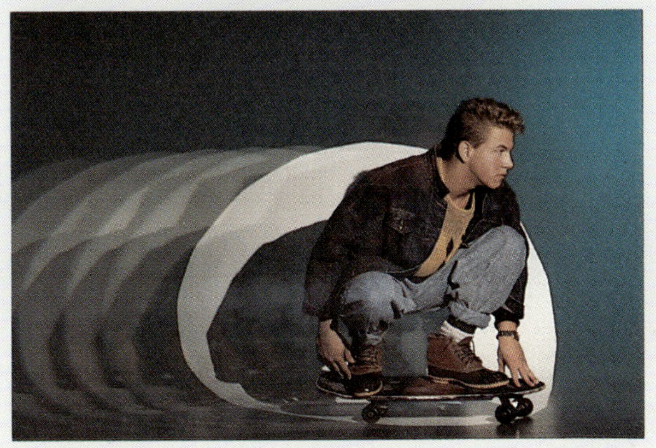

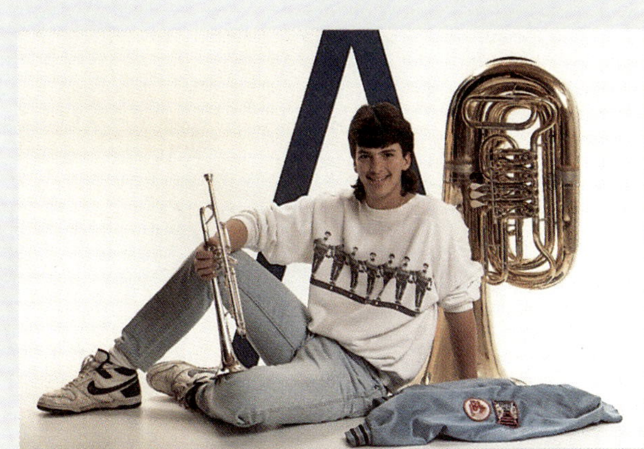

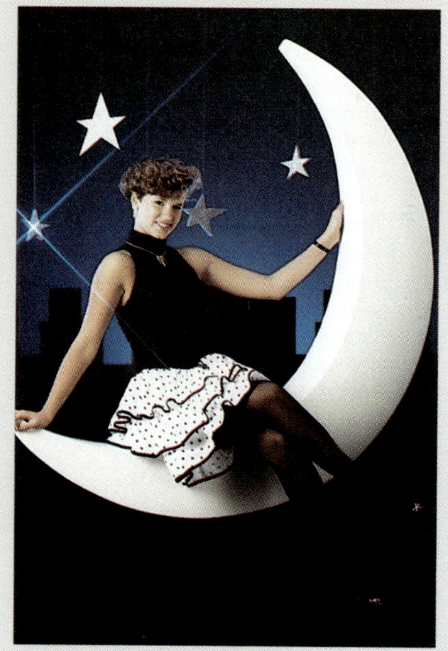

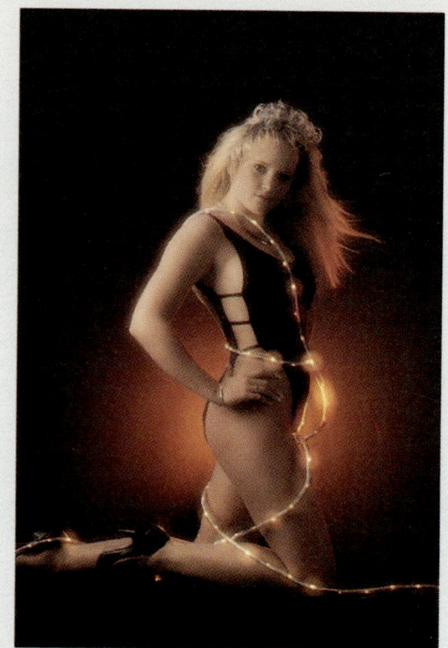

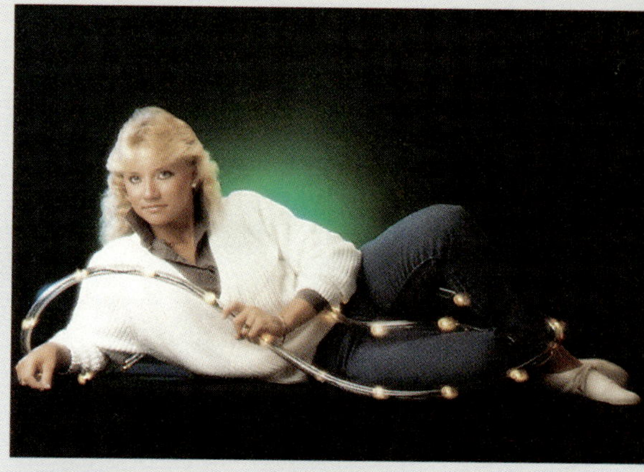

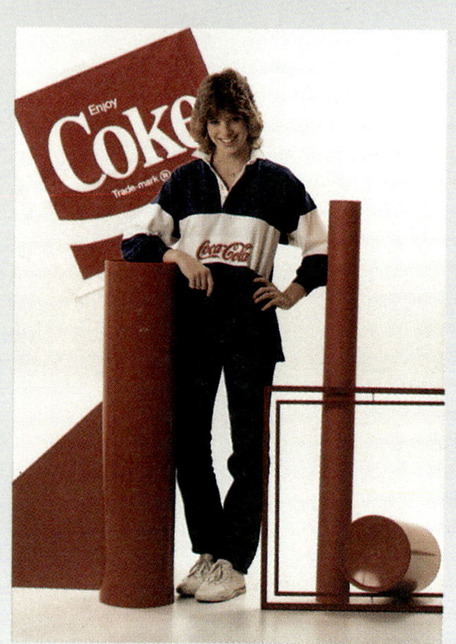

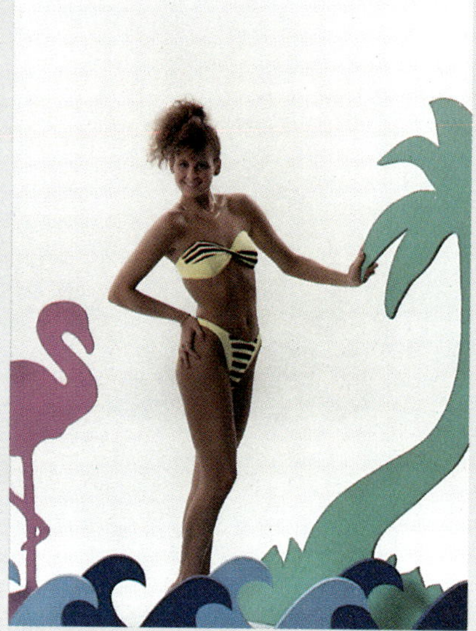

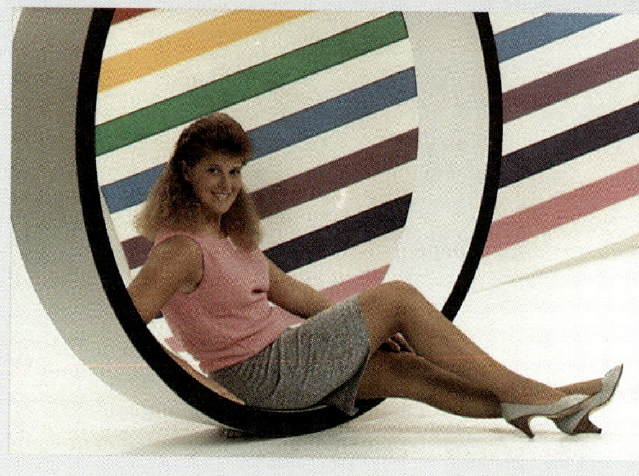

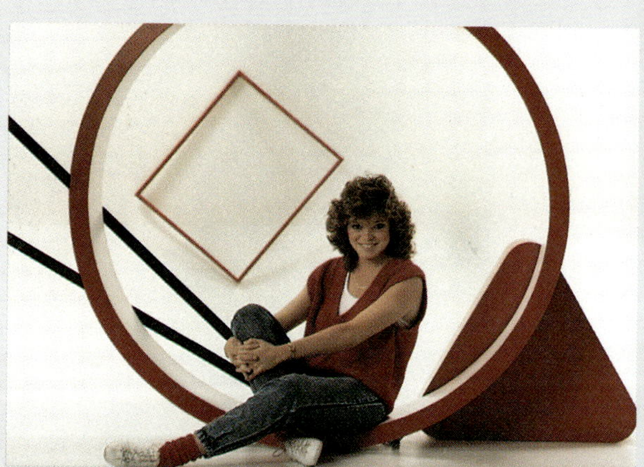

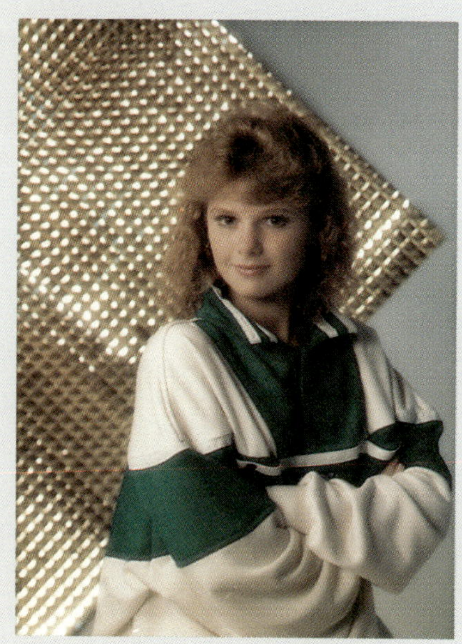

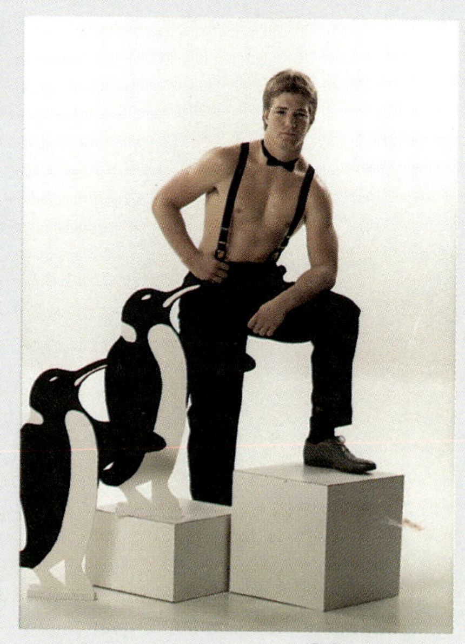

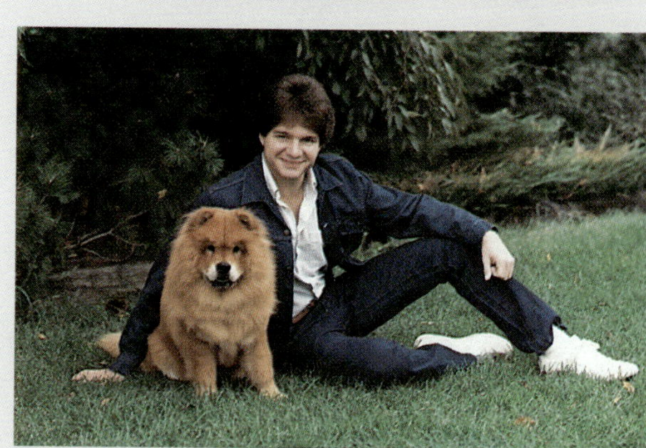

Props

Our new moon prop, the tiny "chase" lights in a plastic tube, penguin and "Florida" cut-outs, fabric backgrounds, even pets all can be used to enhance your senior protraits. Note how well they help to fill the extra space in full length and three-quarters poses.

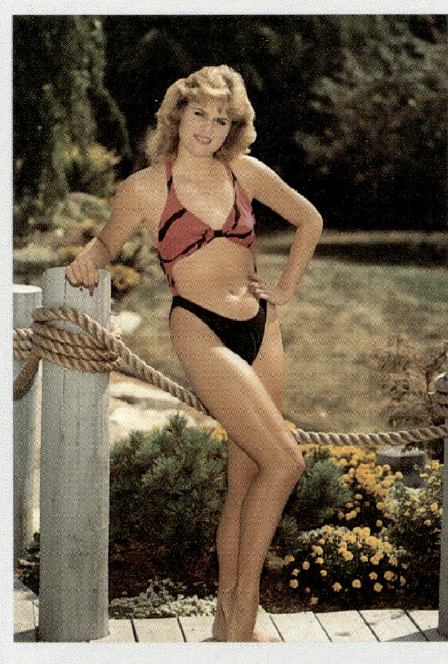

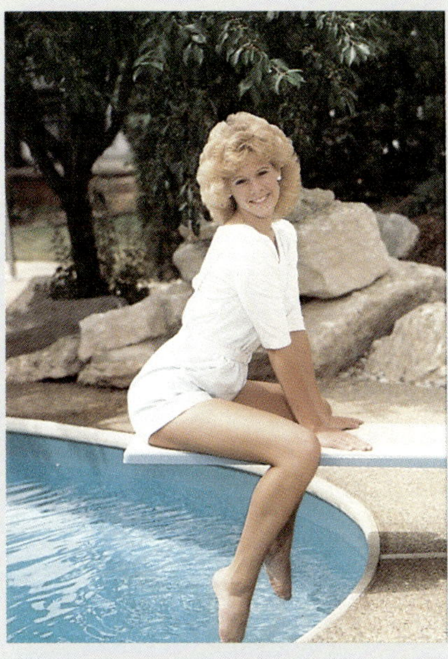

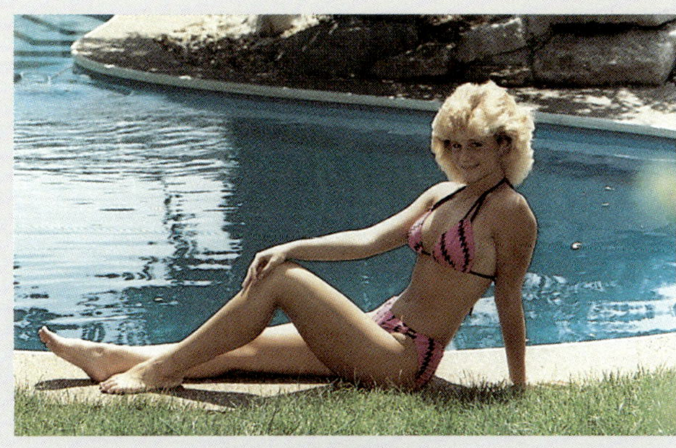

Outdoors

Outdoor poses around our pool and sauna are very popular. Other spots around our grounds and nearby, including the Ohio sky, are also very saleable. Notice just below how a little net and some shells create an instant sea shore.

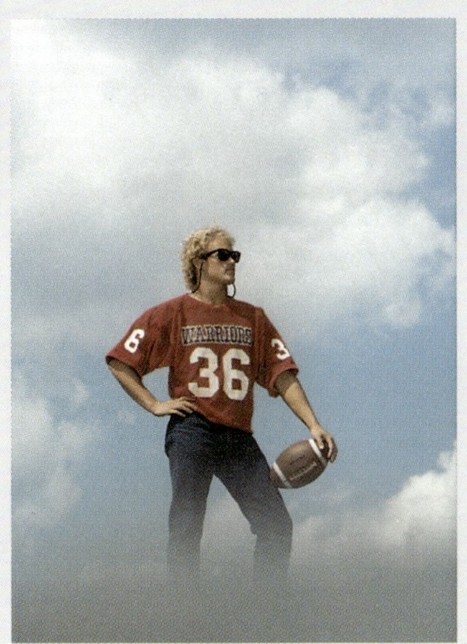

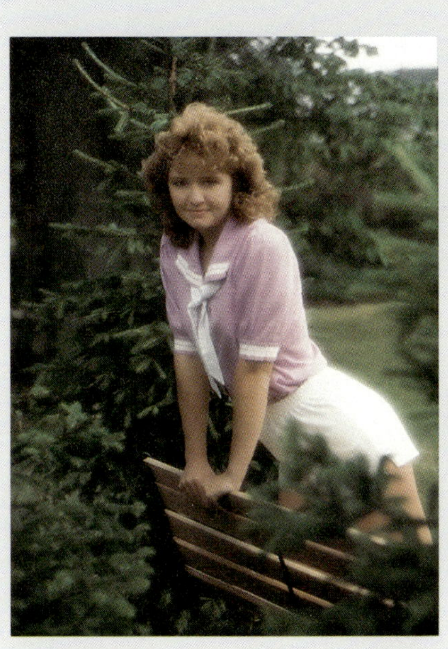

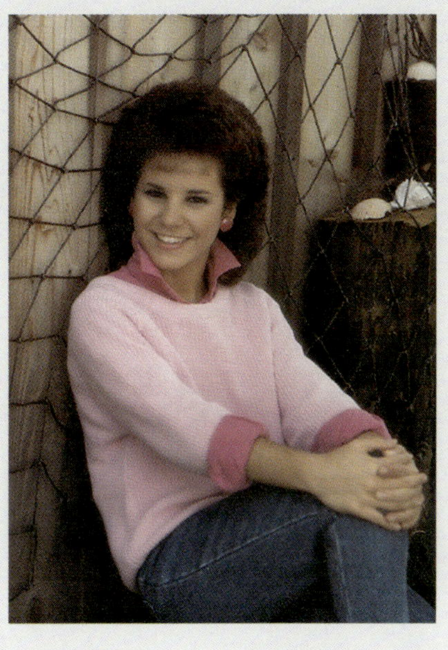

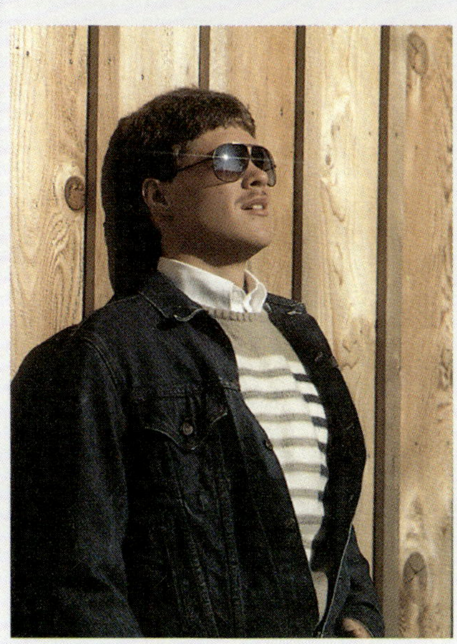

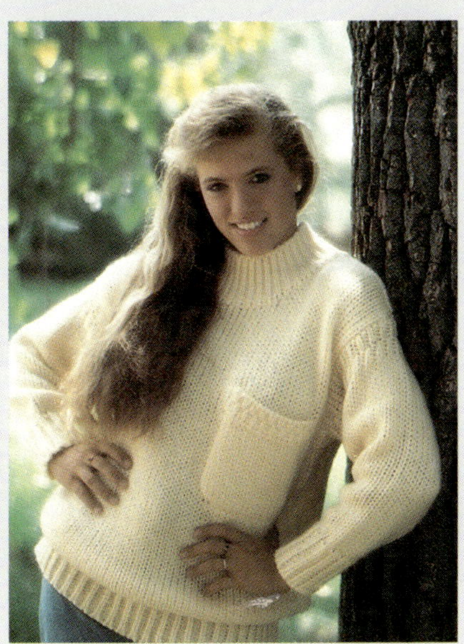

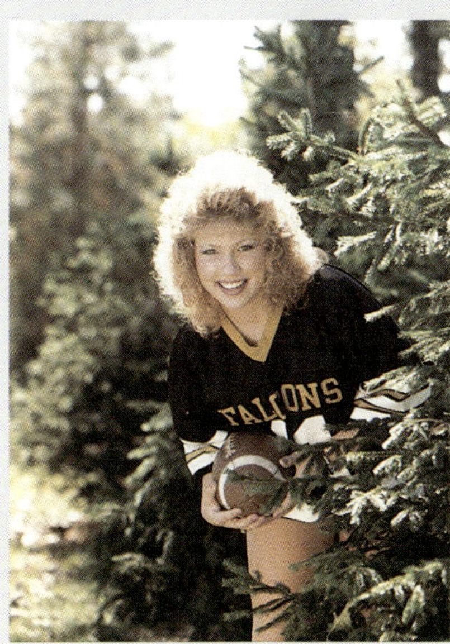

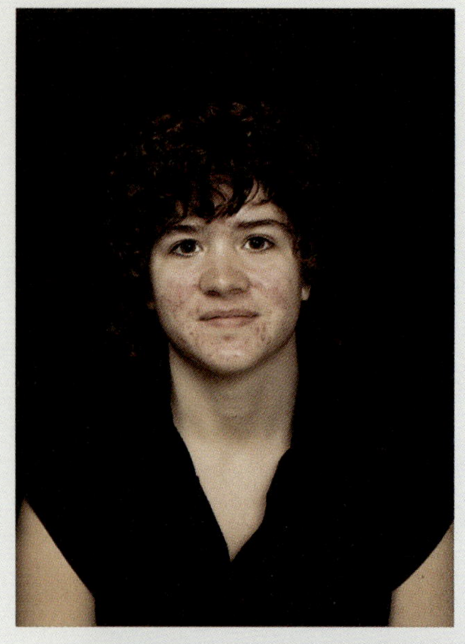

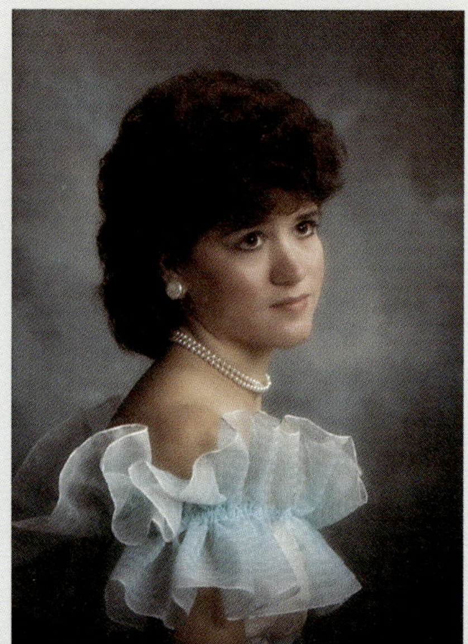

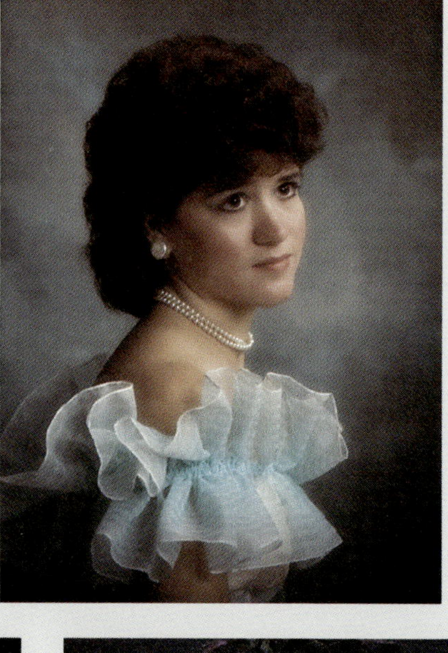

Make-up

I can't say enough for the use of make-up to transform ordinary high school seniors into confident-appearing, stylish young women. The results in sales are outstanding.

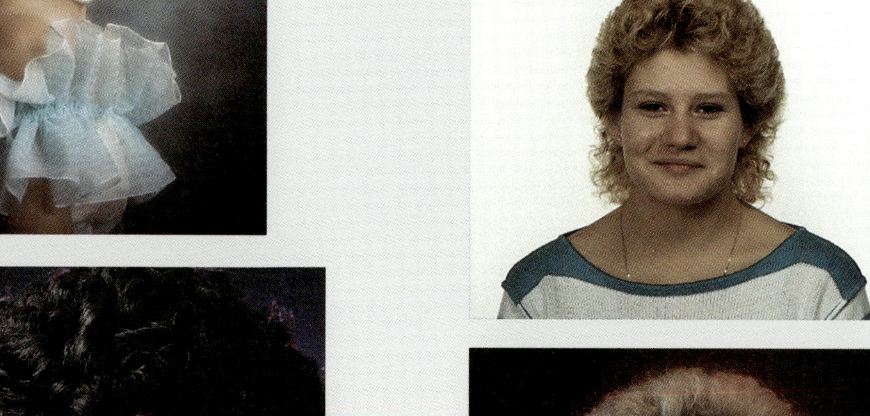

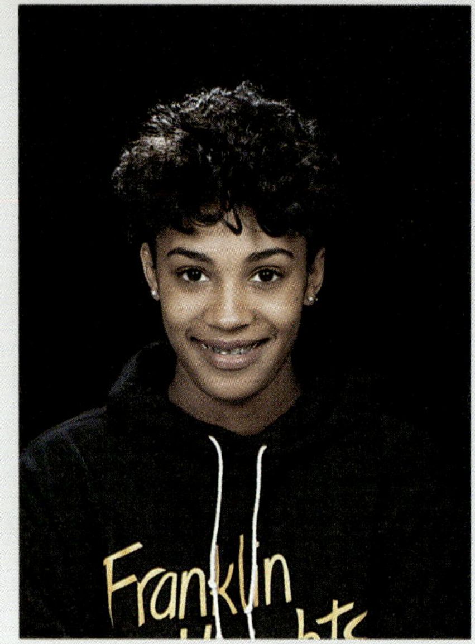

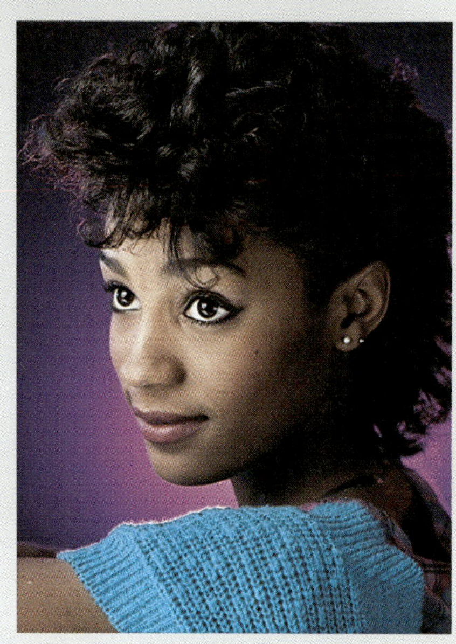

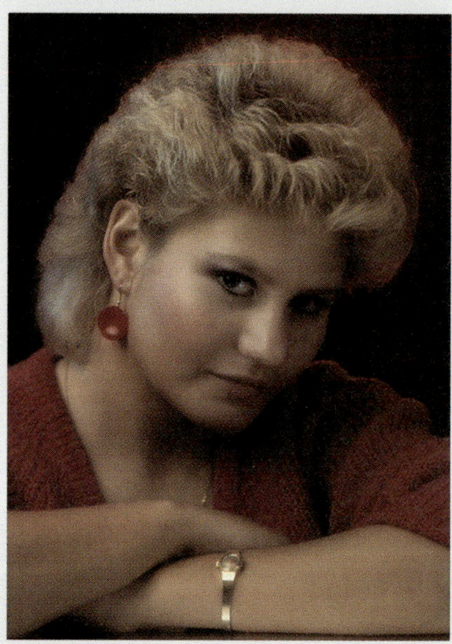

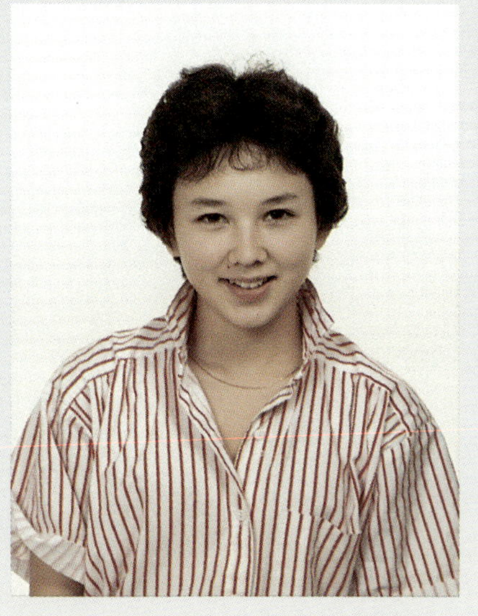

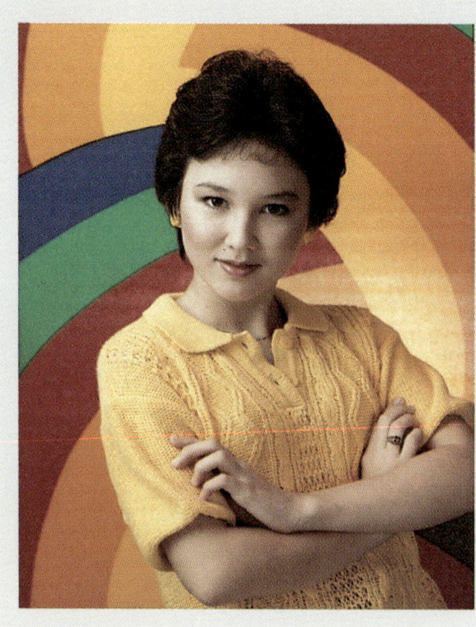

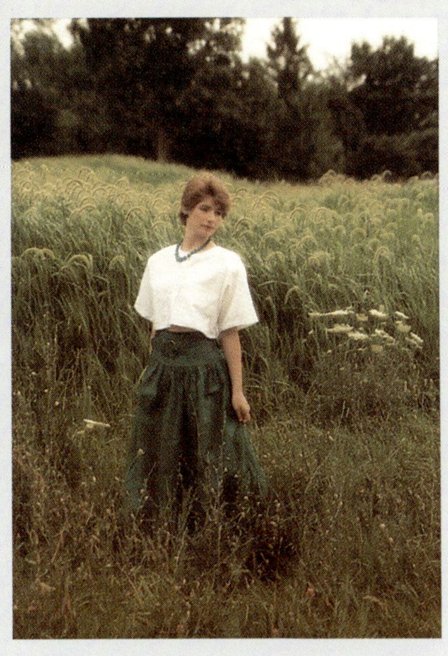
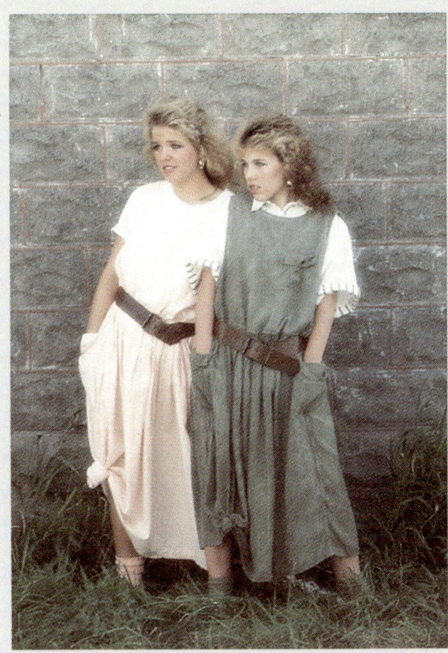
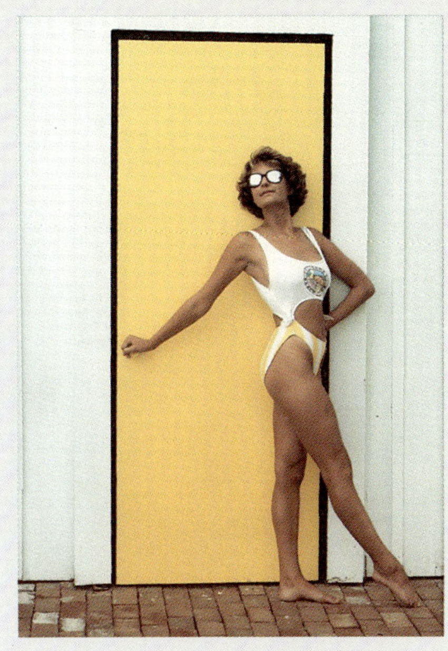

Versatility

Don't get into a rut; become aware of your surroundings and use them to create better portraits. The three pictures above are the result of "seeing" the attractiveness of nearby settings and using them. Below are the use of a fabric background, our barn setting and the revived use of a spotlight with and without a "cookie.'

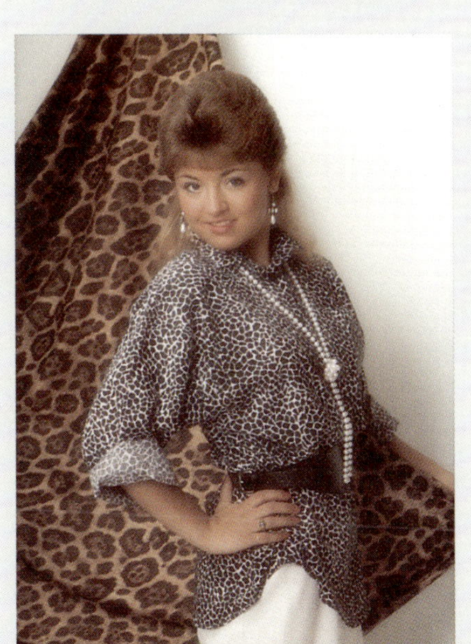
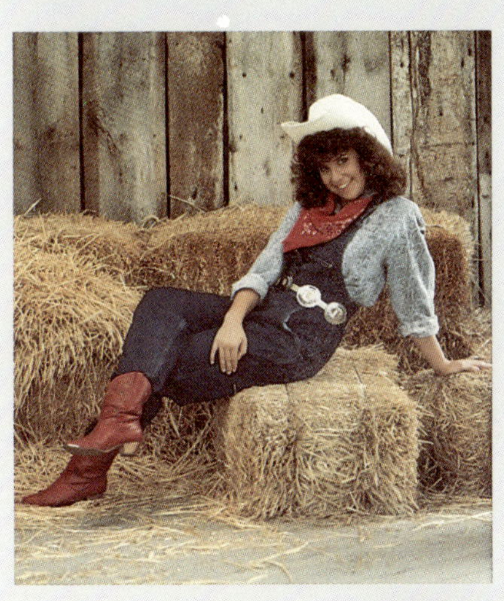
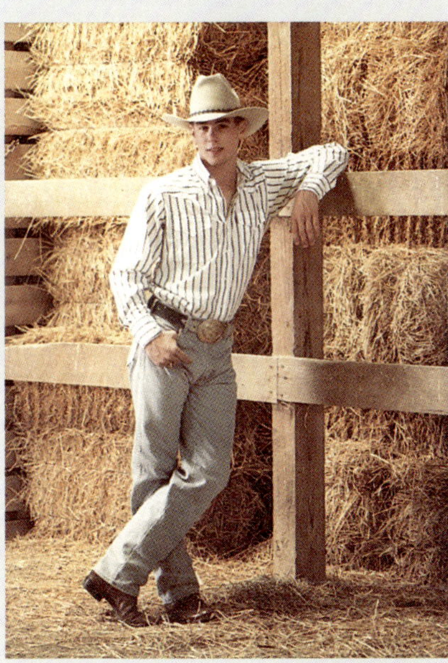
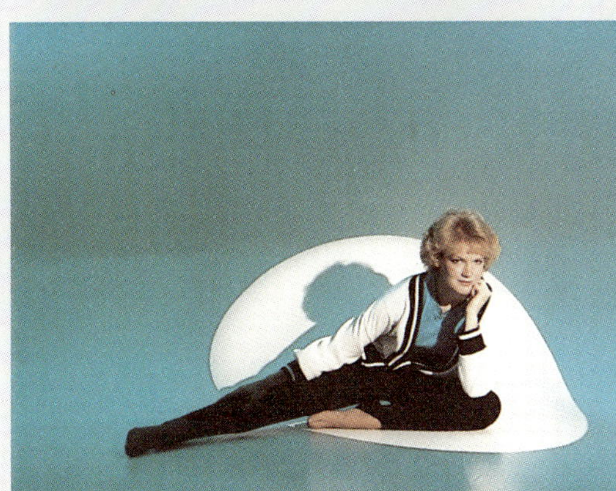
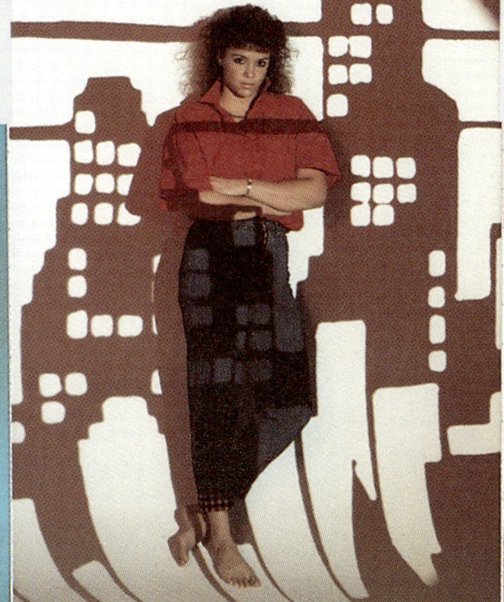
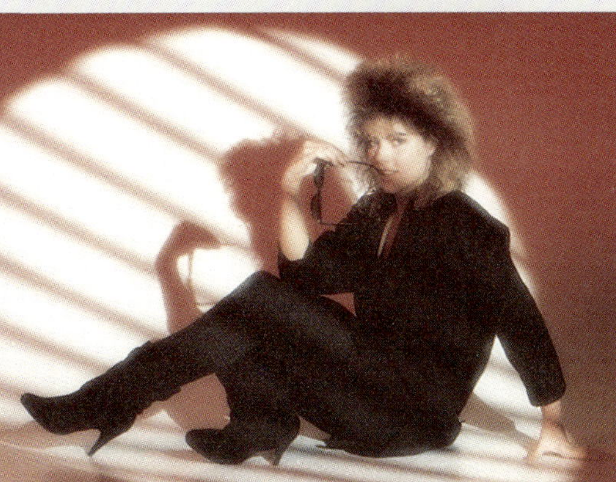

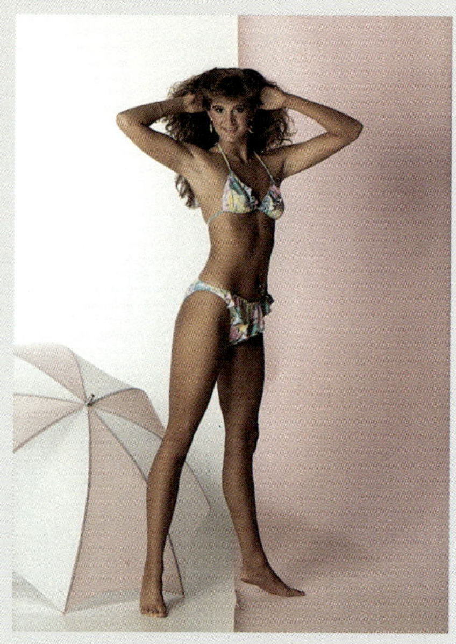
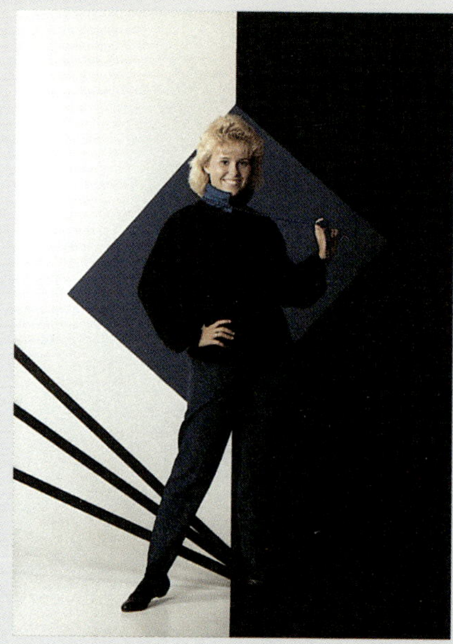
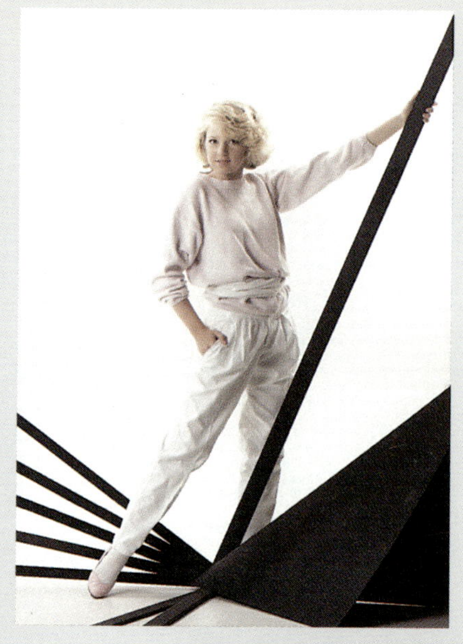
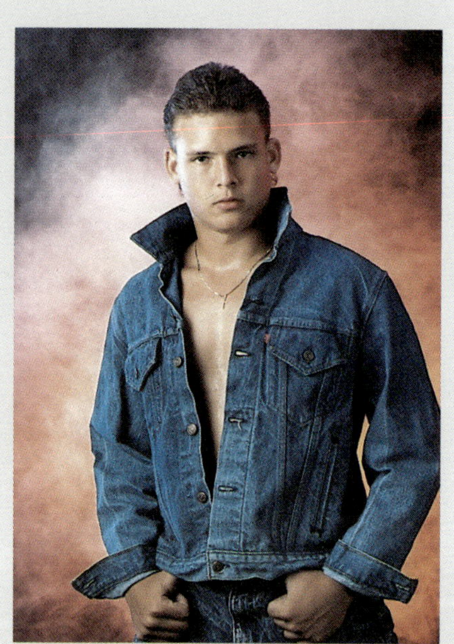
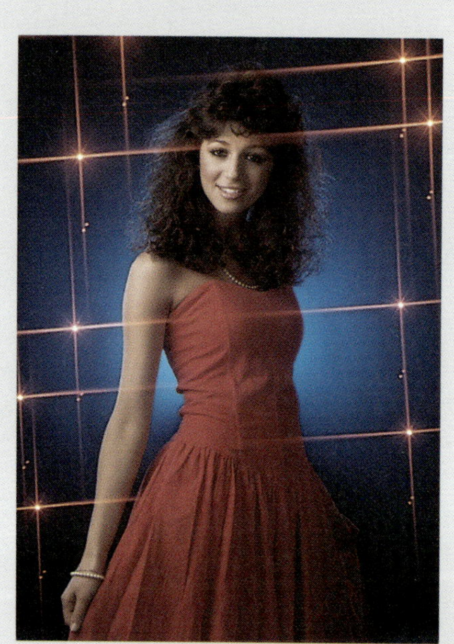
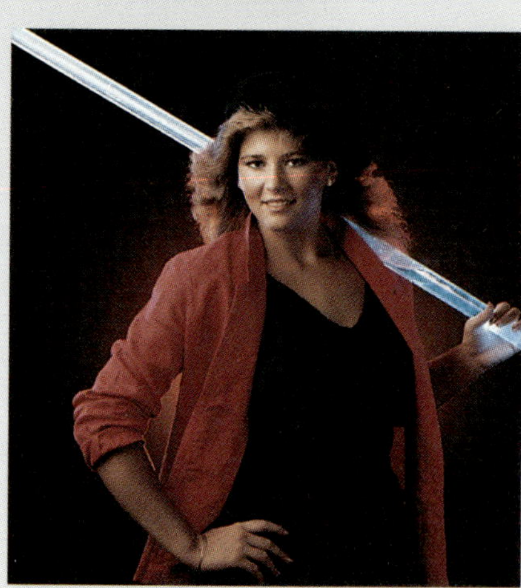
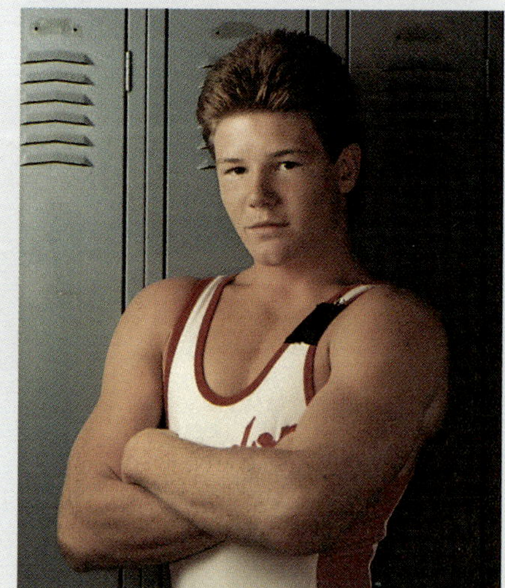
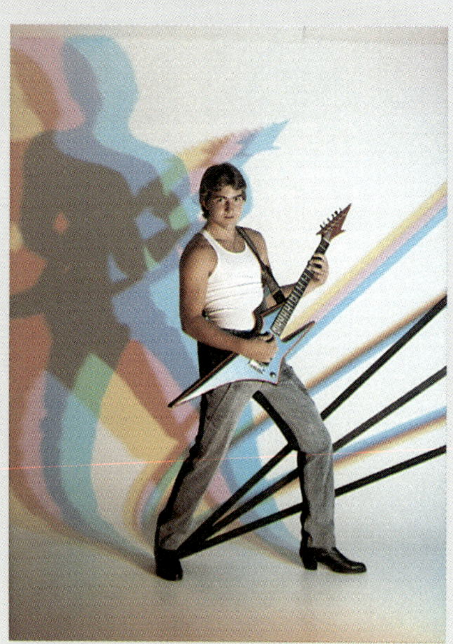
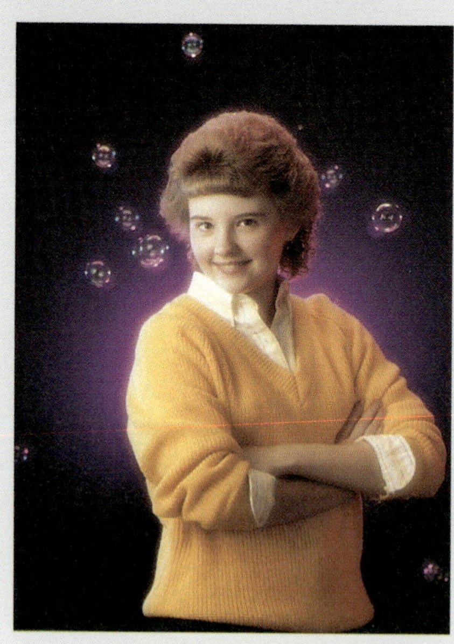

More Versatility

Above are examples of a "split" background, strips of lath painted black, the fog/smoke machine, a star filter, our home-made laser rod and "strobo" images, the bubble machine and a locker background. Remember that it's versatility that sells preview folios: the portraits must all be different to create desire.

Chapter XI

Using Light in Natural Environment

Much of our senior photography is done in the outdoor area of our studio which calls for a whole new set of lighting controls. I believe once you understand how light looks in a finished photograph it makes little difference whether you use electronic flash studio equipment or natural daylight.

To determine the exposure of an outdoor portrait, I use a spot meter and try to set up the pose so there is one f:stop difference from the bright side of the face to the dark side. If everything lines up, set up the pose and take the photograph; but if you can't get the light to conform to the standards you have pre-determined, stop until you pull it into conformity.

Incidentally, the exposure on a Hasselblad lens can be set by using either f:stops or EV (Exposure Value) numbers, and many light meters can read out in either f:stops or EV numbers. After experimenting with both, I found that I prefer the EV numbers because this is a direct metering of light values and the reading can be set directly on the Hasselblad lens. There is no converting from EV to f:stops by going through a chart or graph, hence there is less room for exposure error.

LARGE SCRIMS

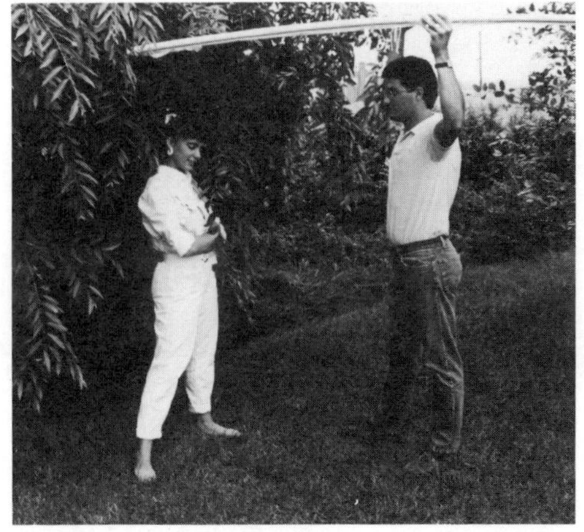

When you have to soften harsh sunlight, one of the easiest ways is to use a translucent panel of some sort to filter the light and diffuse its harshness. These panels are simply held between the sun and the subject. They soften the hardness of direct sunlight while not greatly diminishing its brightness. It is possible to work in direct sun light with just a large scrim because it diffuses the light into the shadow areas and pulls the light and dark areas into a tighter ratio. Properly done, the light area and the shadow won't be much further apart than one f:stop and the background will be within one stop of the light area.

The scrim is commonly used by the movie industry and there it usually consists of a big hoop covered with muslin. You can make one just like it or you can use a translucent sheet of plastic or anything else that will do the job of taking the harsh edge off straight sunlight. That's what a good scrim is supposed to do while reducing the amount of the light by no more than a stop or two.

REFLECTOR FILL

If the scrim is not convenient for you or is not something you can work with easily, you may prefer to use a reflector. Like scrims, reflectors come in all shapes and sizes, and their biggest disadvantage is that the brightness may cause your client to squint. The great advantage of a reflector is that you can see precisely the results on the face. This makes it very easy to get exactly what you want and meter it precisely. As Geraldine used to say, "What you sees is is what you gets." And once you see what you want, all you have to do is meter the set-up, set the camera and shoot.

The use of a reflector permits you to set up a reasonably good outdoor lighting at any time of the day, but a reflector does not limit you to just a soft fill. You can create a strong, secondary side light, or you can use it to backlight the hair, and you can move the reflector in and out for more or less brightness. It is also simple to feather the light or to

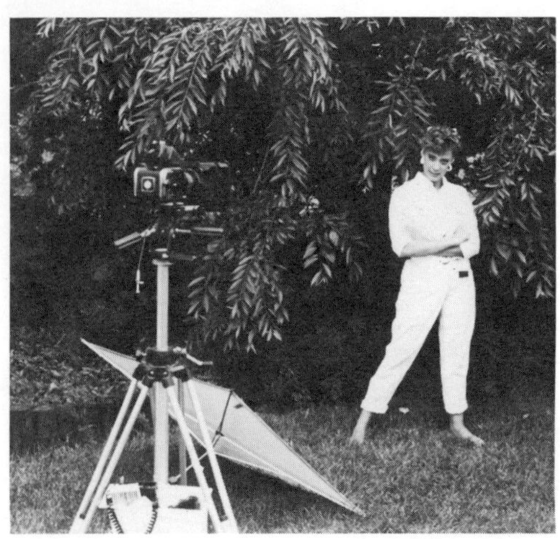

highlight certain parts of the face or body. Experiment to see what looks good by slowly bringing in the reflector until you see a pleasing lighting that does what you want it to do.

If you use a reflector or scrim, you normally have to have an assistant to hold the apparatus, which may present a problem if no one is around. Sometimes you can use a stand to hold your light control gadget, but not if it is a windy day. It would take a very heavy stand not to fall over in the wind and its very weight might persuade you not to use it. Portability is a factor.

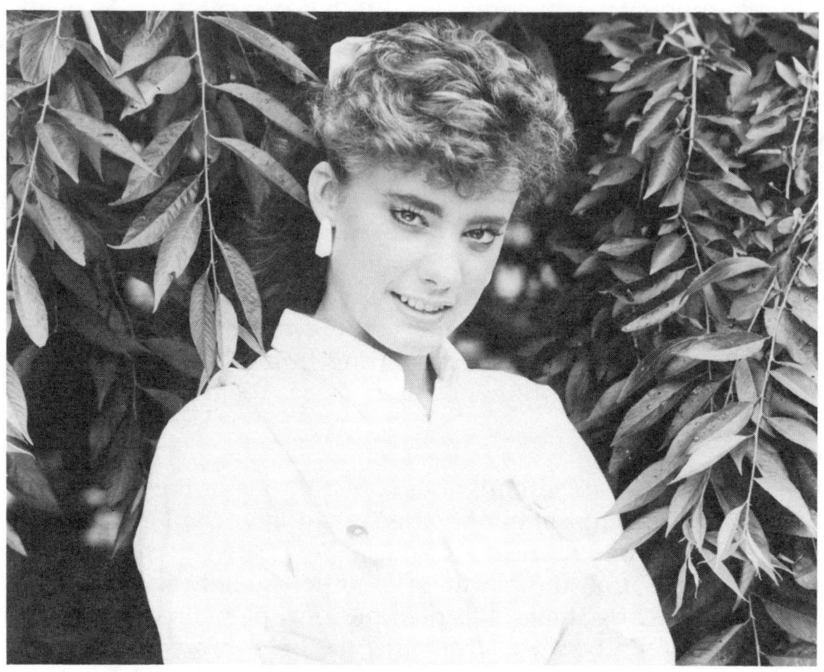

Notice the difference in the intensity of the light from the far reflector and the near one.

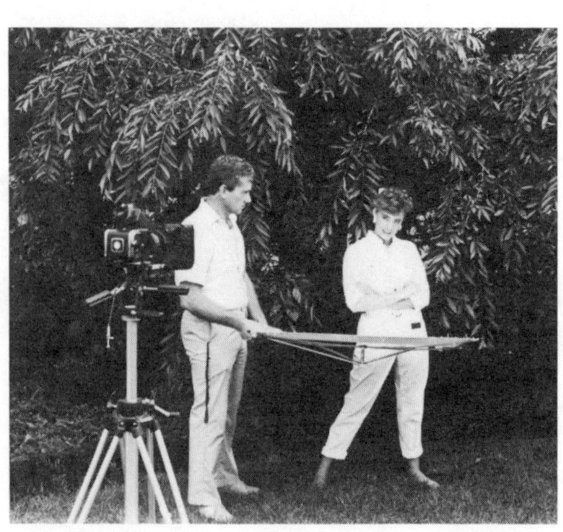

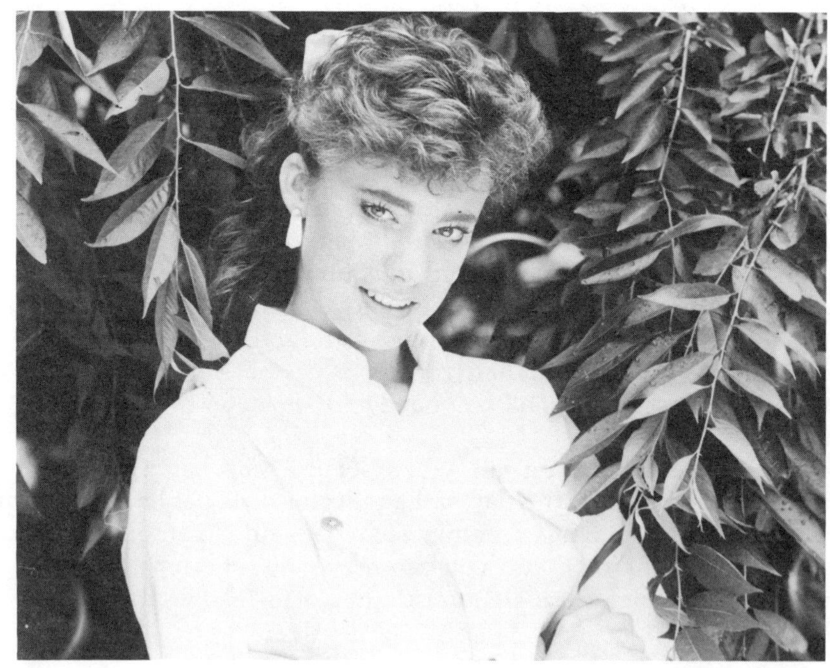

FILL FLASH

Another method for controlling outdoor light ratios is a flash fill. The flash is the most lightweight and portable method for tempering harsh sunlight. The biggest obstacle is learning to control it so you get neither too much nor too little fill. Electronic flash, when used as a fill light, is extremely difficult to determine predictably at first. Sometimes reflected sun light will adversely affect the automatic feature of an electronic flash and render it useless. It goes back to metering. An electronic flash can be set strong enough so that it will actually appear to be brighter than the sun; it may also cast unusual shadows on your subject that will look odd.

The size of the flash reflector is important; a small reflector tends to harshness and it may even cast its own mini-shadows. You can get around this by using a larger reflector, but that may require a bigger power supply than is really portable.

The correct use of flash fill can add that subtle hint of light which creates just the correct amount of fill. It also adds a highlight to brighten the eyes when the main light does not penetrate into the eye sockets. This is especially desirable when you backlight your subject with sunlight; if you don't fill this portrait, you may correctly expose the face, but the hair will be about four stops over-exposed and look exactly like glass wool. A well-exposed flash fill can bring the face and the hair into a much better 2:1 ratio and make your portrait much more saleable.

You'll probably have to use a flash meter outdoors - at least at first - to get a predictable ratio, and something which should not be overlooked when doing flash fill is the full range of shutter speeds. What I do is determine the brightest part of the photograph first. Then I calculate a fill flash that is one stop under this bright area and that's the f:stop we set the camera at using the EV numbers.

Next, I determine how much power is required to provide a good fill flash and I adjust the power setting on the flash to coincide with this number. It may be necessary to meter the flash output to insure its accuracy. Then go ahead and shoot.

Dramatic effects can be achieved at dusk by setting the camera for the flash and using a fast shutter speed to underexpose the background. This technique tends to deepen the color of sunsets and provide dramatic lighting when you normally could not take an existing light portrait. Off camera flash is best when used in this manner.

There are other times when an off-camera flash can add dimension and dramatic life to the portrait, but that's beyond the scope of this book. However, I urge you to experiment with this technique because it will give a different and very saleable look to your portraits.

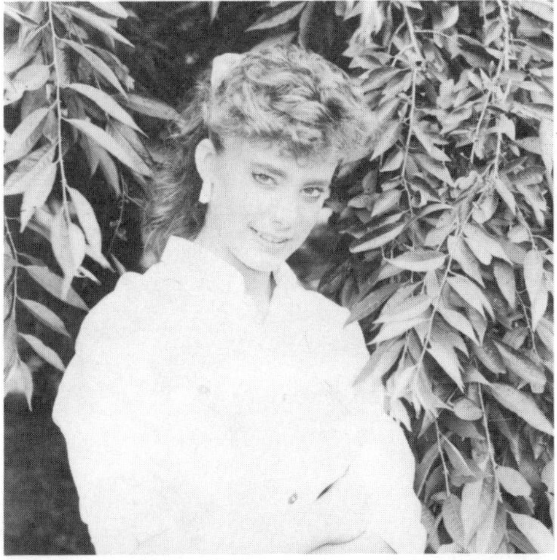

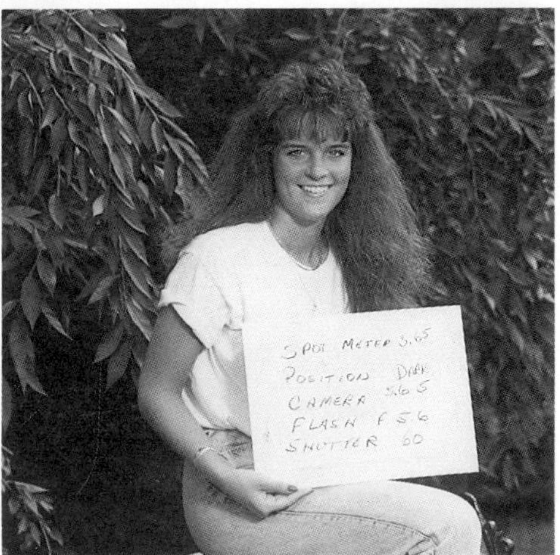

Fill flash not only balances the light and shadow, it adds a brilliant point of light just above the pupil of the eye, giving more life to the expression.

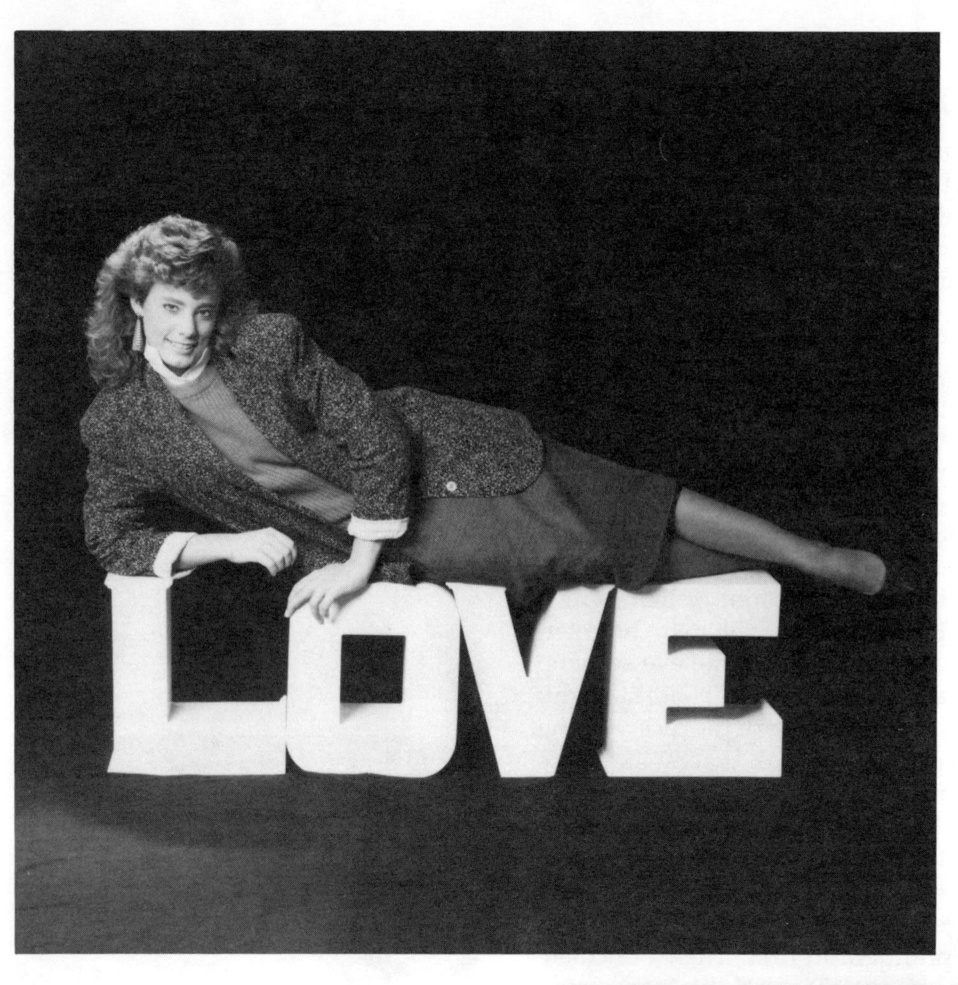
LOVE

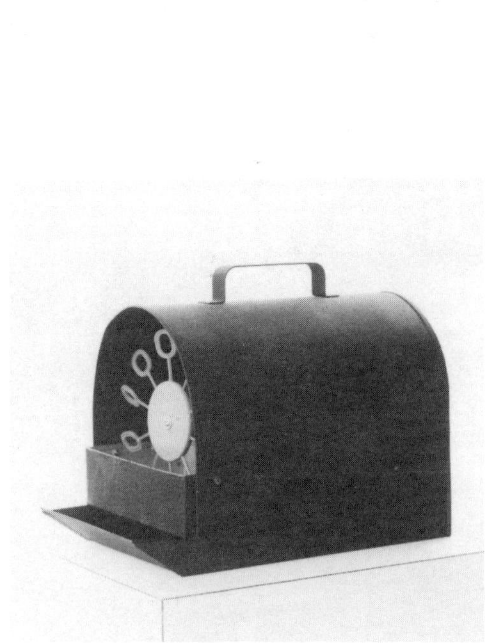

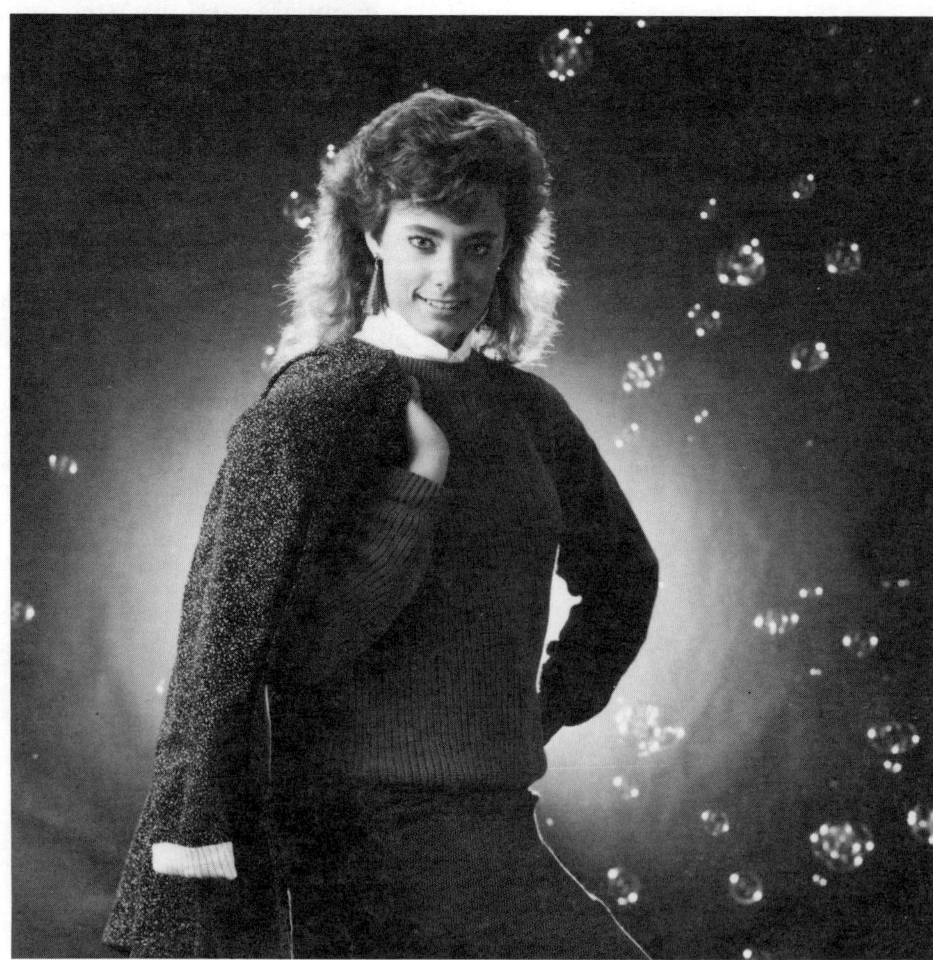

Chapter XII

Props That Attract Seniors and How to Use Them

LARGE NUMBERS TO INDICATE THE GRADUATION YEAR

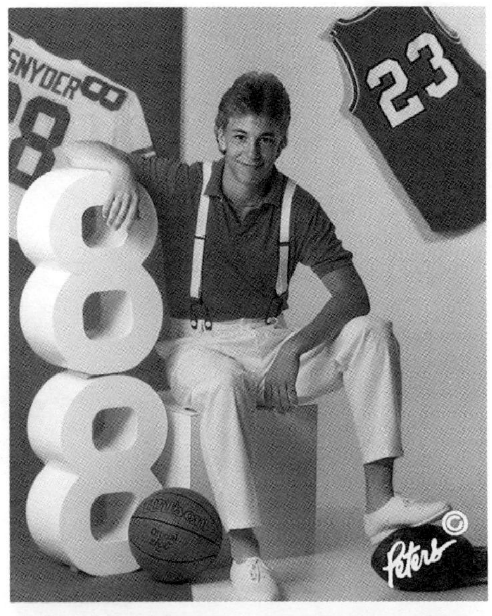

In 1985 a friend of mine visited our studio for a seminar I was holding. At that time we were using the LOVE prop as large black letters for students to lay on, lean against, and stack up. He felt it was a great idea and gave it some in-depth thought. A month or so later, he sent me a Polaroid of an idea that was outstanding and which we instantly adopted. We now use large numbers that indicate the year of graduation for the students to pose with. Many suppliers have picked up on the idea lately and manufacture similar numbers of foam plastic or wood. The original numbers were wood which were sturdy enough to sit on, stand on and use indoors or out. When they get scratched, they can easily be touched up with acrylic latex white paint.

We manufacture these numbers for sale to other photographers and we still make them of the original durable wood. This is a tremendous prop that will be requested by senior after senior, and will set you apart from the contract photographer. Having said that, let me add that I believe you can over-use an idea and so it's better to use a prop too little than too much. Don't be limited to the same two dozen poses for every senior: work to develop different poses, lots and lots of them, so your students don't have all the same poses.

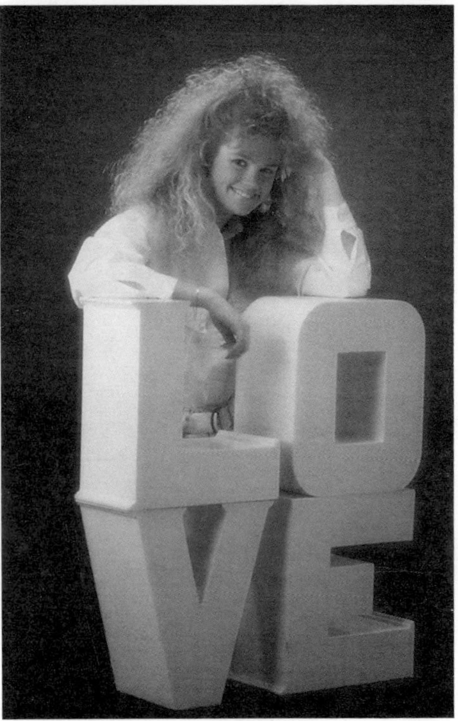

BLOCK "LOVE" LETTERS

The LOVE letters are something I pull out every so often to use with a single girl, a group of children, a couple or even an individual child. We make the LOVE letters of wood also and because of their design they can be stacked in a variety of ways. Most of the large chain school photographers can't offer full length poses, so poses like these will further separate you from the contract shooters in the very important quality department. (If you can design props which are unique to you and your studio, you will attract attention because your style and photography will be different from all others'. On the other hand, if you can't design or build your own props, there are sources which can provide much of what you need. I am now providing a service for photographers by designing new and exciting props and offering them for sale to photographers all over the country.)

Most of the time I use the white block letters and numbers on an all white background, but they can be used with colored papers or you can use gels on your background lights to get strong separation.

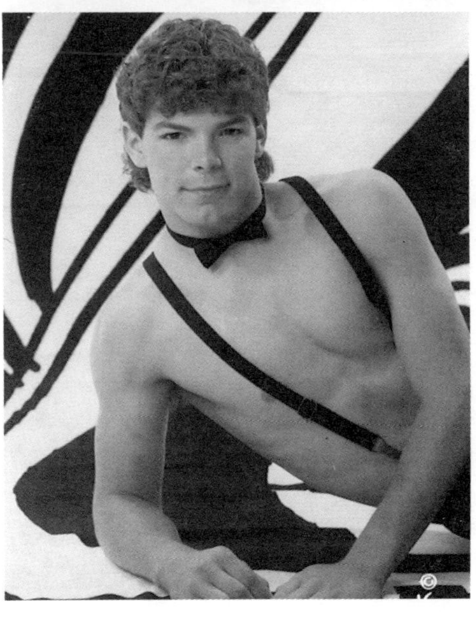

FABRIC BACKGROUNDS

There are an unlimited number of fabric designs available for use as backgrounds, but the line I like best is MARIMEKKO. You can find it in many stores that offer designer wall hanging products. It has very large designs and it comes in four foot widths so you can easily mount it on a frame to hang behind your subject. This provides a large enough background for half-length poses. It is also possible to get longer lengths of this material that can be pinned to the wall and draped to create a sweeping background of exciting color.

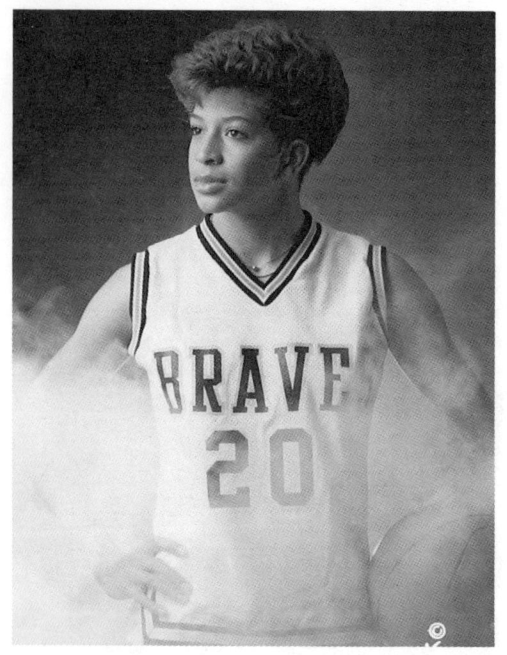

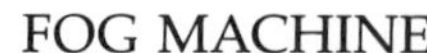

FOG MACHINE

I use a commercially available fog machine manufactured by Rosco. This fog generator creates a very realistic looking smoke effect when used properly. I use a gel, usually amber, on the background and a fan to create a slight breeze on the person. I have found the best position for the machine is on the floor pointed toward the subject's back from about six feet away, with the front raised approximately two inches above the floor. I use a fan in front of the subject to create a slight breeze which will keep the fog behind the subject. The fan also lessens the amount of fog needed to create the image that looks best. When used correctly, the fog machine is turned on for just a few seconds, then turned off. The fan will blow the fog to fill the area behind the subject and that is the instant the photograph should be taken. Because it takes approximately five minutes to clear the fog from the room, I recommend the fog photograph be taken just before the subject makes a clothing change.

THE BUBBLE MACHINE

When it comes to making different settings and backgrounds, there are many more gadgets available today than in the past. We recently came across a fairly inexpensive machine that creates a "bubble" background. Yes, bubbles, and they sure are fun to work with. I like to use them with a dark background and colored gels. The gelled backlights are partially refracted when they hit the bubbles and they show up as many different colors.

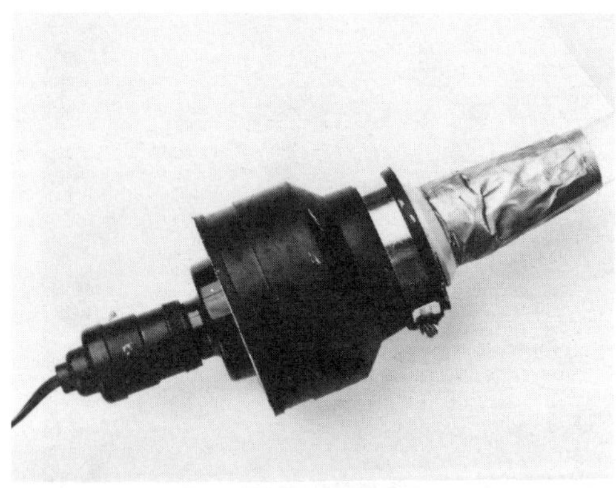

Most bubble machine manufacturers supply a bubble mixture that is added to water to make a working solution. We suspend the machine from the ceiling so that as it operates, the bubbles drift to the floor, filling the area between the student and the background with delightful little spheres of color.

This machine is not for every student, but occasionally someone comes in who smiles all the time, someone with a real "bubbly" personality, and that's the one we use the bubbles with.

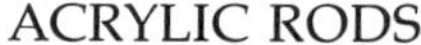

ACRYLIC RODS

Sometimes, in keeping with modern trends of movies, videos, and such, a flash of inspiration can come out of nowhere. A couple of years ago such a bolt hit me as we were hunting for that something different. I don't know how this idea came about, but it works and here's how. We take seven feet long solid acrylic rods that are one and one-half inch in diameter, and fasten a tiny AC flash unit to one end of it. This is one of those units that has a built-in slave and sells for about $20 - $25 dollars. We fasten it to the rod with a PVC plumbing fitting and duct tape to fasten it to the rod, but before you tape the light in place, fasten a gel of any color over its lens. (What did we use before there was duct tape???)

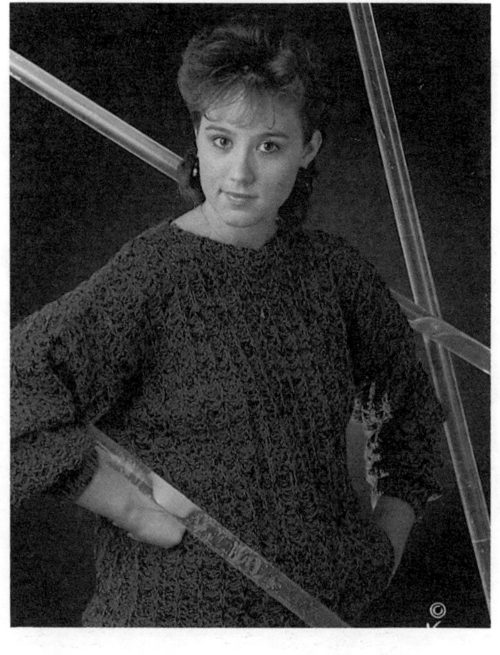

This simple set-up works great. We place several of these behind the subject so they are slightly out of focus. When the main flash fires, so do the lights in the rods and the rods look like laser beams flashing across the scene. (The kids even call them laser rods.)

We find that the best lighting set-up is a soft-box used as a side light with a reflector fill. This is because light coming more or less from the front tends to wash out the color of the rods. A side light - especially a well feathered side light - is not as likely to do so. A large fill light also tends to wash out the color of the rods, so we use just the reflector to fill our "laser portraits". The slightly more contrasty lighting seems to fit the futuristic effect very well and the kids like it.

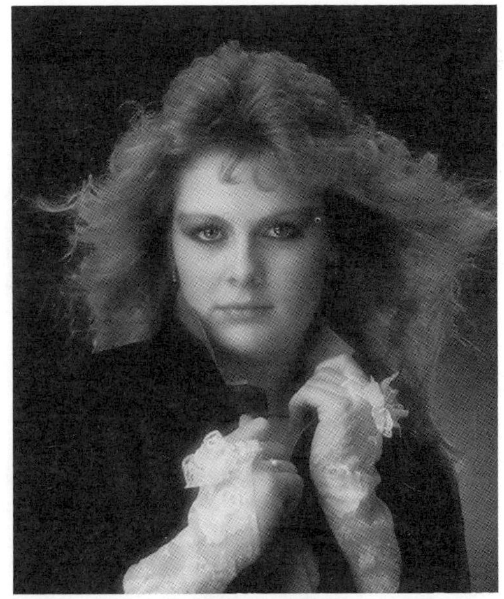

FAN

Every portrait studio dealing in contemporary portraiture needs a fan and it should be very directional and have variable speeds. This means I can direct the stream of air exactly where I want it and also control the amount of breeze it puts out. The fan we use is the BOWENS WIND MACHINE.

The fan is a tool for creating mood. A gentle breeze on the subject will help to put her at ease, make her feel more like a model and produce a really good look on her face. The purpose of the fan is to blow her hair, but the stream of air should be directed toward her chin. This means that you will get the desired movement in the hair beside her face, but you won't blow bangs or the carefully coiffed hair on top of the head. Careful adjustment of the air flow will cause the side hair to look like it's floating.

A back light tends to bleed right through the blown hair and you can get exotic effects by gelling the light. Seniors love it when we do this high fashion look with their hair.

As I mentioned earlier, we use the fan in conjunction with the Fog/ Smoke machine to keep the fog behind the subject in the form of a rolling cloud.

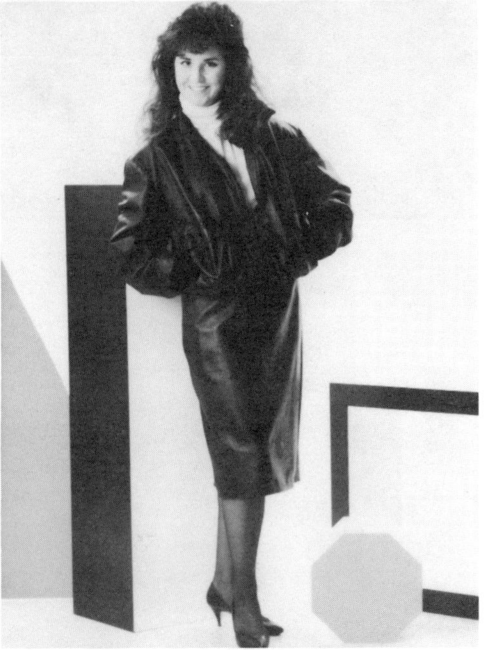

FULL LENGTH POSES

Ever since we started using an all-white background, I have been increasing the number of full length poses I do. This is for two reasons. The primary one, of course, is that I like full length poses because I get certain effects with the props that can only be exploited fully in full length poses. If you do nothing but head and shoulders or three-quarter length poses, the proof set will appear monotonous to your subject. The more variety you get in a proof set, the more poses the client must choose: she just can't do without them or she shorts herself. She has to have those full length poses with the big class number, she has to have the shot with the laser rods and that one with the pyramidal shapes and so on.

The second reason you should offer full length poses is because the large contract operations don't offer them. They do this mainly to save time: it does take longer to set up full length poses and, of course, it takes a larger camera area. A large contract photographer has to work fast and he rarely has the space or the props to do the kind of job you can. Consider full length poses as a way of showing more previews to your clients, of offering a greater selection. With high school seniors, a different look makes your photography seem more creative. No crazy pose, no prop, nor any incredible offer another studio might make, will be able to compete with the creative style of your photography.

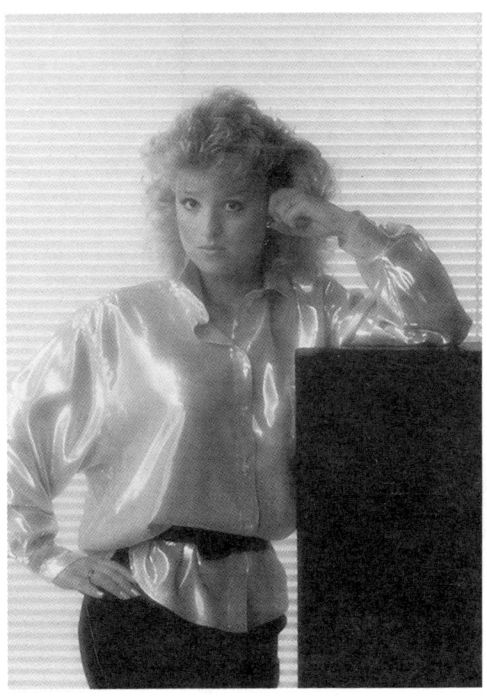

MINIBLINDS

Levelor or any other one inch miniblinds are a standard background used by many studios in our area. They definitely make an interesting but not over-powering background. When used with a gelled background light, black blinds give the impression of little slits of light, a very creative look. The blinds also provide a prop that can be peeked through for a different look. Open them wide enough to recognize the person, however. Another possibility is a pose behind the blind using only back light to create an unusual silhouette. Miniblinds are a definite asset to your background selections.

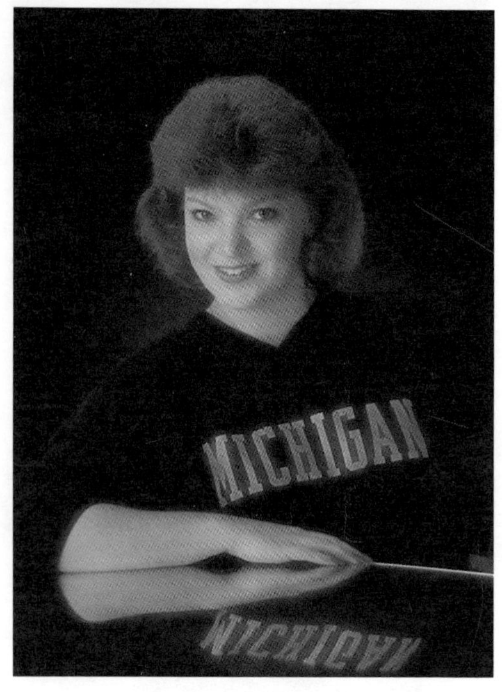

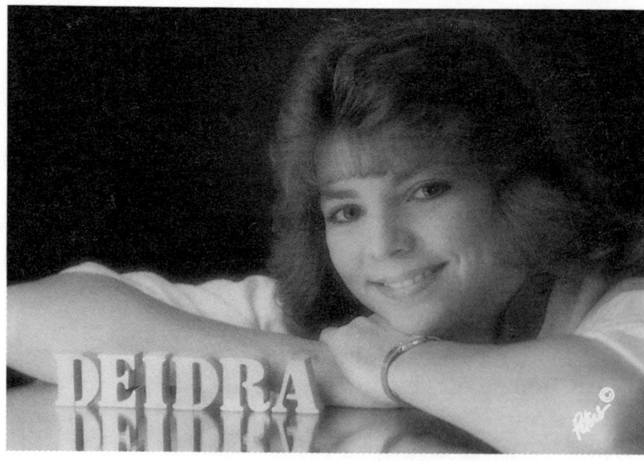

PLASTIC MIRRORS

Using a mirror to show two images of the subject has been done for quite a while, but by using an acrylic mirror you can have your subject lay down across the edge of the mirror and create some great images. But even more, I like the way its reflective surface kicks light back into the subject's face, brightening it and adding additional highlights in the eyes. The size I find most usable is one-fourth inch thick and measures twenty-four by forty-eight inches and you can get it at most plastic suppliers.

Another use for a mirrored surface that has been very useful to use is as a reflector. I use it as a fill reflector under the chin of my subject to fill in shadows under eyes. The lighting is somewhat shadowless, but is very effective for any lighting situation that requires a fashion look. The mirror is normally used with a tight head shot and it is placed in the subject's lap or on a small table just below camera range.

COLORED MAT BOARDS

Mount boards come in many colors and can be used in many ways. Most of the time I use the complete thirty-two by forty inch boards in pairs. I pick two colors that are complementary to one another and that also work with the clothing of my subject. There are a number of ways to use these boards as backgrounds; sometimes I just sit them on chairs, but I may also clamp them to a light stand for head and shoulder photography or pin them directly to the wall of the background with push points or I may hang them using putty. When you use the boards as backgrounds, you can put a design form in your portraits by placing them at various angles or arranging them on the floor to create an interesting image.

With a little cutting and taping, it is possible to create inexpensively a great number of sizes and shapes. These colored shapes will add more dimension and design to your photography. (Note: J.L. Originals also markets some of the above items for your convenience.)

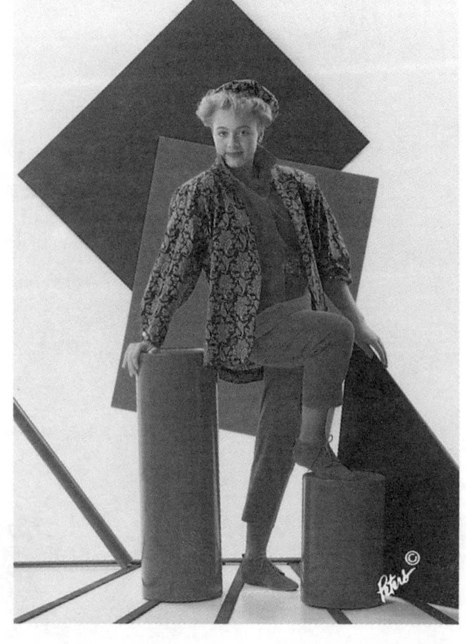

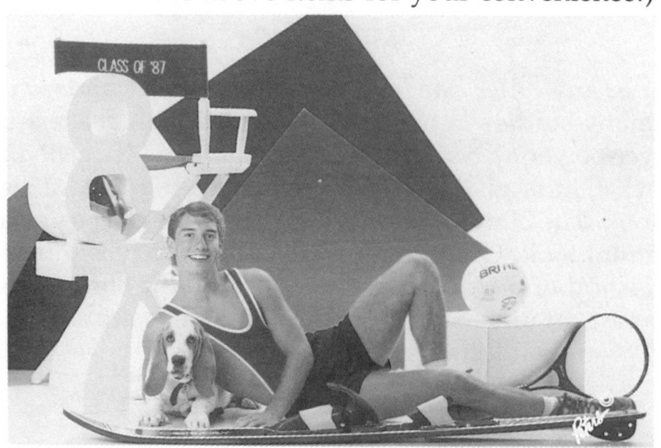

Chapter XIII

Graphic Backgrounds

Over the last several years I have noticed that students like being involved with their backgrounds and props, so we designed and built many props that lend themself to unusual poses. Before very long other photographers saw these props and wanted them for themselves, so we set up a company expressly to make and market these very different items. That company is J.L. Originals, P.O. Box 587, London, OH 43140. A complete catalog is available upon request, so please write. New items are added every year, so stay up with what is happening in high fashion props.

Other manufacturers are now building facsimilies of these props so you should know where the original idea came from, what looks good and what doesn't, the quality of construction and the ease of repair in case of damage. I feel fortunate to be able to come up with designs that flatter the poser, have great graphic appeal and can be used in several different ways. Get the catalog and check out what we have. In the meantime, let's look at just a few of them.

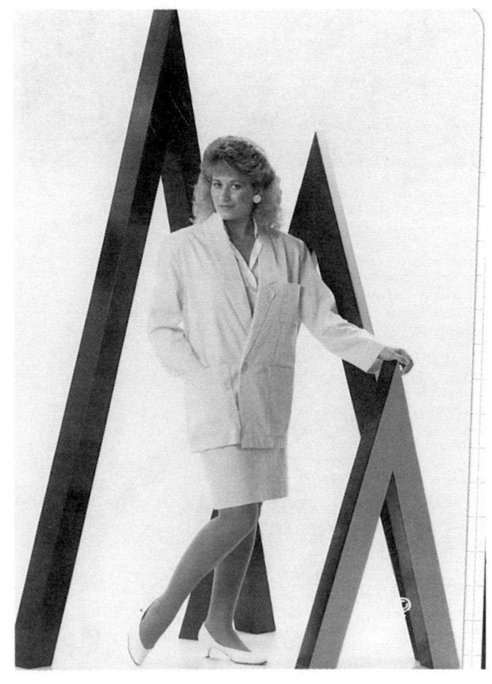

DESIGNER PEAKS

The peaks are inverted Vees, designed in many different colors and sizes and they are black and white on the reverse side. Poses can be done with a single peak or multiples of the various sizes. They are constructed of wood for strength, but covered with Formica for permanent color and ease of cleaning.

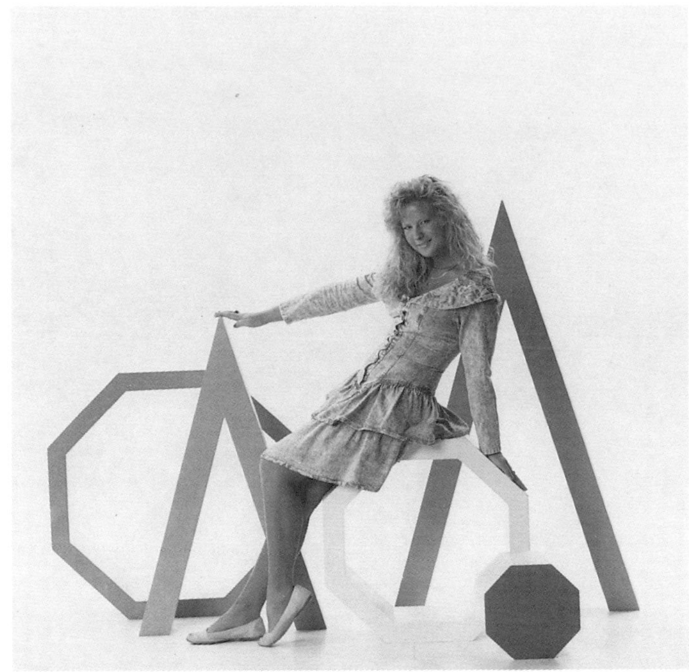

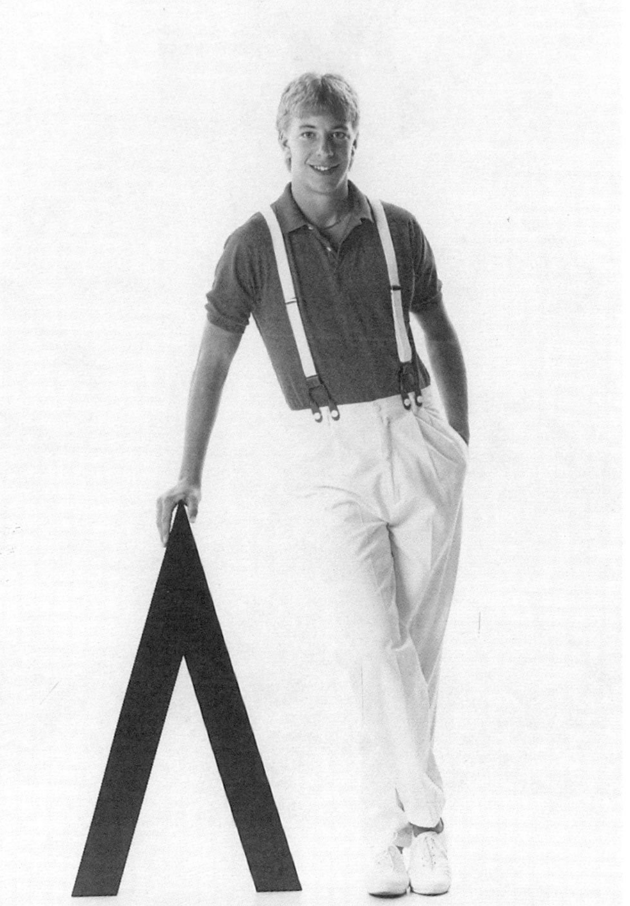

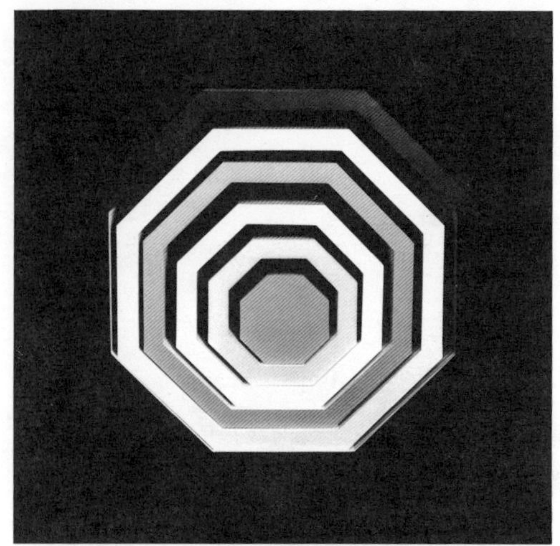

OCTAGONS

One of our more recent designs is the octagon. This prop consists of six octagons designed to nest together one inside the other so you can use all six pieces together or use each one individually. One of the best features of these is that they are finished in pastel colors on one edge and are all white on the other. These finishes make the octagon one of the most versatile props to use.

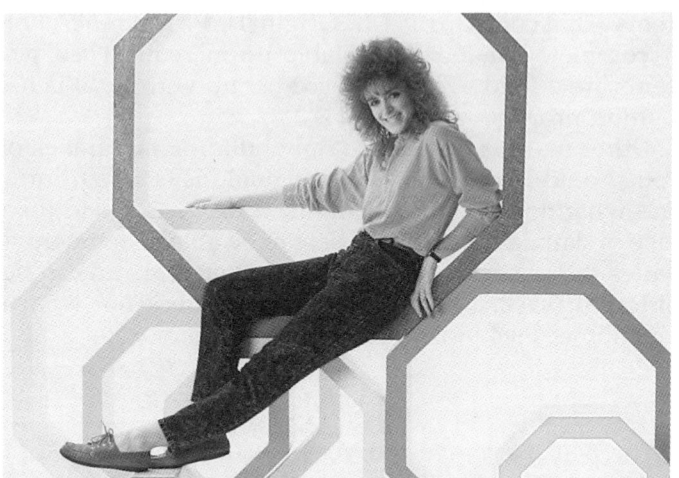

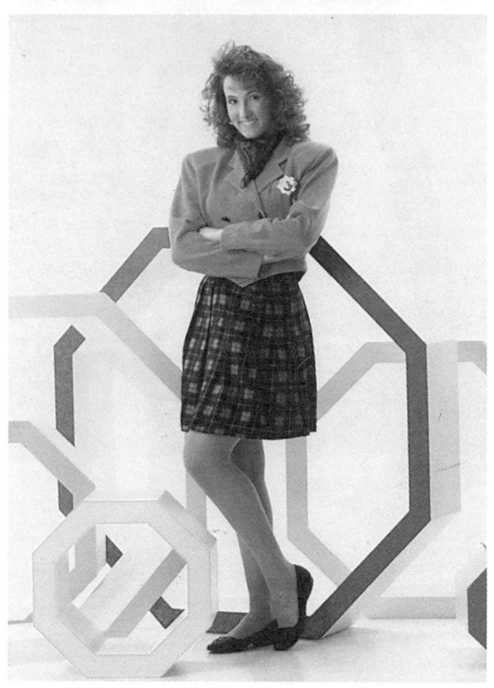

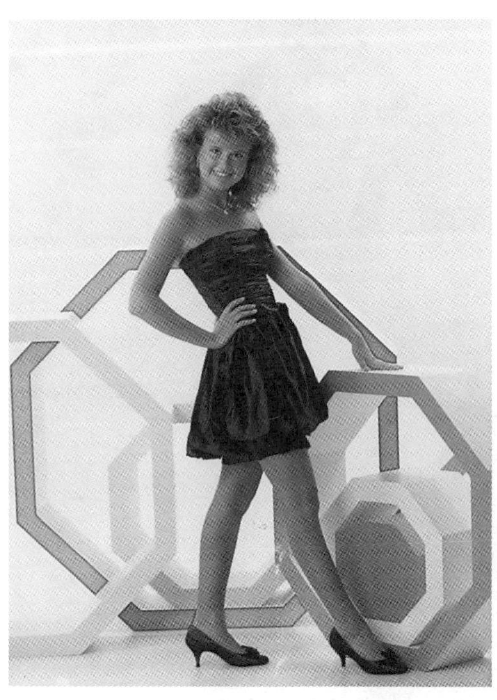

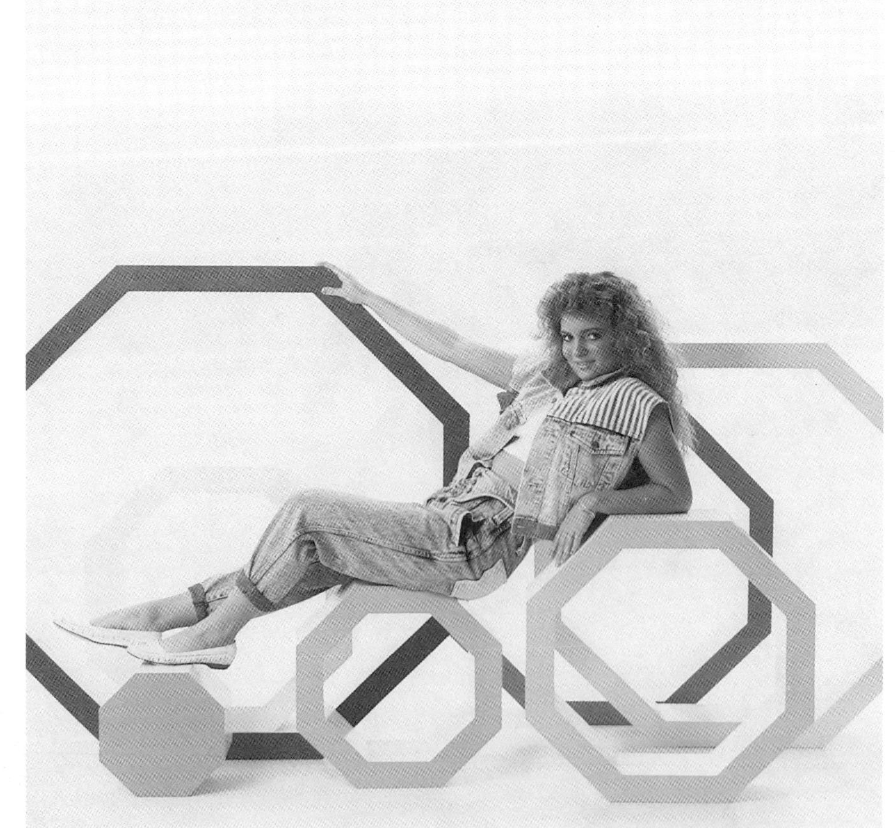

ATMOSPHERES

The Atmosphere is a square with a round opening in the center that has been halved so the two pieces can be used together or separately. It also has depth and is light gray on the front surface, black inside the circle. The circular opening is usually placed behind the head with a light behind it that lights the inside of the Atmosphere as well as the hair. Gel the backlight to add a contrasting color on the opening and the hair, or squirt a spot through the circle to light the hair only. A gelled fill will add another color to the gray front surface, while brackets on the back hold other design elements - discs, fabrics, miniblinds - the list is endless. Put half an Atmosphere on top of tall pedestals to make an ancient archway, which is a great effect for proms. Add a draped muslin of any color and you have a tremendous set. Stack the halves for for spectacular design effects.

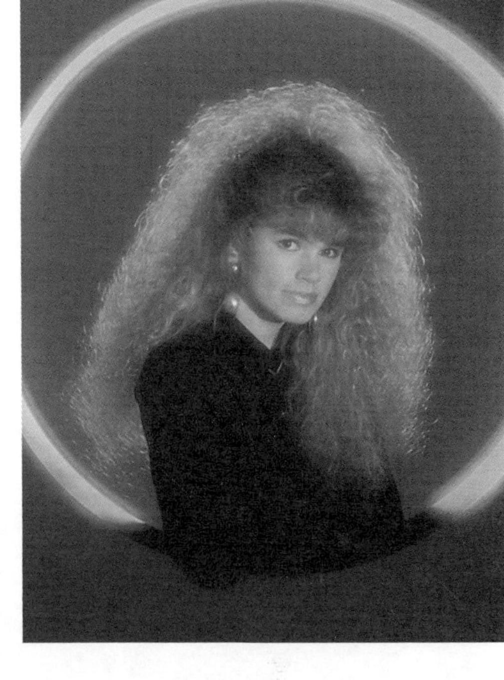

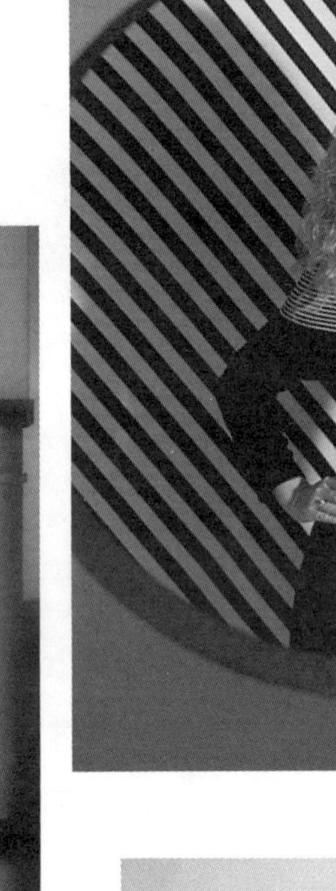

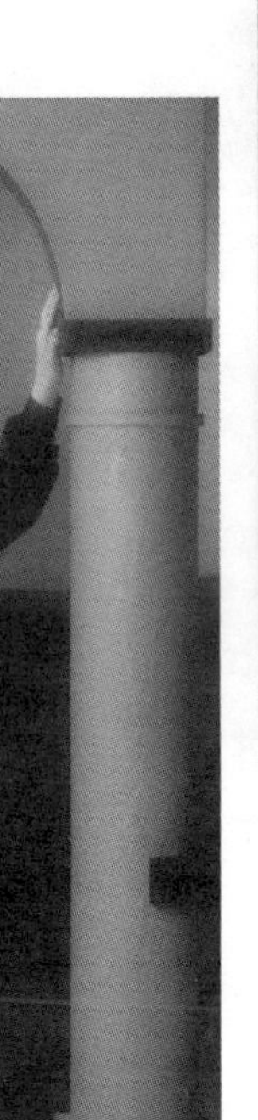

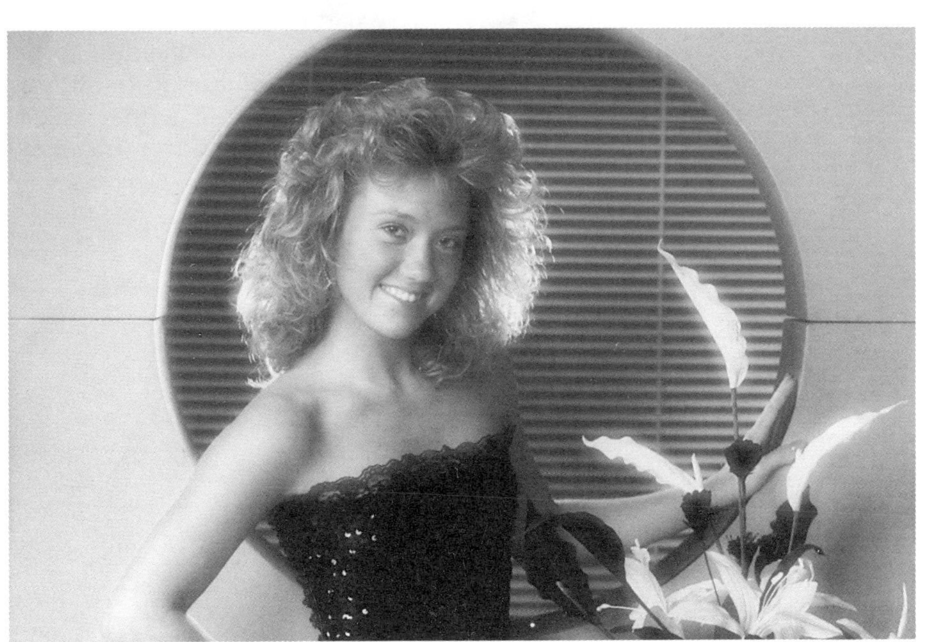

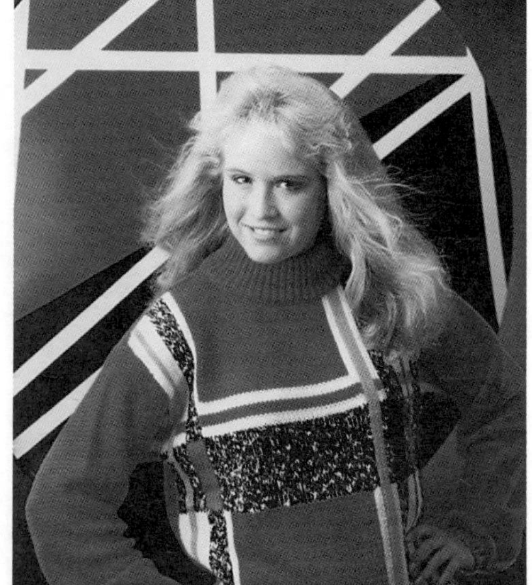

DISCS

High volume studios with limited space will appreciate our new discs which come in eight different patterns and many colors. With their great graphic designs, they are perfect for backing up head and shoulder shots. We use a wooden block with a hole in to mount them on a light stand; the hole fits the stand and a Velcro strip on the block mates with another on the back of the disc. They can also be mounted behind an Atmosphere using the brackets there. A bare bulb flash behind the subject lights the hair, the Atmosphere and the disc for something new and different.

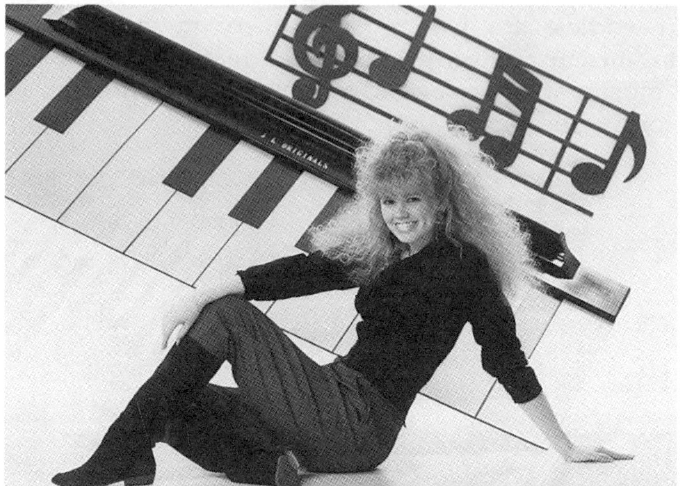

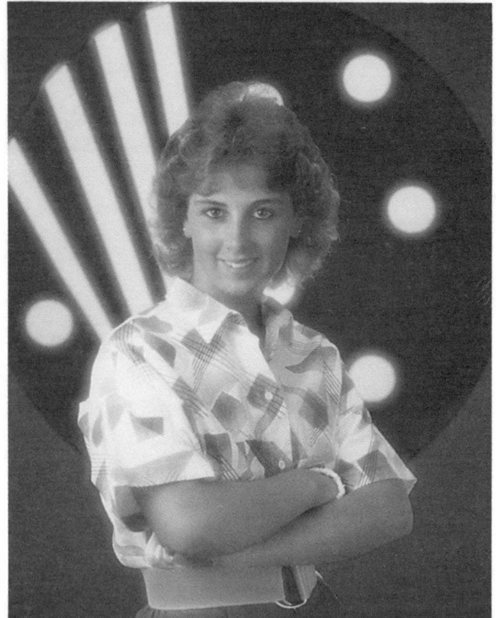

KEYBOARD

The idea for this giant piano keyboard came from the Tom Hanks movie, "Big". Many kids in our area play, so it's a natural prop with them. It's outstanding in b/w where we normally use it in the white room. It can be used in the background either straight or angled, or kids can sit on it. We once made musical notes and a staff from plastic and hung it on the back wall for a very interesting effect.

CIRCLES

The idea came from the "Wall of Fashion", and it's a five foot circle. We had no room for the complete wall so we designed and built a five foot circle that can be hung from the ceiling. It weighs only forty pounds but is strong enough to support ten times that weight. It can also be used on the floor with smaller circles around. A set consists of three circles in various sizes and they are brightly painted in easily touched-up colors.

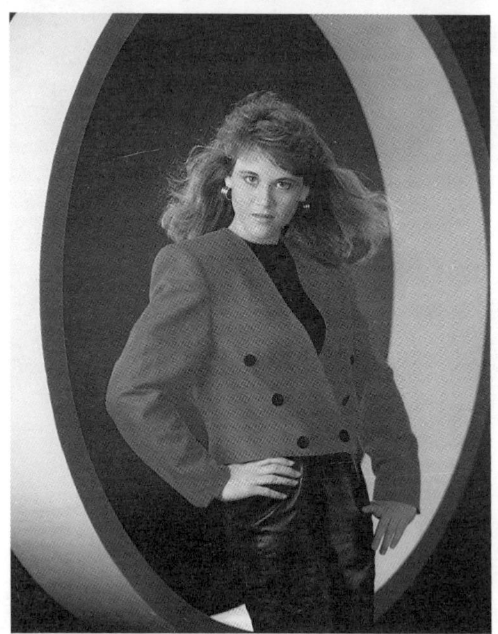

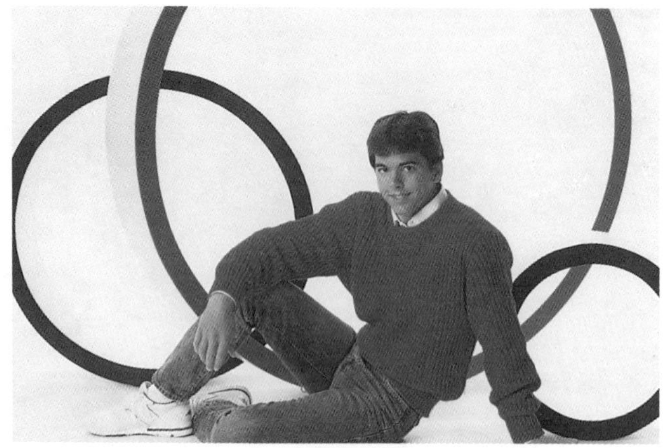

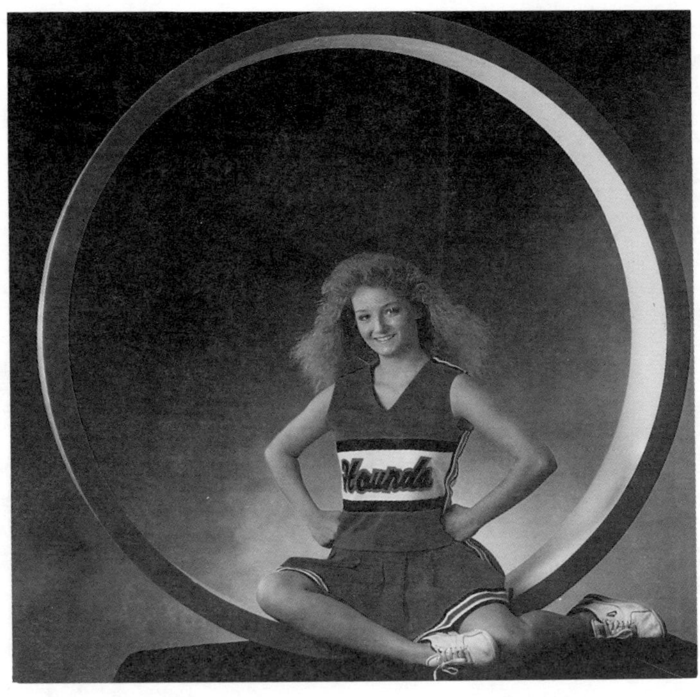

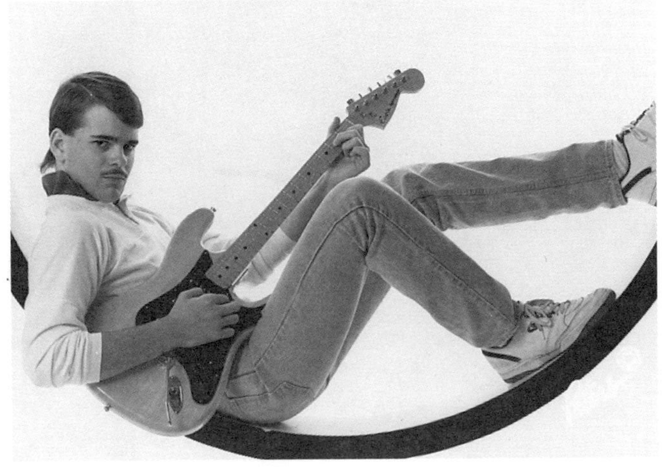

WALL GRIDS

The idea for this prop comes from the displays used in many department stores. I had noticed how a rack was used to hang clothing on and what a nice background it was for the clothing, so we made one with a larger grid and used it for full length poses. Two grids are manufactured, one in white, the other in black.

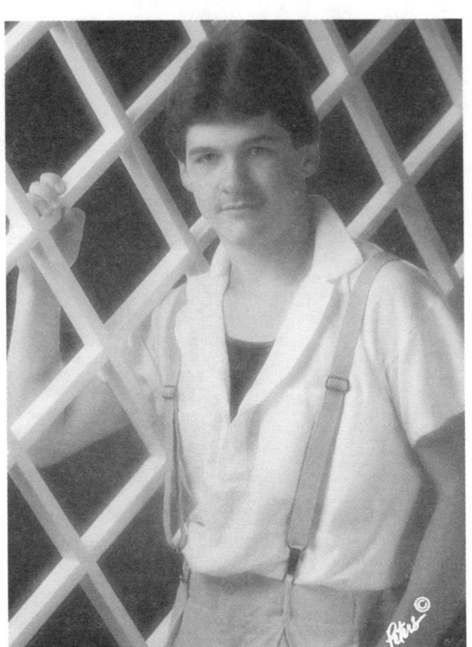

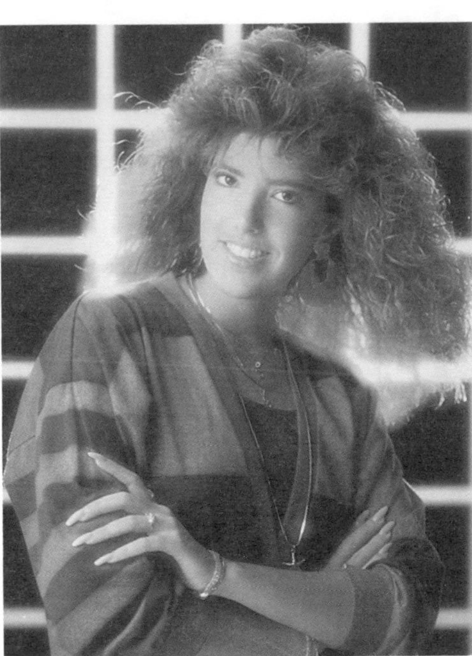

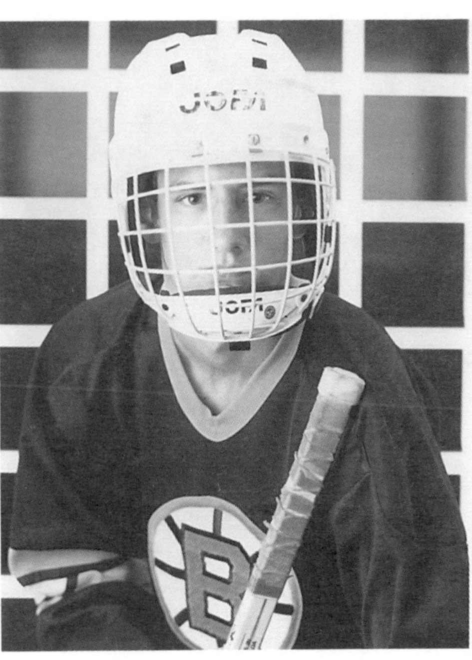

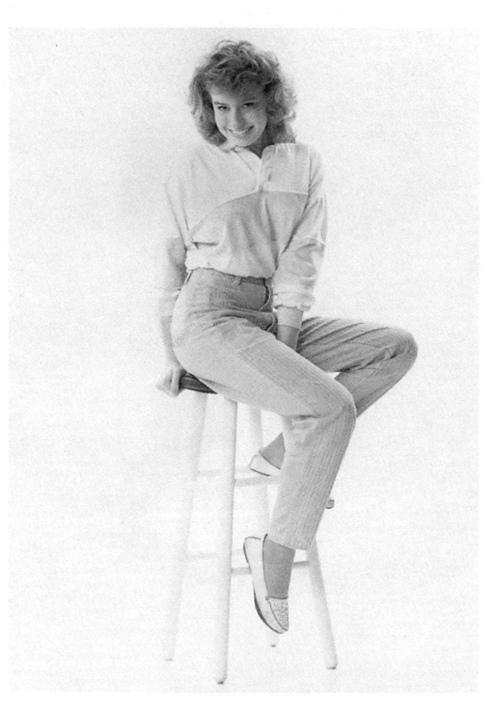

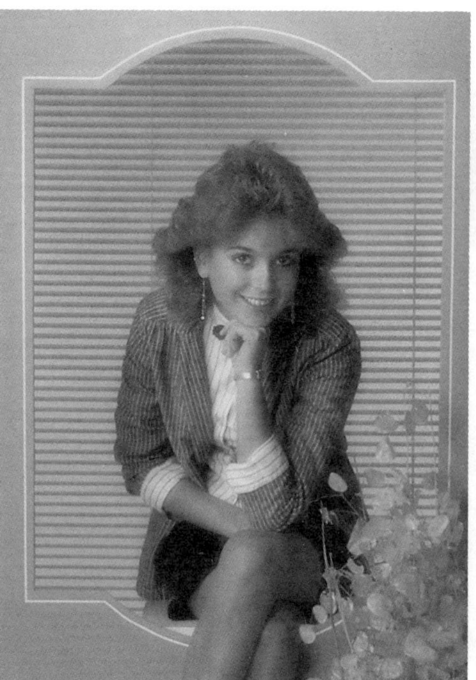

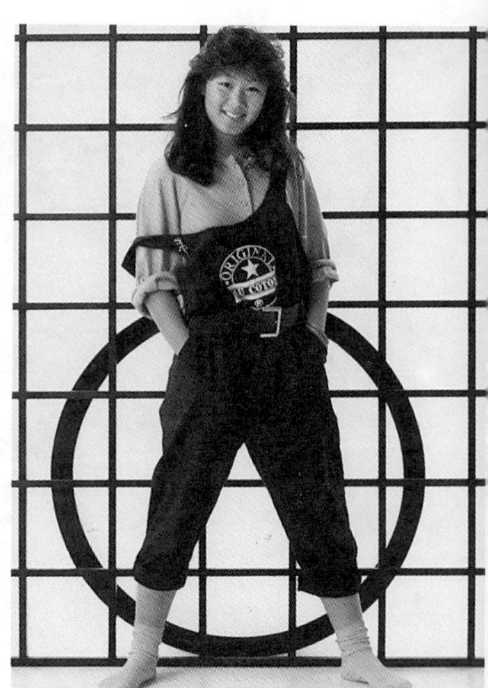

Props can be as simple as the stool shown here, but we keep devising new ones: the mat cut-out above or the cubes and film-strip below. Props can also be mixed and matched as in the three photos at right.

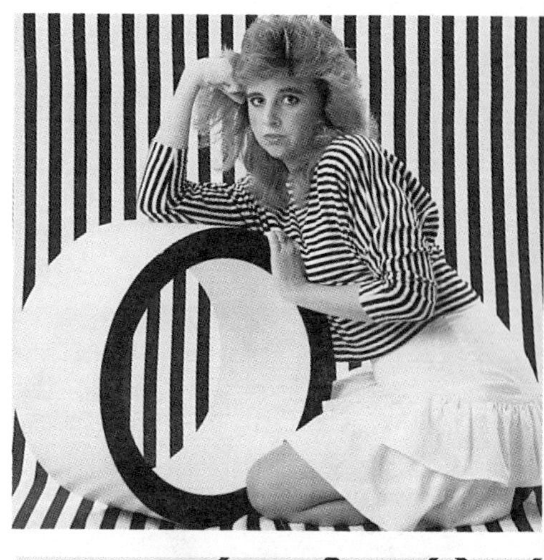

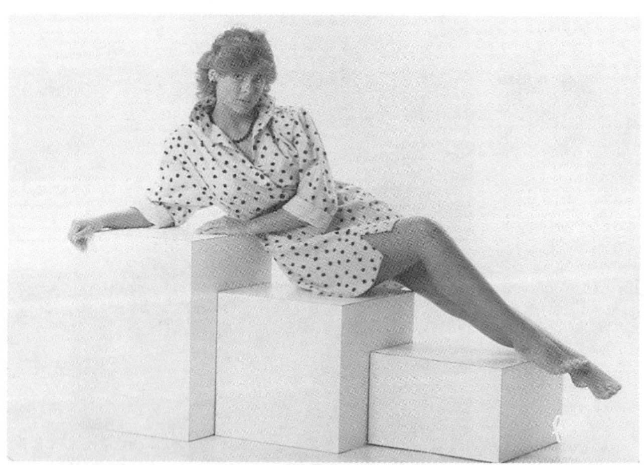

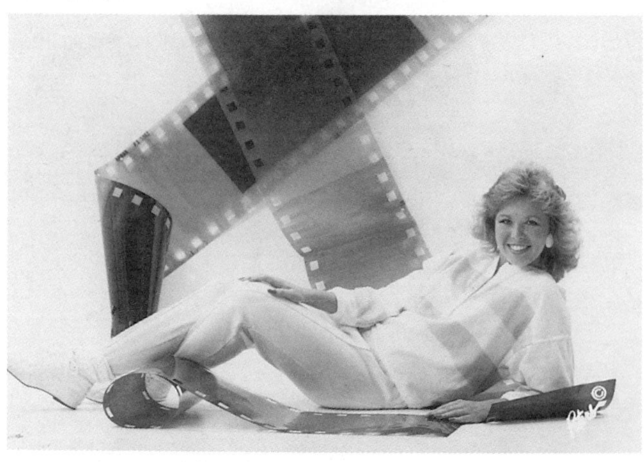

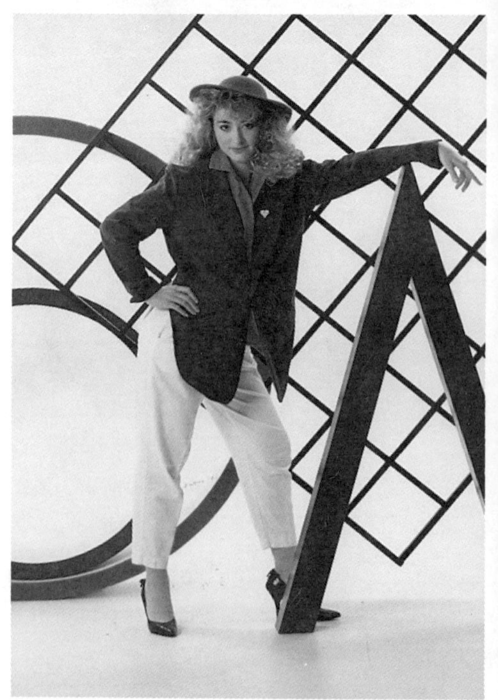

Chapter XIV

Outdoor Photography

When modern photographers began looking for ways to spice up their portraiture, one of the first things they adopted was outdoor photography. This was entering uncharted waters for most of them: their idea of outdoor photography was amateur snapshots, the kind of thing Aunt Nelly did with her Instamatic. Their proper kind of portraits were taken indoors with artificial lights and very often artificial posing. In recent years, however, photographers have refined outdoor portraiture and made it into a product which has proven to be popular with clients in all parts of the country. It is especially well accepted in those parts of the country where outdoor living is easily possible for most of the year and they are among the most popular poses with our senior clients.

Then, after we jazzed up our studio photography with all the new props, backgrounds and poses, we found our outdoor portraits were not comparably exciting. In an attempt to find out what our seniors wanted in outdoors photography, we ran a mini survey among them and found many who like scenic photographs that include open backgrounds, perhaps a field with rolling terrain or old buildings that show the signs of abandonment or are even half fallen down. This comes across to them as a more "creative" look. Brick walls with graffiti have a rebellious look which makes them popular with a certain crowd.

As we have changed backgrounds, we have also changed some of the props that are being used in these photographs. Sun glasses, soda pop machines for a contemporary flair, parking meters, old light fixtures, old cars or new, sleek, hot cars all add interest that appeals to the high school senior.

As photographers, we must look around and see what is available. Things we never would have thought of using are constantly parading before us and we have to become aware of the potential of each one for use as a prop. These props and backgrounds will give your photography a look that's distinct from the look of other less innovative photographers. This is the image you want to portray - an image of being open to creative ideas, of not locking all students into the same dreary pose day after dreary day.

What appeals to the kids is letting them be themselves in their portraits or even to create a fantasy image totally the reverse of their everyday persona, a character perhaps exactly the opposite of their daily style. Be open to using prom dresses blowing in the wind, peasant type clothing worn with bare feet in the grass, leather jackets, swim suits or shorts and, yes, the eternally popular faded jeans.

We have designed and built some photography sets around the studio that we use for outdoor photography. They have proven to be good investments for us, so let's talk about them for a moment.

BARN AND SPANISH SETTING

Very early in our career of photographing seniors we did portraits outside and almost from the first sitting we had a set that resembled the inside corner of a barn. In it we had barrels, a wagon wheel, a window opening the kids could lean through, several items of tack (riding gear) and of course hay, both baled and loose. This "barn" was just two walls put together to form a corner with no roof or floor. It worked very well, but when it rained, the straw got wet and mildewed unless we remembered to run out and cover it with plastic.

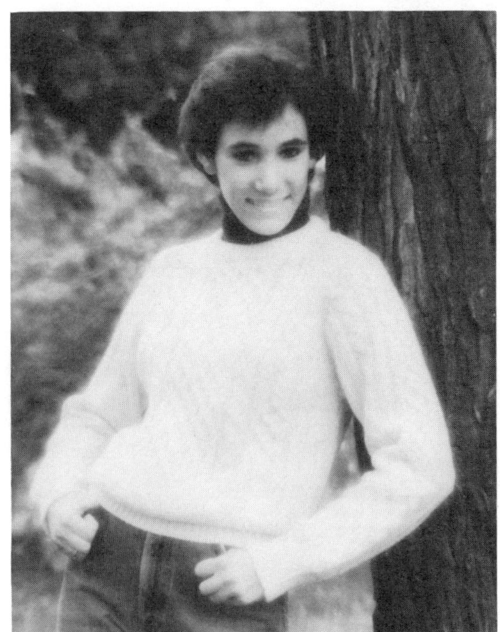

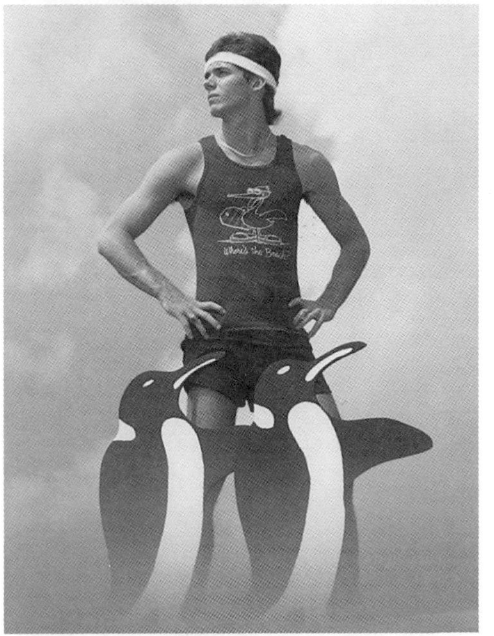

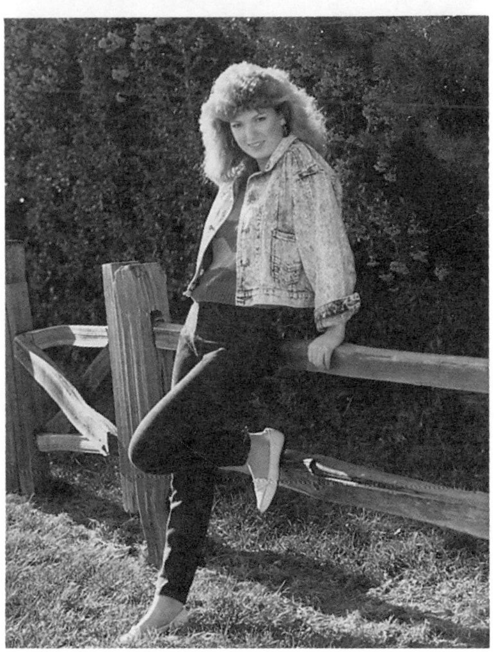

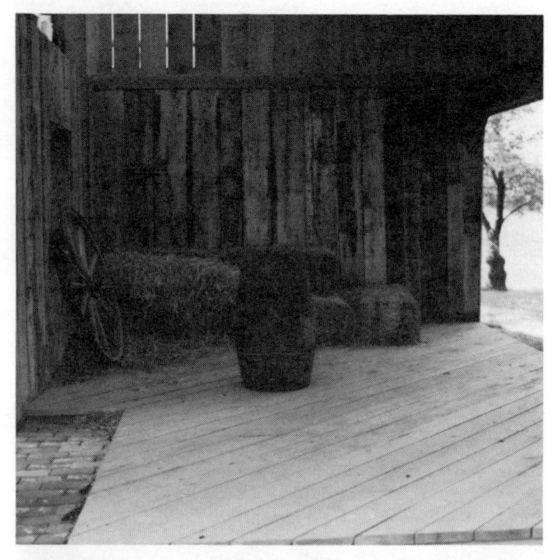

We finally built a barn set that had a floor and roof and is now a lot more than just a barn. It is larger than the first one and it's divided into three areas - the barn setting, a Spanish stucco wall with a brick patio and a one-car garage that is not a set, but is used to store the lawn mower and garden tools for my own uses.

We still get a lot of requests for the barn setting and I suspect that's because we live in an area of farms, many, many farms. There are literally dozens and dozens of poses, from close-up to full length, which can be taken in the barn. The other posing area in this structure is a Spanish-style stucco wall and archway. We added this as a different look so the barn would be more funtional and it is very popular with our students.

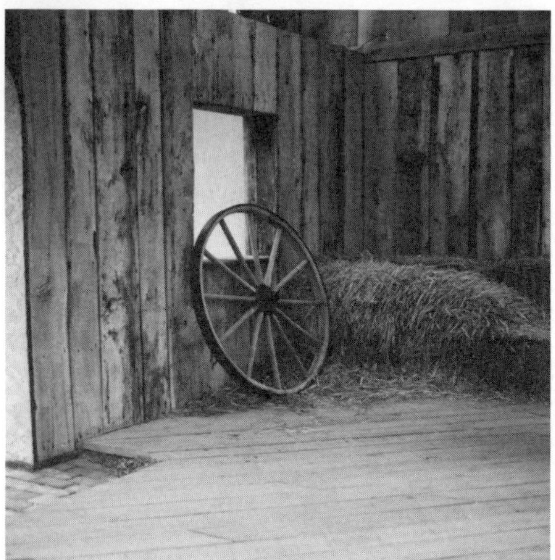

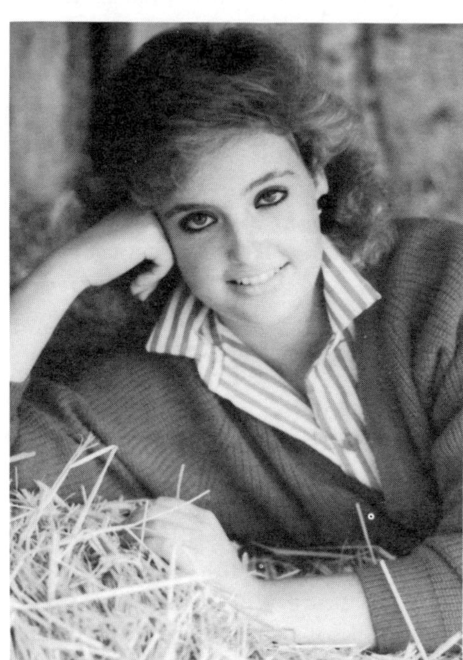

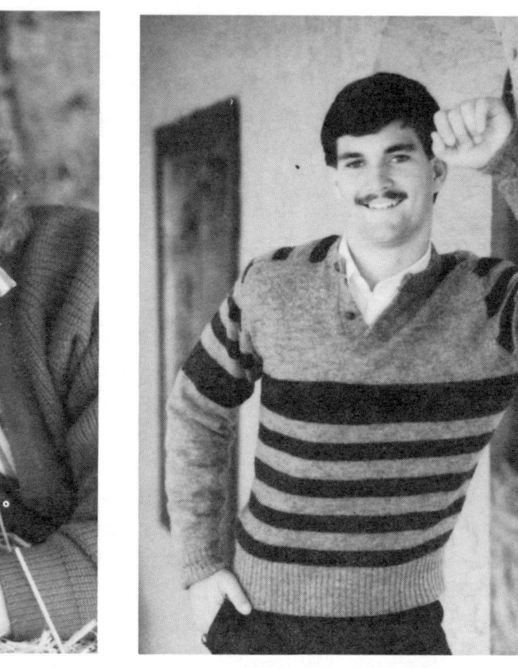

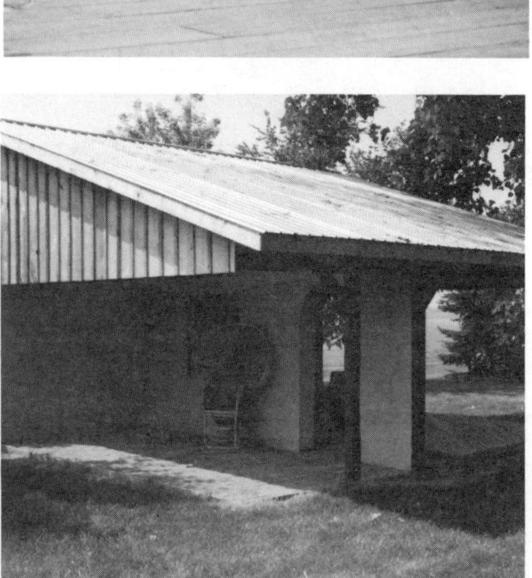

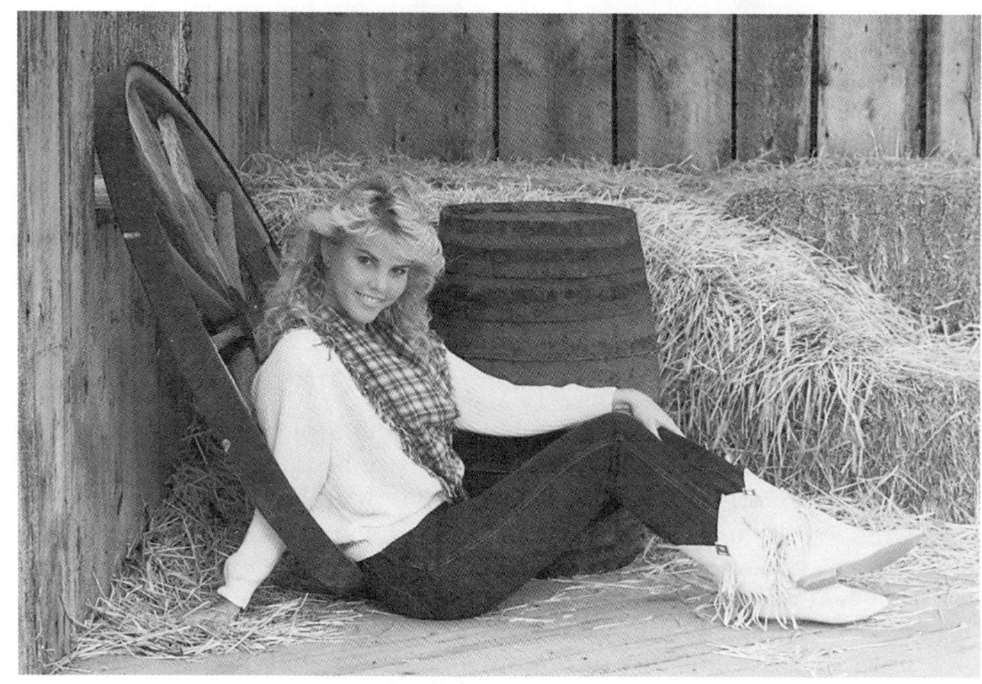

ARCHES AND TRELLISES

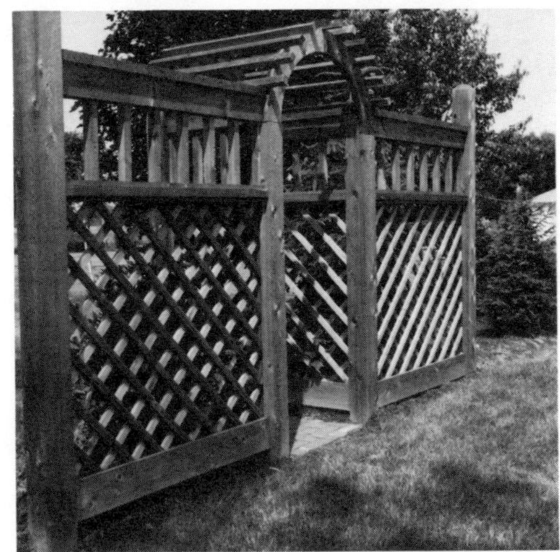

You can incorporate a variety of arches into your garden to use as settings. We had a pre-existing cedar archway and trellis set which was used as a divider in our yard. It became our first arch-trellis background and it was successful enough that we added several others for variety.

There are several ways to finish the wood of these arch-trellis arrangements. The one we have found best is staining because the natural color and texture of wood seems to work better for outside props. I painted one trellis and arch white and found it normally looks very busy in photographs and sometimes even overpowers the subject. There's one exception to this rule and it is to use the white trellis with a prom or other formal dress and use a vignette to soften the background. But for general use with most subjects, I believe the natural finish is more serviceable.

Trellis structures do not have to be huge in size. They actually can be just panels set into the background greenery to give the appearance of a full size trellis.

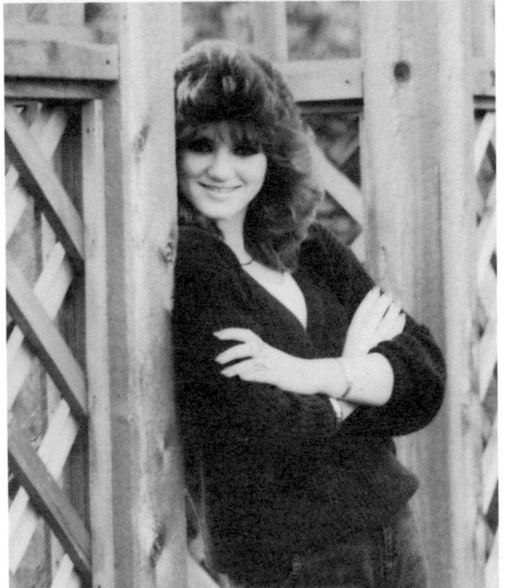

SWINGS

Many props can take a variety of different looks. For example, a swing can be just a rope, a rope with a wooden seat or an old tire, a porch type double swing, or even one made of decorative wicker. Regardless of the type, this prop has about the same effect as a bridge. People love it. As they look at our garden studio, I hear them say, "Look! There's a swing, a bridge and a gazebo". You can be sure the swing is right up there as one of the more popular settings.

One thing that is important in designing an outdoor studio, is location of all of the sets. You want to have as much as possible without making things look junky. You must also arrange your various set items so that, when you're working in one set, the others don't show in the background. Each set needs to have its own distinct appearance without the clutter of other areas.

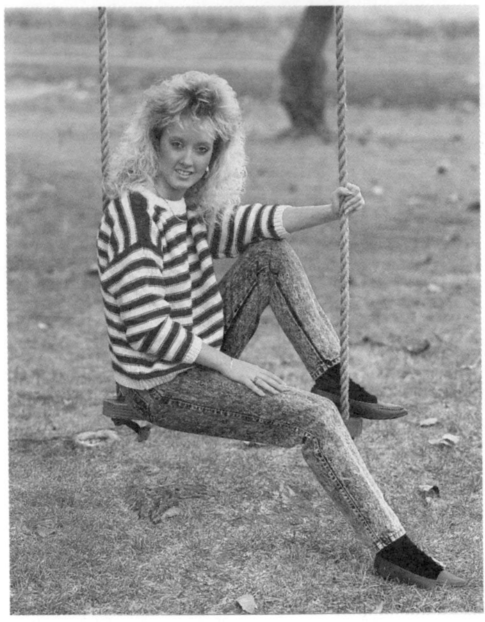

BRIDGE

We have our studio constructed on approximately one acre of property, located on the edge of London. There are no streams of water running through our property, nor are there streams nearby. What I did was build a bridge across nothing. It's quite small with an overall length of about eight feet, and it's light enough so we can move it about the yard. It is made from treated lumber so it will not rot. It was inexpensive to construct, and we left it in a natural wood finish so it blends better into our natural setting. It is quite an attraction and we use it for family groups as well as individuals.

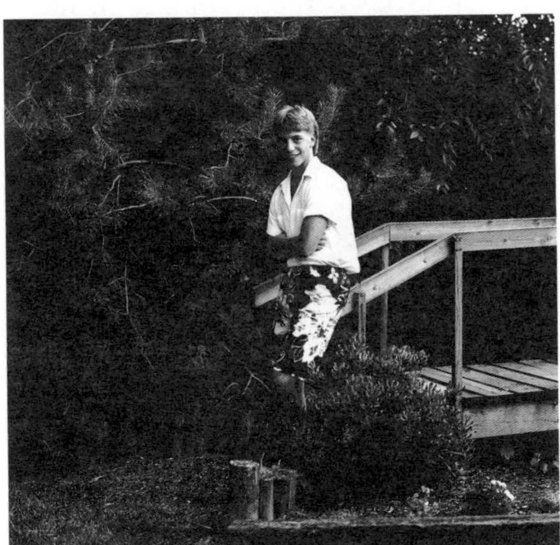

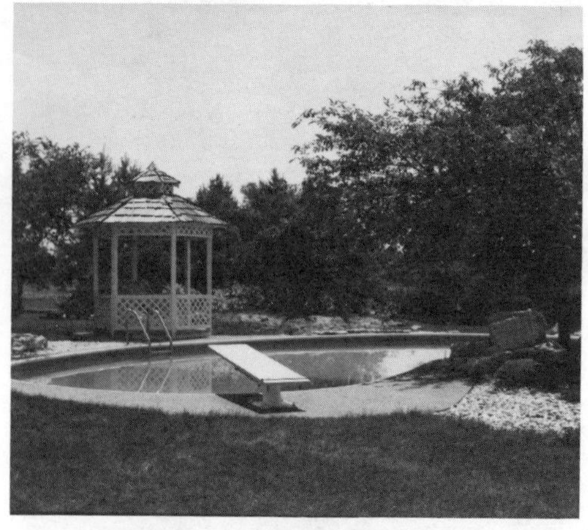

GAZEBO

When we were deciding on the various backgrounds and sets, one of the first we thought of was a gazebo because it was an important American fixture in the last century and the early part of this one. For example, one hundred or more years ago band concerts were one of the principal forms of entertainment and culture and they were often performed from the gazebo in the center of the town park.

Besides its bit of historical interest, the gazebo makes a good background. I like to use this posing area for a girl in a prom or other fancy dress or a guy in a nice suit. I painted the gazebo white and it has a lot of trim on it that can be very, busy busy in the background, so most of the time we use a white vignetter to tone down its brightness.

This gazebo is basically my own design, being a hexagon eight feet in diameter. The roof was the hardest part to contruct. We finished the roof with cedar shakes for an antique appearance and inside is a wicker porch swing. All of this makes an interesting set that has many basic uses and it's a great addition to the variety we can offer in our garden studio.

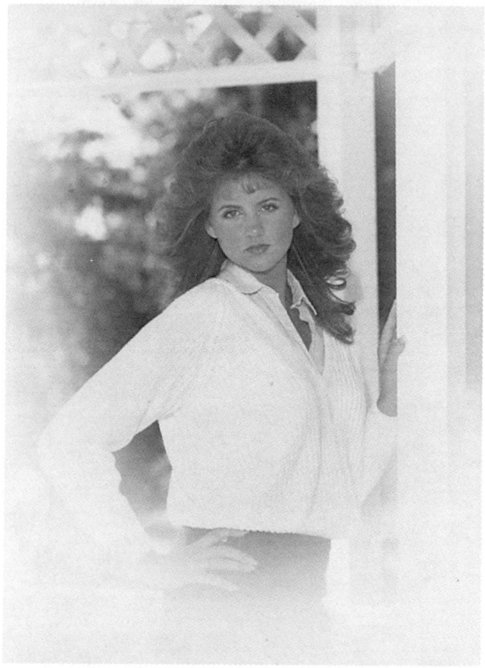

SWIMMING POOL

I always wanted to have a pond to pose people around, but it just didn't come with the house. I checked into having one dug on the grounds, but are several problems with such an idea. First, stagnant water that attracts insects; second, the water tends to leach away and must be constantly replenished; third, the water would have to be aerated with some sort of a pump. With these problems in mind, I started looking into a swimming pool and weighing the options. We settled on the swimming pool and gave it a more natural, pond-like look by designing the area around the pool with stones.

The poses we do around the pool vary from one student to the next. In the summer months almost every student brings a shorts outfit as one clothing change. These outfits vary from a very basic shorts outfit to exotic Hawaiian types. Many girls and boys also include a swim suit as one of their clothing changes.

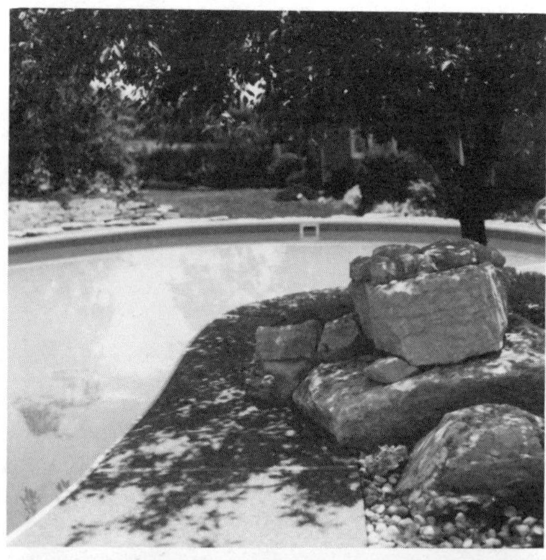

Students today are very health conscious and they often are eager to have a swim suit as one of their changes. Even if they aren't, often their mothers are. We often hear comments from mothers like this, "My daughter looks great right now and I think she should have a swim suit picture made so she can show her children what a cute figure she had in high school".

Fathers are usually not as crazy about these poses, but they tolerate them. It's important that you remember that these students are in high school and the poses you put them in should not be seductive or erotic, even while you are working to flatter them. Have fun with them while you are doing these poses, try to keep them smiling in most of the shots. They probably will not buy large prints from these poses, and frequently will buy nothing but the proof, but you have added variety to their folios and given them the opportunity to express themselves in another way.

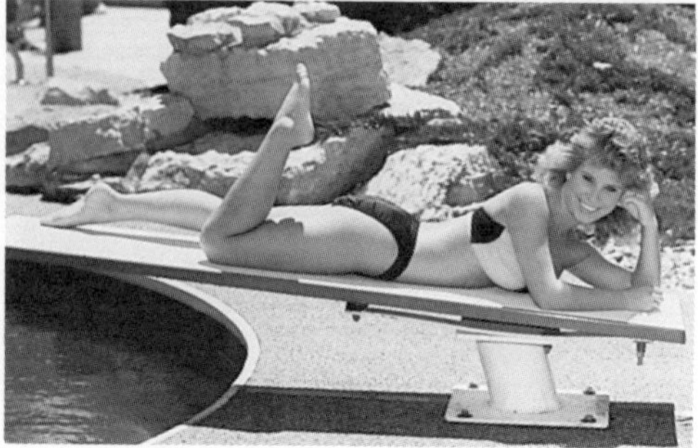

DECK AND HOT TUB

We recently added a large wooden deck to one side of our swimming pool and on one corner of the deck we put a hot tub. The deck has several large posts all of the way around it and they are connected together with a large rope. This "anchor hawser" gives a very nautical look to photographs taken here. The hot tub or spa is built right into the deck and provides another area for swim suit type poses. The pool, deck and hot tub are out in the open with absolutely no shade so we have to soften the harsh sunlight with a silver reflector, a flash fill from a small unit mounted on the camera or an overhead scrim. Any of these methods works quite well so choose the one you like best.

When I set out to soften sunlight, I don't try to overpower the sun with fill light, but only to add enough additonal light in the shadows to bring the ratio up to normal portrait levels.

Common practice is to use the sun as a backlight with sunlight coming from behind the subject and to meter for the hair, which will be the brightest part of the subject. I then set my camera for one f:stop under this reading. This is also the brightness I try to obtain from my fill flash or silver reflector. I prefer to work with a silver reflector although it is very bright and may cause your subject to squint. If this is a problem, switch to a flash fill.

These pool poses are always fun poses which add more variety to the student's portfolio - and maybe to her perception of herself. Each year I try to develop new backgrounds that add more dimension to our senior portraits. We make these additions and changes to keep improving and to keep ourselves alive and alert with fresh ideas.

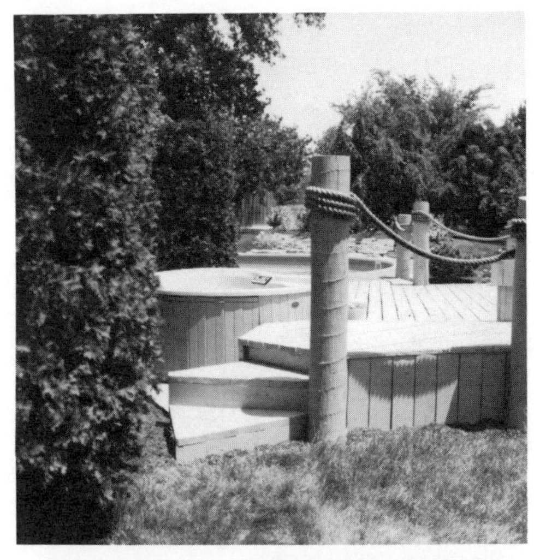

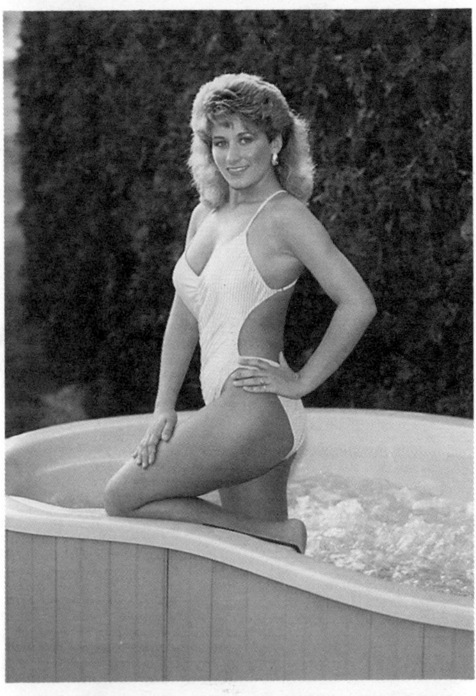

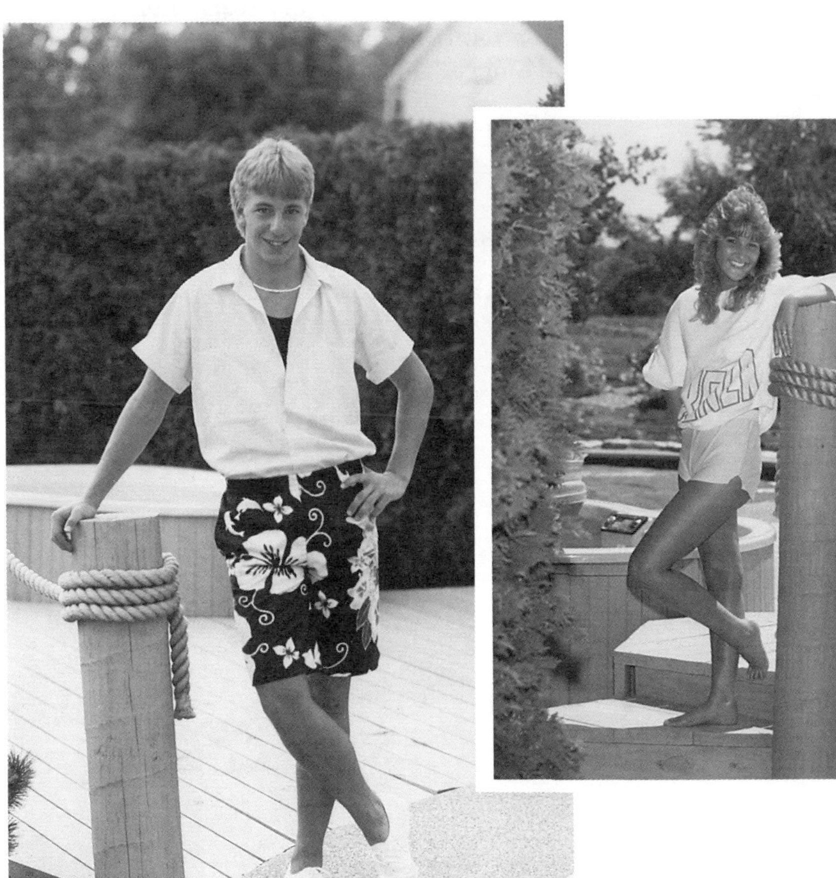

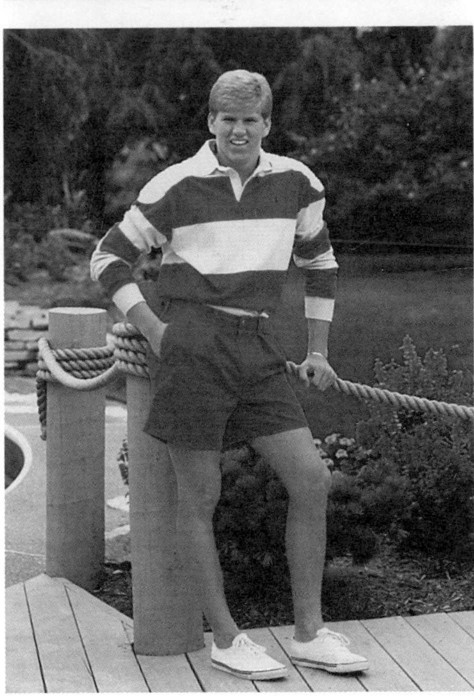

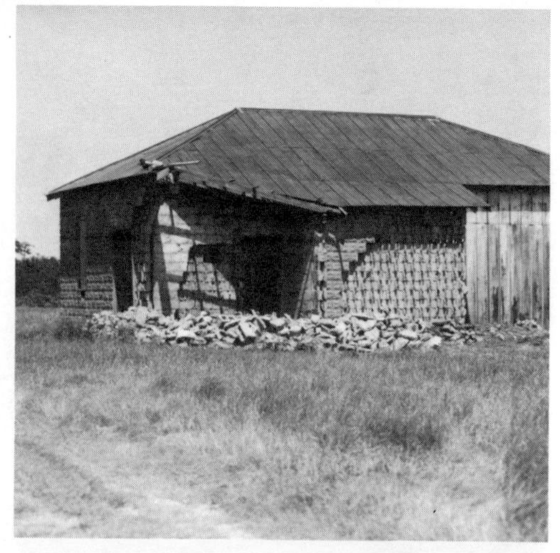

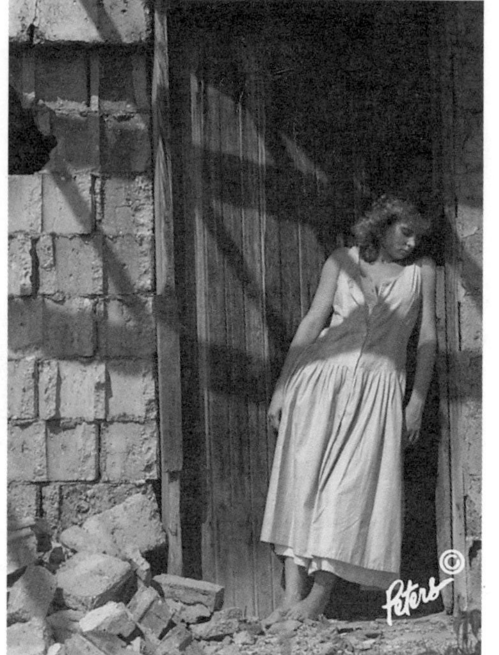

OLD BUILDING AND AWARENESS

In these constantly changing times I find people are leaning toward a more creative appearance in their photographs. I have the great luck to have an old, crumbling, half fallen concrete building just a short walk from my studio. What is so great about this old crock is that every side of it is photogenic and one side of the building is always in the shade, so posing around it is great. I try not to use it for every student I photograph, just those which have clothing that will either blend with it or contrast with it. I want the images I create here to make distinctive statements, not just be echoes of every other portrait.

There are old wooden and weathered doors, and the building has a corner that has been torn partially apart, so it lends itself to a concept that almost seems like Greek ruins. It is totally unlike any other background in this area and it is this uniqueness that makes it so appealing. Are there similar places that you walk by daily and take for granted that have the potential to be some of the best backgrounds you can imagine? These settings may lead to unusual images which can be sold for large wall portraits simply because they are so unusual. The poses are usually full length and incorporate more of the environment than a normal senior pose.

You need to look at what is at your disposal for backgrounds. For example, last summer I walked by an area where the grass had grown very tall. It had dried but it had not yet fallen over. Beyond this field was an old tree with very low branches and it's whole aspect was very appealing. It was ideal for outdoor poses.

The reception of these poses by seniors was unbelievable. Who would ever think that portraits done in a field of weeds could be acceptable, let alone a smashing success. The fact is, they are very well accepted, and are actually becoming sought after. I suggest you look around and open up to backgrounds you have never thought about using before. Your possibilities are endless.

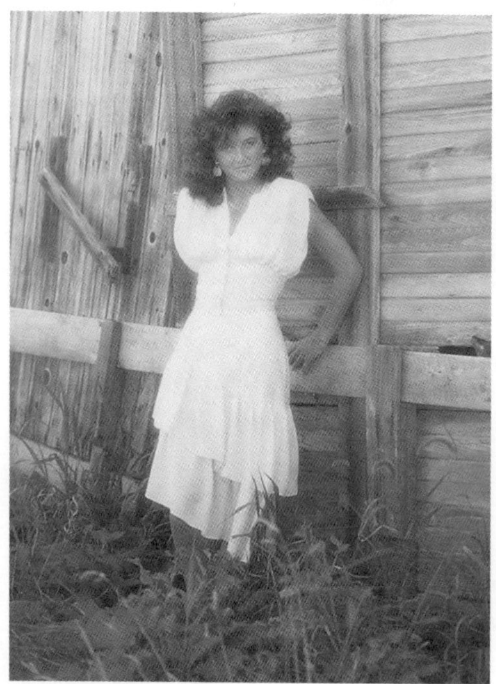

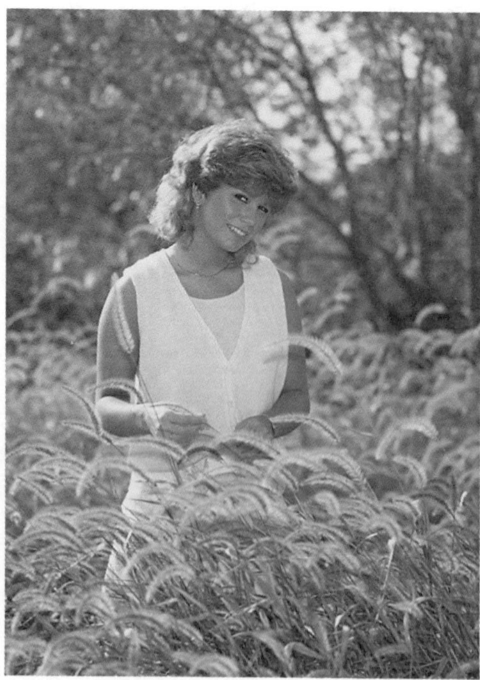

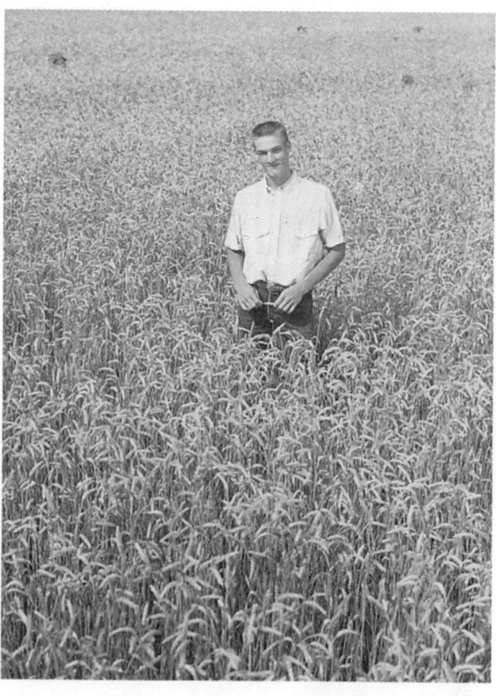

Chapter XV

Expressions

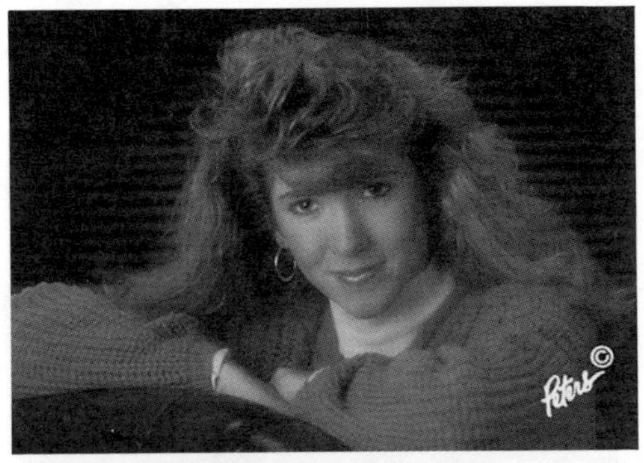

After you establish the pose and set the lighting, there's still one thing left that determines whether the portrait will be a much loved winner or a loser that spends the rest of its existence in your files. That thing is the expression of your subject. There are many factors that decide the type of expression needed and most of them are your responsibility: you must know what the portrait will be used for and you must make the exposure at just the precise instant.

The ability to catch good expressions at their peak is so important that this one thing can make or break your business. Imagine for a moment the different expressions that would be appropriate when a passport photo is taken, when a business portrait is made, when a photograph is used just for a record, for a gift, for the senior annual, or any of a dozen purposes.

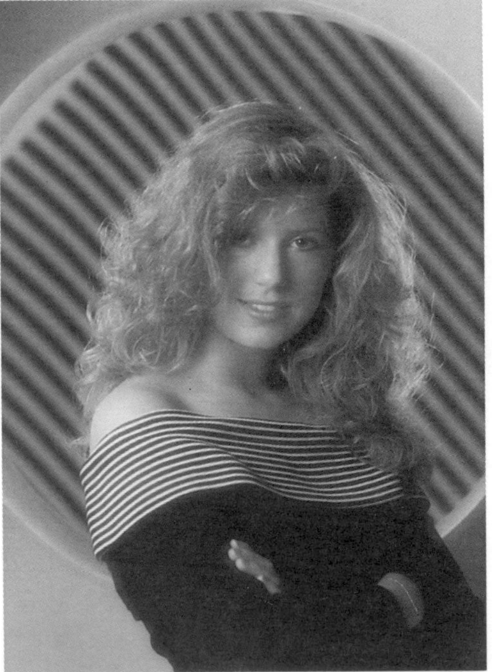

You must evaluate the situation, determine what the subject wants, then capture the desired expression on film - and do it all in a moment of time. Many photographers go wrong because they don't know how to get past the defense mechanisms of the subject nor when to press the shutter release. To catch a smile at its peak can be learned by most people with practice, but breaking down defense mechanisms is quite different. Let's look at some of the ways you can do that.

One of the best ways is to have all kinds of music available and let the subject select the kind. You need both soft and hard rock, instrumental, country, rhythm & blues, rap, dance tunes and classical, a little something for everyone. The moment we enter the camera room we ask our subjects what kind of music they like and they usually reply, "I don't care", or "Whatever you've got". They say this because they don't think I have what they want to hear.

Once you know the type of music they want, give them the names of the albums you have in that field. They are usually impressed by the large variety we have of "their" music and this reacts in our favor. It's like magic when we play their music and toes begin to tap or they lip-synch the song that's playing. Once this happens, you can usually do whatever you want with that person and his/her expression.

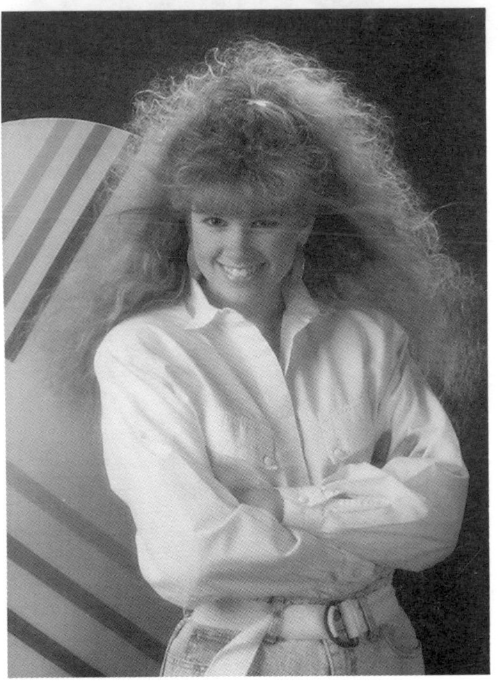

What is your customer expecting in the way of expression? The best way to find out is to ask. It doesn't take much discussion to pick up some pretty strong ideas about what is wanted. During this time I get a chance to express myself, too. I tell them that a large smile is not expected and is rarely the best expression; that a pleasant, happy look is near ideal, although most of the guys want to look cool by not smiling. If you get one of these, you can usually induce a pleasant expression by showing him pictures of other cool guys who smiled or looked happy for their portraits.

Expressions like these will usually fill the bill, but be sure to listen carefully when they tell you they don't want their crooked teeth to show, or that their smile shows an inch of gums or they close their eyes when they laugh. Many people feel strongly about these minor defects and it's your responsibility to observe their wishes as much as possible.

Even so, you can't just let the subject sit there expressionless or you have a losing sitting. Occasionally I get a person who honestly looks bad when she smiles and they hate to do it. With them I say, "Just think about smiling; don't let it quite happen, but let the corners of

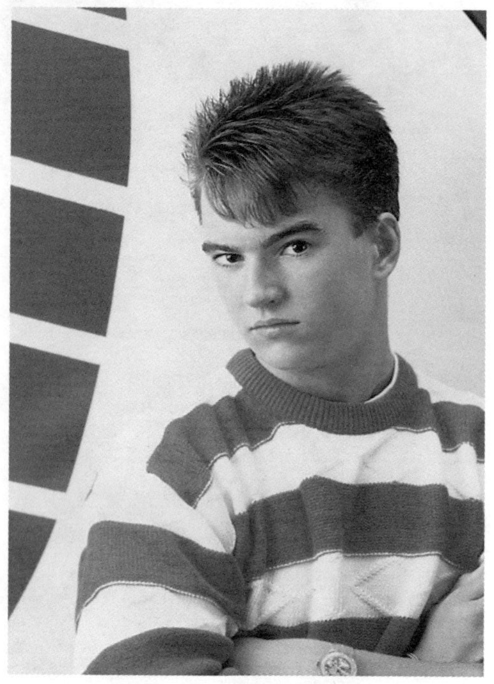

your mouth turn up a little while keeping the mouth shut." Sometimes it's better if the lips are parted just slightly, not enough to show the teeth.

Either way, you get a pleasant look and it's often all that's needed for the person who won't smile. The subject must be told there's no need to smile to have a good portrait and that if he forces a smile, it won't look right. A fake smile shows only in the mouth, while a real one involves the whole face, especially the eyes. It's a rare subject who looks good in a full laugh. Save the belly laughs for snapshots; keep it more restrained in a portrait. Don't be afraid to tell a subject to relax and enjoy himself.

Let him know you will help him get through the portrait experience with his ego and self-esteem intact. Tell him just to watch you and your expression will tell him whether to smile or be more serious. Watch the shoulders; don't let nervousness pull them so high your subject seems to be neckless.

Stay in control through eye contact. Block out other distractions by giving them the expression you want to get back, then pop the shutter. A sure-fire relaxer with boys is to tell them, "I'll bet your mother told you to smile for me, didn't she?" Then, "Okay, let's get the smiles over with early in the session, then you can get into casual clothing and be yourself with the expressions you want. Smiles aren't for every photo, but if I don't have a few in here, your mother will hang me out by the ears. After we get the smiles in the suit for the family, you can be yourself."

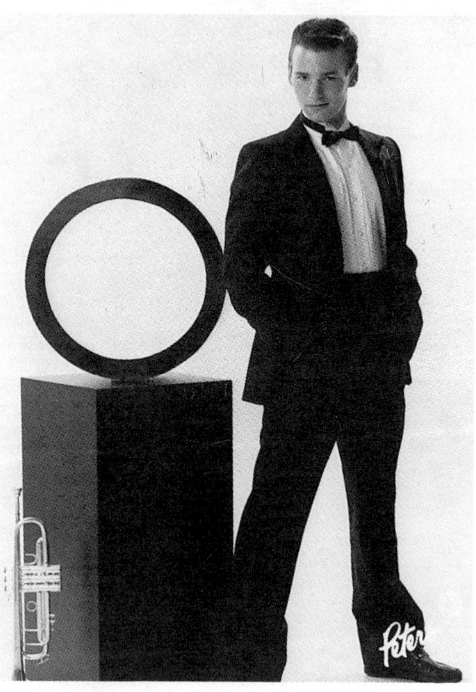

You have to follow through on this promise; after he gives you the smiles for his "family" portrait, let him be the way he wants to be in the next few poses. He'll soon begin to trust you and be more relaxed and willing to follow your lead during the rest of the session. Music helps with most guys, too, but what will really get the expressions for you is to have his girl friend there. I usually place her where I would stand and I tell him to watch her. She will always smile encouragingly at him and this pulls a real smile out of him.

If I am posing a girl, I know I can wink at her or flirt a little (as much as a man twice her age can do!) to get the expressions I need: with a boy, there are definite limits to what is appropriate to do. But a girl - any girl - can turn him on to a smile. Amazing! I have sometimes stepped out into the waiting room and grabbed any girl who was there and used her to get a reaction from Mr. Stoneface. Maybe I should hire a pretty, sweet sixteen girl just to smile at the big, tense guys who can't relax.

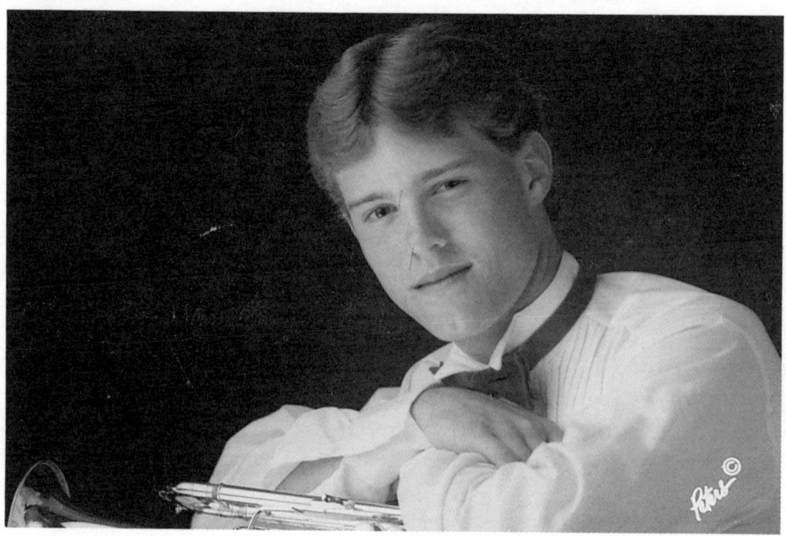

Look at the series of photos here. The girl didn't know what the signs said and the expressions are the result of her reacting to my commands or to my winking, smiling or whatever at her. All of which proves that you can get the expressions you need. So when do you push the button? When your own sense of what's right and good tells you the moment is here. You're in control, so don't fire if the face is a blank mask or when the smile is too big. Look for what a famous photo-journalist called the "Decisive Moment", then take your portrait.

Would you like to know how much control you have as a photographer? Try this: catch the undivided attention of your subject, then open your mouth as is you are saying "oooooooh" and watch your subject mirror your image. Or smile and watch the smile come back to you. But if you're feeling bad today, stop before you start another sitting and pull yourself together so you don't drag your subject down into a bad mood, too. That's too much like having heart surgery from a surgeon who's worrying about his golf game.

You are building a relationship - however temporary it may be - so leave your troubles at the camera room door and come in with a smile. Smiling at another human being is rewarding and you owe your subject the best you've got. Enjoy the music, hum along with it, give your client a lift and you'll feel better yourself.

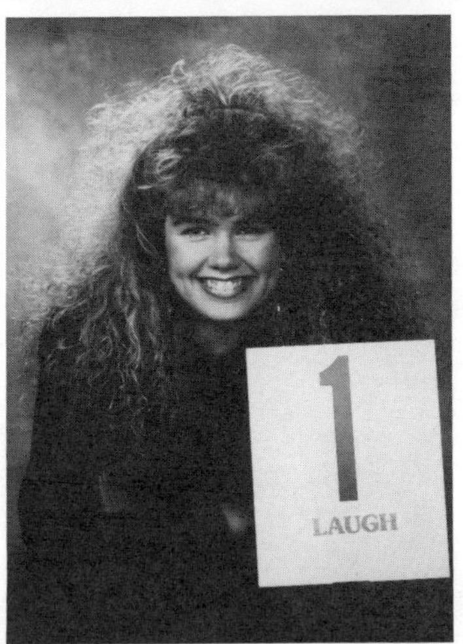

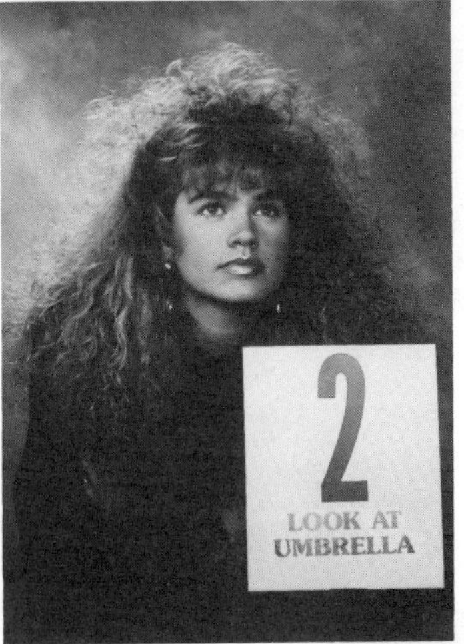

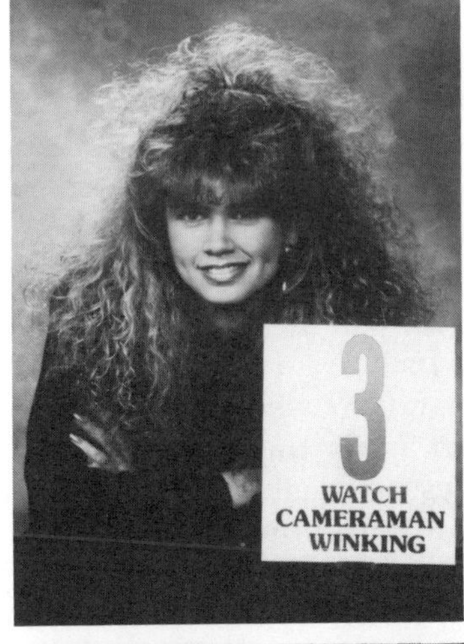

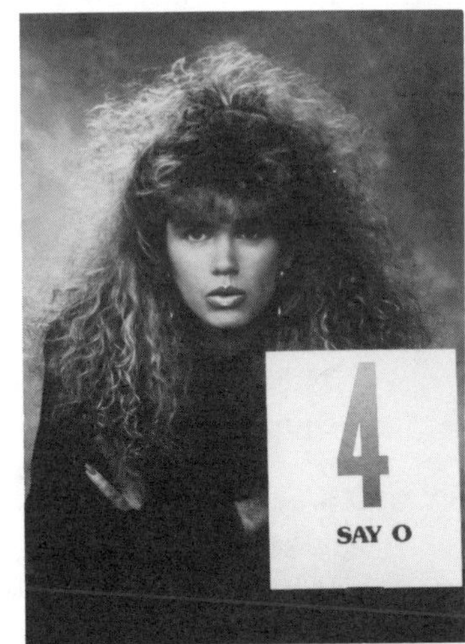

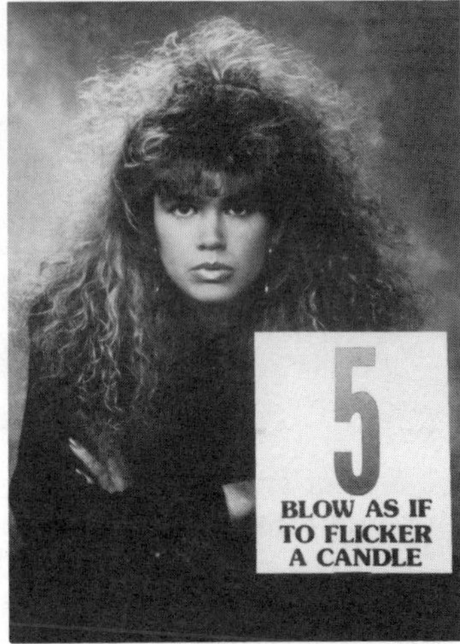

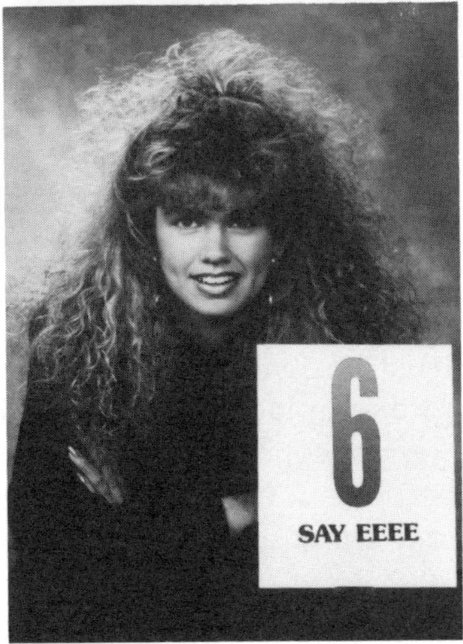

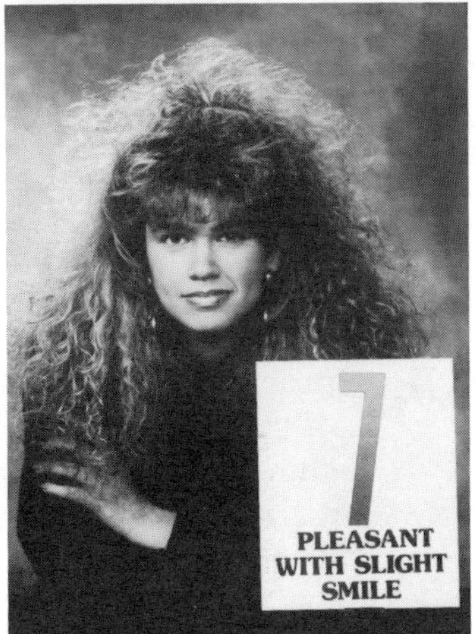

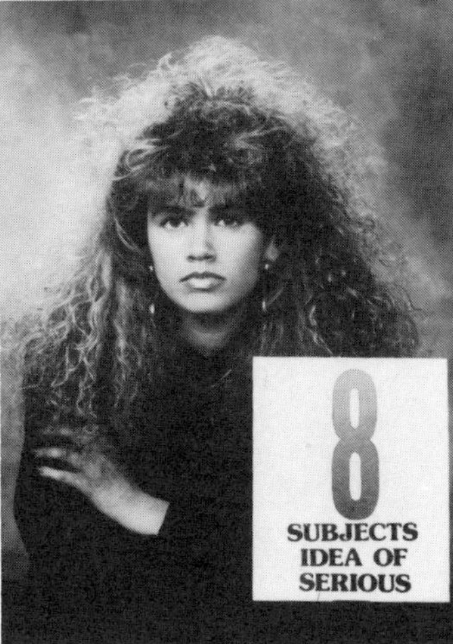

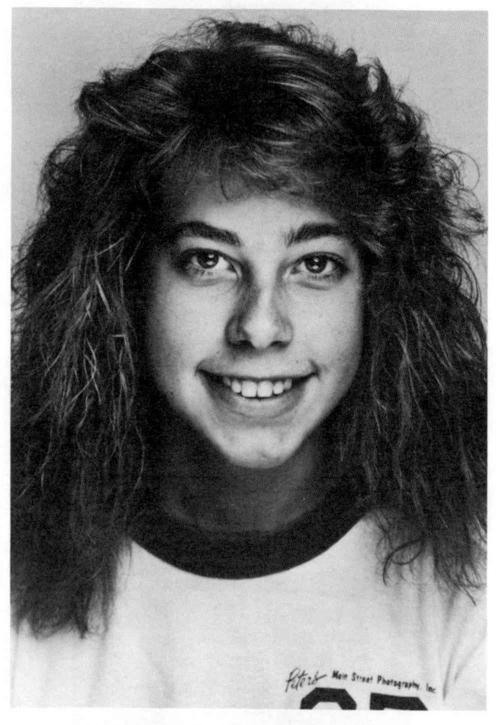

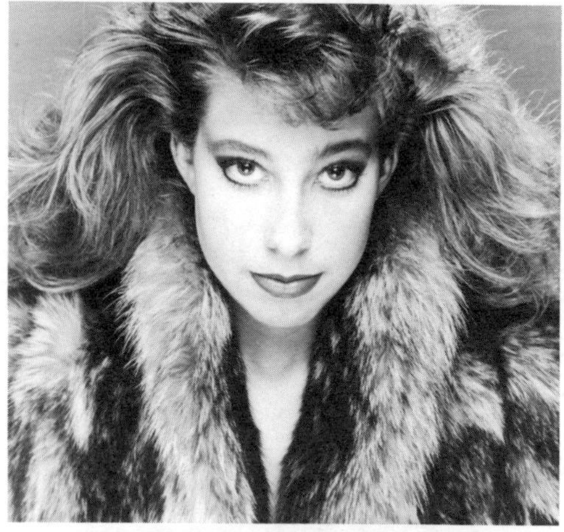

Before and after make-over. This senior came in a plain, shy little girl, but when we photographed her a few minutes later, she was a chic, stylish, confident young woman. You know she'll buy lots of the new look, don't you?

pronounced in b/w than in color. The photographers who specialize in this treatment make high contrast images which are artistic in appearance, very permanent and more flattering than any other form of photography.

4. How about a location sitting? We hear some photographers charge as much as $125 to take a senior into a scenic area (mountains, lake or sea shore, or other interesting area) to be photographed. On a designated day, he may transport four or five people in his van to a unique setting for their senior portraits. Look at the potential within an 80-100 mile radius of your own community for unusual walls, stairways, garage doors, and buildings that lend themselves to creative uses. Airports, shopping malls, or a famous tourist attraction can all provide that something different students are looking for.
5. Studio photographers are fast becoming set designers. As education increases, seniors want more for their image than just painted backgrounds and wicker chairs. The photographer is actually creating surrealistic backdrops and creative graphic designs that involve the student. The student is posed right in the middle of all these items and becomes a part of the entire environment. The set can be built from artboard, wood, foam core, or other materials that are unique to the individual. They can be colorful and show shapes from triangles, to circles, to squares and the like. But they are real and they involve the students who love the idea of having something created just for them.

As more people become educated to what creative make-up, correct color of clothing and proper hair styling can do to create a total image, these things must be incorporated into your senior photography. I suggest working with someone in your area who can educate you and your staff on the techniques of color analysis so you can help students pick the right colors of clothing.

There are books available (Carole Jackson's Color Me Beautiful, for instance) which are very helpful in selecting the colors they will look best in. Many make-up people, such as Mary Kay salespeople, would be delighted to work with you in developing your knowledge of color. This is something they use on a regular basis in their business which they can teach to your staff. (I also know a photographer who uses a Mary Kay consultant to apply the make-up at his studio. She's very good at this and he pays her well for her expertise.)

Make-up is an area of exteme importance to the portrait photographer. When used with b/w photography, you can actually change the way a person's face looks. Bone structure, size of eyes, nose, mouth and height of forehead, are all things which should be analysed. An excellent textbook for this information is Michael Maron's **Makeover Magic.** This book will show practical uses for corrective make-up and how to use it in color photography to conceal blemishes and add color and life to an otherwise plain face.

I recommend doing before and after photographs of everyone you make up. The dramatic changes really show up in the comparison. Many times the improvements occur so gradually during the make-up process that even the artist applying the cosmetics has no conception of the changes that have taken place. Only the before and after images show what has really taken place. These photographs provide you with a great advertising aid because you are able to show what make-up can do to change and enhance the appearance of even very plain people.

Chapter XVI

What Are the Future Trends?

Many students are looking for new ideas for their portraits - a new look, a now image, a great background. Keep your mind open to new ideas. My personal feeling is that it is our responsibility as photographers to initiate new concepts in portrait photography. The photographer who is inventive and who maintains an open attitude about props, backgrounds and poses will always be the one who has the most business. High school students want to be distinctive within certain limits and they will actively seek out the studio which offers the new, the different, the unusual, and avoid follow the leader clones.

Isn't this true with all business? If you develop a new idea or product and promote it, clients will respond. If you do nothing with your thoughts, you get stagnant, go nowhere and always wonder what it would be like to be on top. I believe you are better off to develop something new and to actively promote it. If it succeeds, great! And if it fails, you have learned a lesson in persistence that should make you a better judge of the next new idea.

Successful people have many failures along the way. What makes them successful is being able to accurately evaluate what went wrong, correct the problem and go on from there. If your studio is the one others look to for leadership in new ideas and new types of thinking, in backgrounds and props, remember they will be copying you just as fast as they can. The answer to continued leadership is in your imagination where you can develop ideas that will set you apart from others.

Let's share some new ideas:

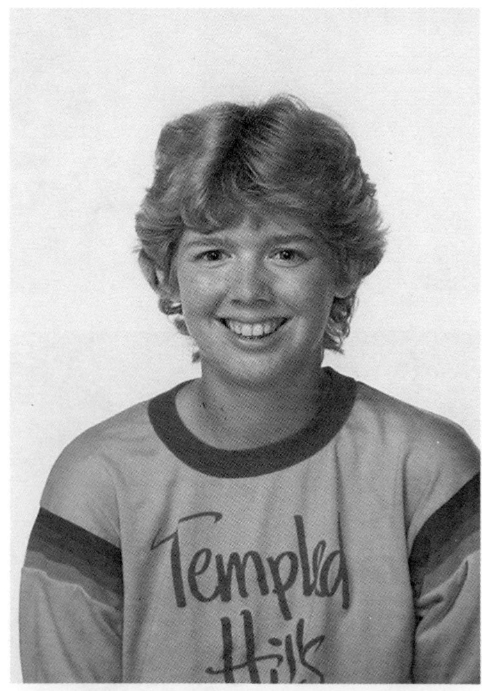

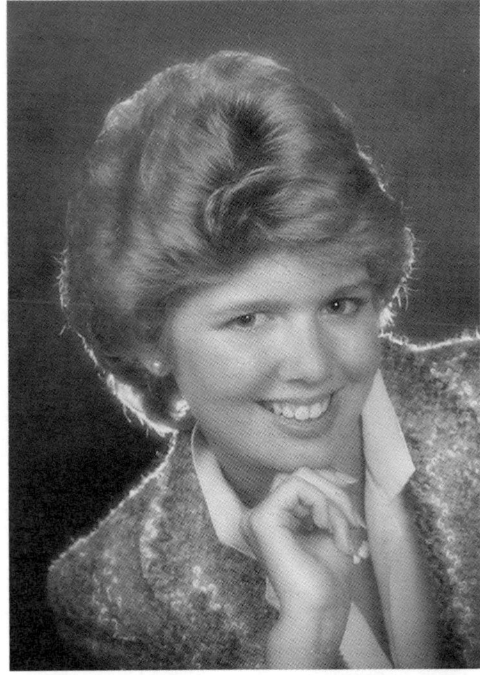

1. The latest trend in photography is education. Why not set your studio up to educate clients as to correct make-up, clothing colors and styles with each type of prop you are using. You could set up an area in your studio where you would use an audio-visual presentation to give every client a pre-appointment consultation. To avoid spending an extra hour or more with every client, you might hold an hour-long group session once a week at a designated time. Have your make-up artist and hair stylist there to suggest what is new and what is expected from these students when they arrive for their portrait session. This is a great way to promote a new type of photography session or to get students to bring more or different props than usual.
2. Offer make-up and hair styling with your best sitting (for an extra charge). There are several ways to do this. Your own staff can be trained in corrective make-up applications, or you can acquire the services of a professional in the industry. Hair styling should be left to a professional person. You could send your clients to a particular hair stylist or even make arrangements for the styling to be done in your studio. This added attention will generate additional interest and profit for your studio. It is simple coordination but worth the effort.
3. How about a black and white session which includes a corrective make-up to reshape a person's face through proper contouring and highlighting? Black and white lets you actually change the total appearance of a person. The results of corrective make-up are more

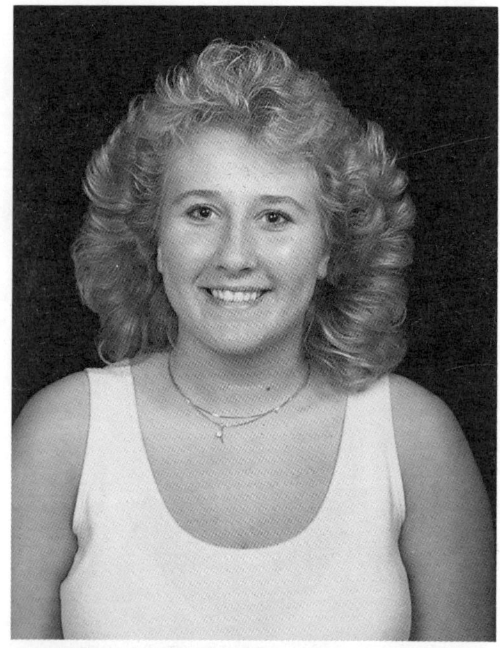

This is especially effective when the person seeing the photos knows the subject. Do you suppose this could be beneficial to your business and its bottom line?

The application of make-up needs to be handled carefully. We don't have a licensed cosmetologist on our staff, but that may be necessary in the near future. The laws very from state to state, so before you train your receptionist to do make-up, call the state board overseeing cosmetology to learn about the laws that govern who can do make-up.

The rule here in our area states that if don't sell make-up or have a specific charge for its application, it is okay for us to use it to enhance our finished portrait. However, we do get a written release from each person saying she has given us permission to "help" her apply cosmetics. Most senior girls have a pretty good idea of how to put on make-up, so we just act as a coach telling them how much to use, where to apply it, and what colors are best for them. There are always a few who just don't understand make-up at all, so - with their permission - we make the applications as required.

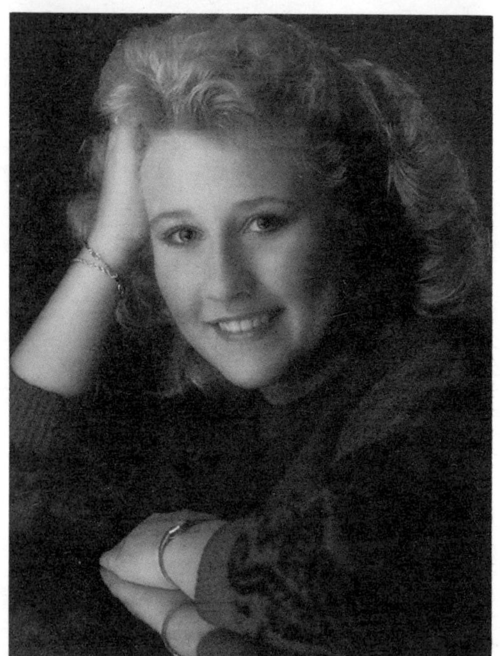

The requirements in different states vary from requiring a licensed cosmetologist to allowing anyone to do the work. If anyone can do it, get someone on your staff trained as soon as possible, but if the rules are tough, you can have the young woman apply it herself under your direction. Do what you have to as the enhancement of your finished photographs is definitely worth the effort. Our experience is that when you improve her appearance through make-up and hair styling, you will get a much larger order.

You may have to find ways to accommodate yourself to the laws of your state, but do it whatever it takes - even to hiring a cosmetologist to do make-overs - because it is *profitable* and your senior girls will love it and they will buy, *buy*, BUY! You can cover the cost of the cosmetologist by adding a fee for the make-up. Most studios charge only what their artist charges and usually the senior pays the fee directly to the artist.

We have considered making our best portrait session a complete makeover session, including a tanning session at the local salon, a conditioning exercise program at a local spa for total body conditioning, an application of sculptured nails, a gorgeous make-up and hair style, along with a great photography session.

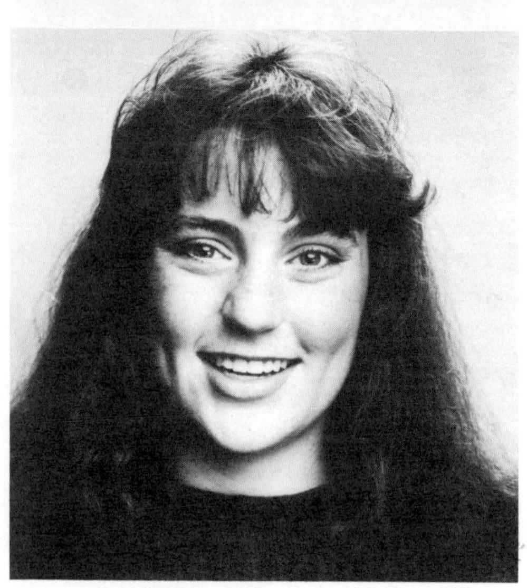

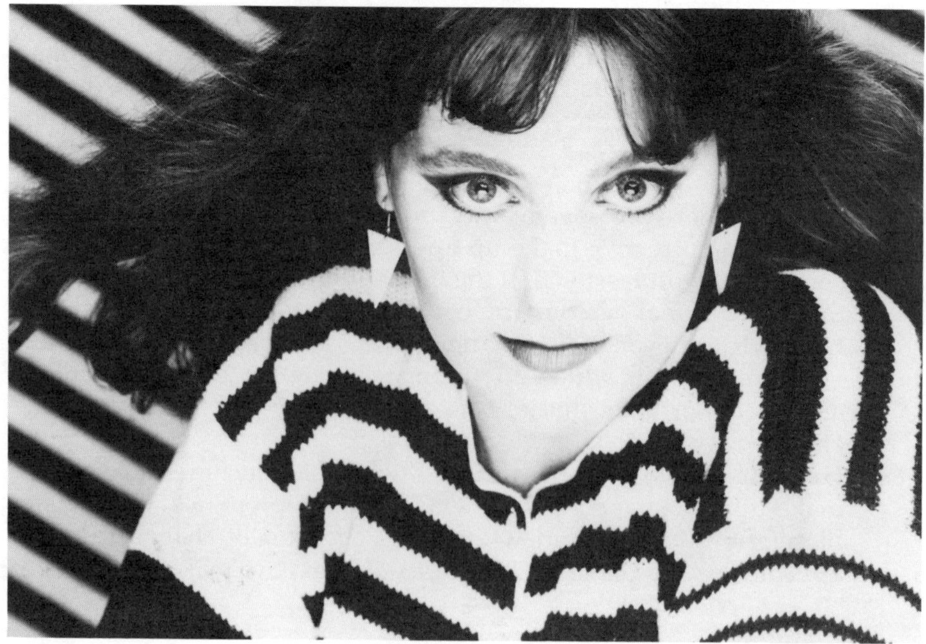

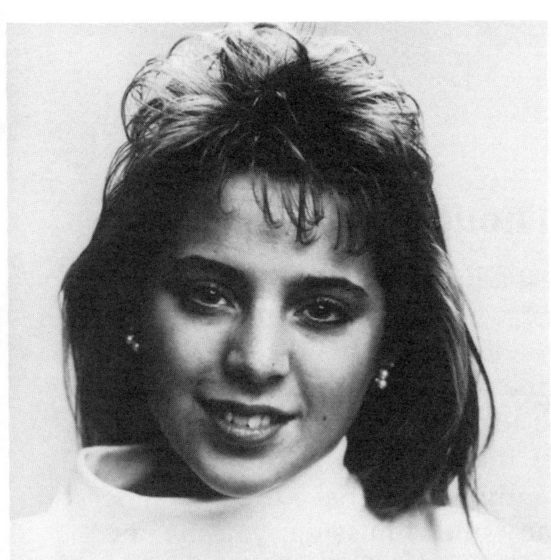
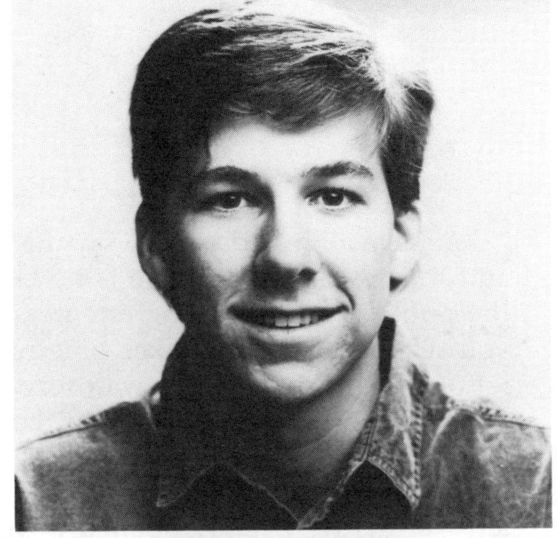
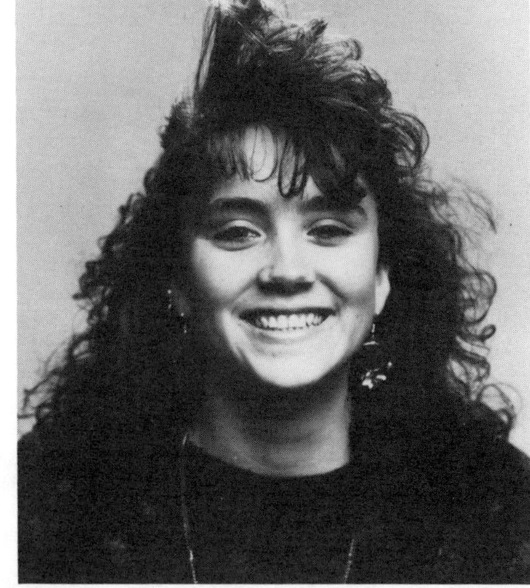
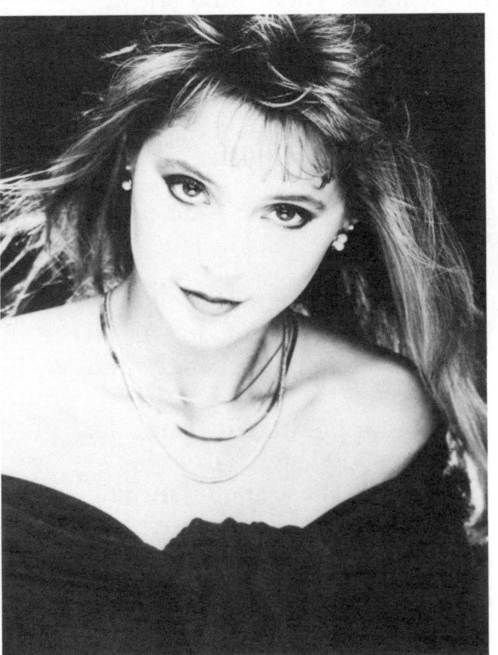
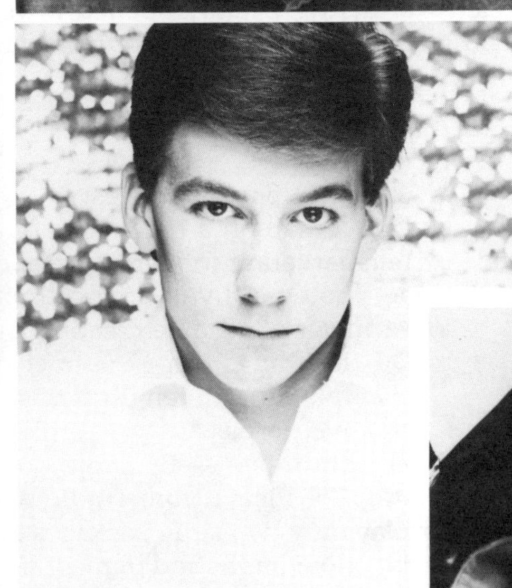
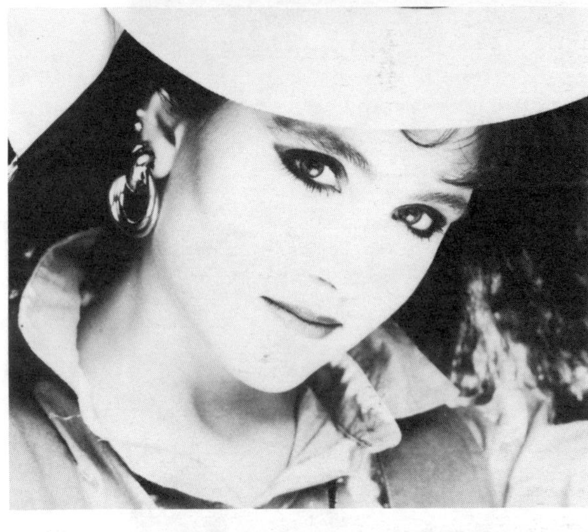
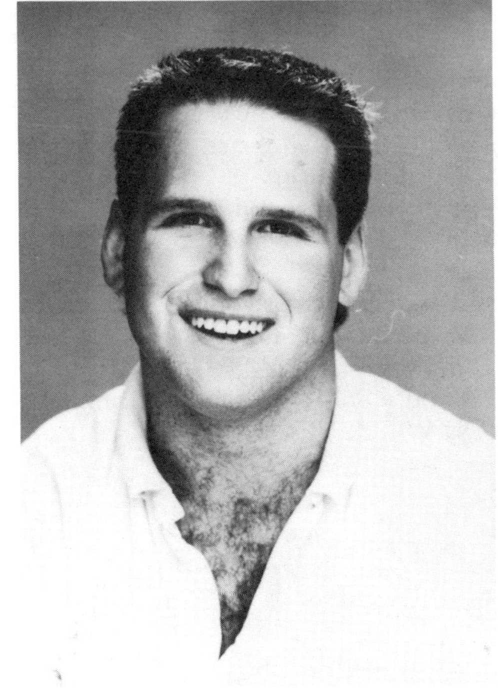
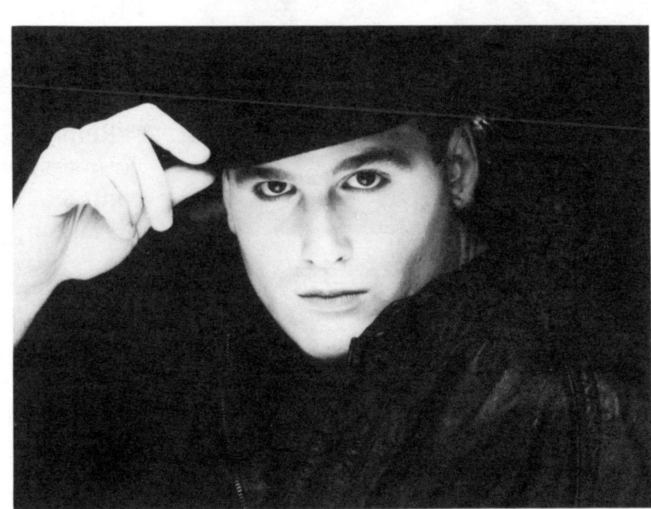

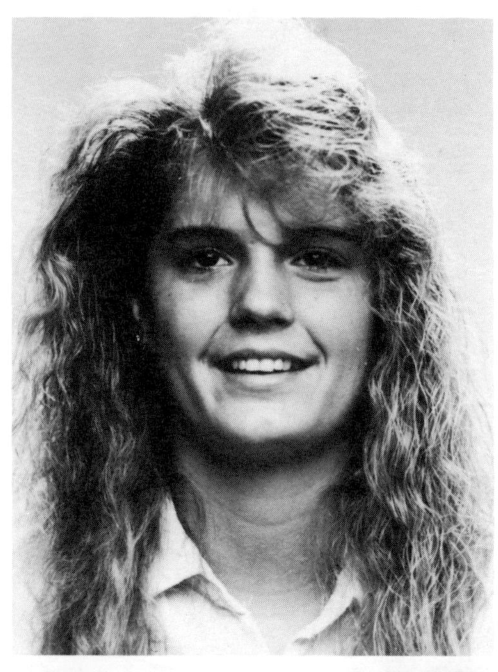

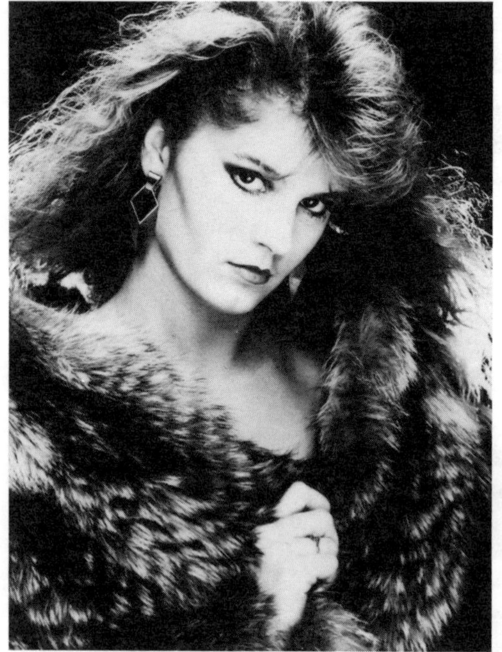

Concluding Thoughts

We have all heard people say the best advertising is Word of Mouth and that's very true. There is no better way to get your name before the public than by having one person tell another good things about you. Unfortunately, it takes time for the word to spread, time and a lot of good PR, so if you wait for that to happen in a new business, you will go bankrupt. It is my belief that to build a strong senior photography business there are several things that have to happen or which you must cause to happen. If any one is missing, you may be left wondering what happened to your business. There is no one key to success, but this list deserves your most serious consideration.

1. A clean, comfortable facility.
2. An advertising campaign.
   Including:
   a. Student Representatives
   b. Direct mail on a regular basis
   c. Telemarketing to increase response
3. Good photography in an incredible variety.
   a. At first, spend time creating truly unique photography.
   b. Do the things large contract photographers cannot do. As an example, do full length poses with lots of clothing changes and creative props.
4. Show the previews by projection and by appointment. Don't let photographs leave your studio without this vital step.
5. Display only two large packages on your wall. These should include all the photographs and frames one would normally need to purchase. And when the client spends X number of dollars (you pre-determine the amount), they get the proofs free.

Any one of these things will increase your business, but tying them all together will bountifully bolster your bottom line. Once you start to do these things you will get even more excited about photography. I believe with the proper planning you can determine exactly how much you make. Do not guess about business practices: plan and set goals, then work your plan!

The senior market has been the backbone for most of the photography studios in existence. Why not use this to your advantage and grow financially and in popularity?

Remember that profit is not a dirty word! Making a good living is your responsibility. Your life should never be controlled by a school contract.

Wake up and take charge of your life and business. It is not by luck nor is it by chance that you succeed, but only by careful planning and carefully working the plan.

Above all, if you want it, if you sacrifice and make strides to work your plan, YOU WILL SUCCEED!

If you have enjoyed this book, remember that STUDIO PRESS publishes other books exclusively for professional photographers. We'll be glad to send you a catalog of them. Just call (800) 445-7160 toll-free in all states, except California which is (209) 533-4222. Or you can write STUDIO PRESS, USA.

STUDIO PRESS
P.O. BOX 160
SOULSBYVILLE, CA 95372
(209) 533-4222

"The Two Best New Portrait Styles Since The Boudoir Portrait"

The Madonna Portrait by Lynne Jerome

The *Madonna* PORTRAIT

by Lynne Jerome

Madonna Portraiture is not a new concept; mother and child portraits have been common for more than 1000 years. Lynne Jerome's mother-baby portraits are classic in both style and the setting: the mother is garbed in a flowing, non-revealing gown, the baby is totally nude and they are in a bedroom setting. Raphael or Michaelangelo would have been very comfortable with these portraits.

What's new is the name — Madonna Portraits — plus Lynne's marketing methods. During the very slowest time of the year Lynne offers Madonnas at special prices, turning an excellent profit during normally profitless times. After just eight years of promoting Madonnas, they have become so popular that many women do not always wait for the annual special, but call to set an appointment at full price as soon as their pregnancies are confirmed. The result is an annual net on Madonnas of between $13,000 and $15,000.

The classic style of these portraits calls for a large framed print on the wall. Because of this and because she markets wall prints as part of her packages, Lynne sells an unusually high number of large prints on her Madonna sittings. She also successfully markets Folios and gift sizes, as well.

This small book contains Lynne's marketing plan, camera room procedures, and sales steps so you can install this great new promotion in your studio without delay.

Paperback, 6 x 9", 48pp, fully illustrated, just $12.50, plus $2 to pack & ship. Californians, please add 78¢ tax. Thirty day money back guarantee.

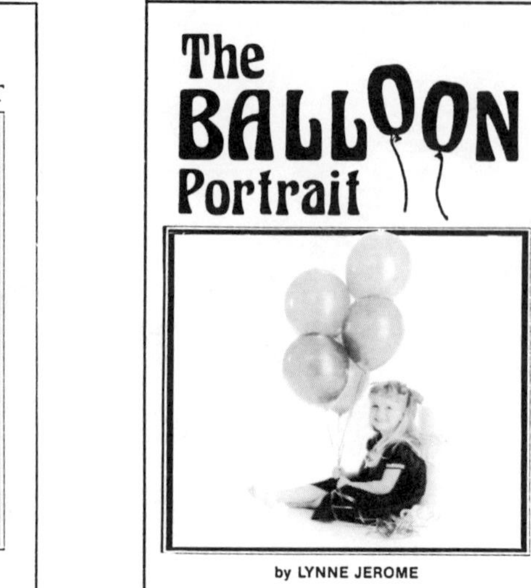

The Balloon Portrait by Lynne Jerome

This outstanding new portrait style from Lynne Jerome will positively bring the children back into your studio. It's different, it's something the store-shooters can't do and it provokes expressions like no other type of portrait. The first studio in your area to offer Balloon Portraits can quickly lock up this new market.

Look at the advantages:

1) It can be done only in a permanent studio with a white background, so the store-shooters can't ape it.

2) The portrait is actually *more* than full length so it demands a wall size, framed print. You will find sales of wall prints and frames zooming when you do Balloon Portraits.

3) The situation is cute — kids with balloons — the expressions are incredibly alive, and the whole high key look is so different that Mom has to share them. The sale of gift prints is excellent.

4) It is simple to do ten or fifteen different poses in five to ten minutes. They are all so cute that Mom has to have every one of them. You will sell Folios of proofs from almost every sitting.

5) It's a perfect portrait to offer during any slow time and it turns times of loss into times of profit. Lynne offers it for only two days of sittings in July, yet she nets (that's NETS) $3000 — $5000 every time it is offered.

Paperback, 6 x 9", 28pp, fully illustrated, just $7.50, plus $2 to pack & ship. (Californians, please add 47¢ tax.) Thirty day money back guarantee.

Save $6.50 on our Special Offer.

Buy both of these great new promotions and save $6.50. Purchased separately, the books, plus shipping, cost $22. Buy both today and pay just $17.50 including the shipping. (Californians, please add 97¢ sales tax.) Order today from Studio Press, Twain Harte, CA 95383-1268. Or ***call toll-free (800) 445-7160*** and order using your Mastercard or Visa.

Paul Castle says: *For a number of years I wrote a column in The Rangefinder on portrait promotions, yet I never found a single one as good as these two from Lynne Jerome. They are about as good as you'll ever see. What makes them so great?*

First *of all, they get a lot of the children out of the hands of the store-shooters and back into your studio where they belong, and it's because this style can't be done in the middle of the grocery store.*

Second, *the style of portraiture — from three quarter poses to more than full lengths — almost* ***demands*** *that the client order at least one wall portrait, and perhaps several, and Lynne includes big prints in her offer. This may be the first time a mother has ever ordered a wall portrait, but it surely won't be the last.*

In addition, Lynne almost always sells gift prints for the grandmothers and other family members and many, many Folios for the parents. With portraits like these, it's easy to build high average sales.

Third, *Lynne* ***nets*** *between $3000 and $5000 every time she offers Balloon Portraits and even more from Madonnas. This is for just two days shooting time during the dog days of July, the slowest time of the year. Balloon Portraits are offered only during the slow period; Madonna Portraits are offered at special prices only at this time also, although they are available all year long.*

Fourth, *because the quality of the portraits is distinctly superior to that of the store-shooters, mothers are reluctant to return to the sameness of Pixie Pinups. The moms who buy these specials become long-term clients, not one-time bargain hunters who disappear when Sears runs their next special.*

Fifth, *Lynne is located in a rural/small town territory, yet these portrait promotions draw people from more than 100 miles away. Her fame has spread and her market has grown with each offering of Madonna or Balloon Portraits.*

Sixth, *the appeal of both promotions is universal: how can you beat a mother-and-child in a classic pose or cutely posed kids enchanted with their balloons? These two concepts will do well anywhere. Not just California razzle-dazzle, they can be transported instantly to Punkin Center, Iowa, or Moosejaw, Alaska. Wherever there are mothers and kids, these promotions will make money — lots of it — for forward-thinking portraitists.*

Seventh, *the cost of these two small books — just $17.50 postpaid — is nothing compared to their potential for annual added profits in the thousands of dollars. Besides, they are guaranteed to work or your money will be refunded. Order today while this money-saving special is still available.*

Mail this coupon to: STUDIO PRESS, Twain Harte, CA 95383-1268

Mail to: STUDIO PRESS, Twain Harte, CA 95383-1268

YES! Please send me the following book(s) with the understanding that I may return them within 30 days for a full refund of the purchase price.

( ) One copy of **THE MADONNA PORTRAIT** @ $14.50 (includes shipping. Californians, please add 78¢ tax.)

( ) One copy of **THE BALLOON PORTRAIT** @ $9.50 (includes shipping. Californians, please add 47¢ tax.)

( ) One copy of **EACH BOOK** for just $17.50 (includes shipping. Californians, please add 97¢ tax.)

My telephone number is ( ) ____________

(In case of a question about your order.)

Name ____________

Address ____________

City ____________ State ______ ZIP ______

Yes, you may use your VISA or Mastercard.

Card # ____________

Exp. Date ____________ Amount authorized ____________

X ____________

(Signature required on all credit card orders. If the signature is not the same as the "name" above, please print the signature, too.)